The Animal Question
in Deconstruction

This book is for my parents,
John William Turner and Leonie Joan Turner,
gardeners extraordinaires

The Animal Question in Deconstruction

Edited by Lynn Turner

EDINBURGH
University Press

© editorial matter and organisation Lynn Turner, 2013
© the chapters their several authors, 2013

Edinburgh University Press Ltd
22 George Square, Edinburgh EH8 9LF

www.euppublishing.com

Typeset in 10.5/13 pt Sabon by
Servis Filmsetting Ltd, Stockport, Cheshire

A CIP record for this book is available from the British Library

ISBN 978 0 7486 8312 3 (hardback)
ISBN 978 0 7486 8313 0 (paperback)
ISBN 978 0 7486 8314 7 (webready PDF)
ISBN 978 0 7486 8315 4 (epub)

The right of the contributors
to be identified as author of this work
has been asserted in accordance with
the Copyright, Designs and Patents Act 1988.

Contents

Acknowledgements	vii
Notes on Contributors	viii

Introduction: The Animal Question in Deconstruction   1
Lynn Turner

1. A Refugee   9
   Hélène Cixous

2. Swans of Life (External Provocations and Autobiographical Flights That Teach Us How to Read)   13
   Sarah Wood

3. Love of the *Löwe*   34
   Marie-Dominique Garnier

4. Insect Asides   54
   Lynn Turner

5. Sponge Inc   70
   Laurent Milesi

6. Elephant Eulogy: The Exorbitant Orb of an Elephant   89
   Kelly Oliver

7. Troubling Resemblances, Anthropological Machines and the Fear of Wild Animals: Following Derrida after Agamben   105
   Stephen Morton

8. Derrida, Rousseau, Cixous and Tsvetaeva: Sexual Difference and the Love of the Wolf   124
   Judith Still

9. Deconstructing Sexual Difference: A Myopic Reading of
   Hélène Cixous's Mole   142
   Marta Segarra

10. Your Worm   158
    Peggy Kamuf

11. Mole   177
    Nicholas Royle

Index   192

Acknowledgements

My heartfelt thanks go to Johnny Golding who responded to ideas and drafts from the beginning and heard it through until the end. Jackie Jones (Edinburgh University Press) and Wendy Lochner (Columbia University Press) gave immediate enthusiastic support that brought this project to press and at relative speed. Thank you also to the anonymous reviewer whose excellent suggestion made this a better collection. Jorella Andrews granted some much appreciated teaching relief in the last leg of putting it all together.

The editor and the publisher would like to thank the following: Éditions Galilée for permission to publish the first English translation of 'Un Réfugié' by Hélène Cixous (first published in *L'Amour du loup et autres remords*, Paris: Éditions Galilée, 2003); Nicholas Royle for permission to reprint 'Mole' in this volume (first published in English in *The Uncanny*, Manchester: Manchester University Press, 2003). Additionally, extracts from the works of Emily Dickinson are reprinted by permission of the publishers and the Trustees of Amherst College from *The Poems of Emily Dickinson*, ed. Thomas H. Johnson, ed., Cambridge, MA: The Belknap Press of Harvard University Press, Copyright © 1951, 1955, 1979, 1983 by the President and Fellows of Harvard College.

Notes on Contributors

Hélène Cixous is the author of innumerable works complicating genres in drama, literature and philosophy. Among her most recent publications are *Double Oblivion of the Ourang-Outang* (2013), *Eve Escapes* (2012) and *Hemlock* (2011).

Marie-Dominique Garnier has published numerous essays on literature and philosophy (especially on Derrida, Cixous, Deleuze, Woolf and Joyce), including in *Demenageries: Thinking (of) Animals After Derrida* (2011). Her edited collections include *Jardins d'Hiver: Littérature et Photographie* (1997) and *Cixous sous X: D'un Coup le Nom* (co-edited, 2010). She is preparing an annotated translation of Madeline Gins's 1994 *Helen Keller or Arakawa*, and an edited volume on Cixous's 1976 *Partie*. She is Professor of English Literature, Paris 8, where she also teaches at the *Centre d'Etudes féminines et d'Etudes de Genre*.

Peggy Kamuf publishes on literary theory and contemporary French thought and literature, particularly regarding the work of Derrida and Cixous. She has also translated a number of their texts including Cixous's *Love Itself in the Letterbox* (2008) and Derrida's *Without Alibi* (2002). Her recent books include *To Follow: The Wake of Jacques Derrida* (2010) and *Book of Addresses* (2005). She is Marion Frances Chevalier Professor of French and Comparative Literature, University of Southern California.

Laurent Milesi publishes on literary theory and contemporary French thought and literature including on the question of 'the animal', particularly in relation to the work of Derrida and Cixous. He has translated several of their works including Cixous's *Zero's Neighbour* (2010) and, as co-translator with Stefan Herbrechter, Derrida's *H. C. for Life, That Is to Say . . .*, (2006). His work is included in the French publication arising from the 1997 Cerisy-la-Salle conference *L'Animal autobiographique* (1999), and he is also the editor of *James Joyce and the Difference of Language* (2003). He is Reader in English Literature, Cardiff University.

Stephen Morton's books include *Gayatri Spivak: Ethics, Subalternity and the Critique of Postcolonial Reason* (2007), *Salman Rushdie: Fictions of Postcolonial Modernity* (2007) and *States of Emergency: Terrorism and Colonialism in Literature and Culture 1905–2005* (2013). He is Senior Lecturer in English, University of Southampton.

Kelly Oliver publishes on continental philosophy (especially Nietzsche, Derrida and Kristeva), film theory, feminism and 'the animal'. Her recent books include *Knock Me Up, Knock Me Down: Images of Pregnancy in Hollywood Films* (2012), *Animal Lessons: How They Teach Us to Be Human* (2009) and *Women as Weapons of War* (2007). She is W. Alton Jones Professor of Philosophy, Vanderbilt University.

Nicholas Royle's books include *Telepathy and Literature* (1991), *After Derrida* (1995), *The Uncanny* (2003), *In Memory of Jacques Derrida* (2009) and *Veering: a Theory of Literature* (2011), as well as the novel *Quilt* (2010). He is Professor of English at the University of Sussex.

Marta Segarra has edited numerous books on literature, sexual difference and 'the animal' including *Demenageries: Thinking (of) Animals After Derrida* (with A.E. Berger, 2011), *The Portable Cixous* (2010), *Rêver Croire Penser – Autour d'Hélène Cixous* (with B. Clément, 2010), and *L'Événement comme écriture: Cixous et Derrida se lisant* (2007). Her recent books include *Traces du désir* (2009) and *Nouvelles Romancières Francophones du Maghreb* (2010). She is Professor of French Literature and Gender Studies, University of Barcelona.

Judith Still is the author of *Justice and Difference in Rousseau* (1993), *Feminine Economies* (1997), *Derrida and Hospitality* (2010) and *Enlightenment Hospitality* (2011). She is the editor of *Men's Bodies* (2003), and her co-editing includes *Intertextuality* (1990) and *Textuality and Sexuality* (1993) with M. Worton. She is Professor of French and Critical Theory, and Head of the School of Cultures, Languages and Area Studies, at Nottingham University.

Lynn Turner has published on deconstruction and animals, feminism, science fiction and visual culture in journals such as *Humanimalia*,

Mosaic: journal for the interdisciplinary study of literature, Camera Obscura and Derrida Today and in books such as Animality and the Moving Image (2014). She is the co-editor of a special issue of parallax called 'bon appétit' (2013), the co-author of Visual Cultures As . . . Recollection (2013) and the author of Machine-Events: Autobiographies of the Performative (2014). She is Lecturer in Visual Culture, Goldsmiths, University of London.

Sarah Wood is one of the founders of Angelaki: Journal of the Theoretical Humanities for which she has edited 'Home and Family' and 'Hotel Psychoanalysis'. She is an editor of Oxford Literary Review, and has edited issues on 'Writing and Immortality and 'Deconstruction and Poetry'. Her books include Derrida's Writing and Difference: A Reader's Guide (2009) and Blue Guitar, co-written with Jonathan Tiplady (2007). She is Senior Lecturer in English, University of Kent.

Introduction: The Animal Question in Deconstruction

Lynn Turner

> Rather than developing [a] fabulous bestiary, I gave myself a horde of animals, within the forest of my own signs and the memoirs of my memory. I was no doubt always thinking about such a company [. . .]
> (Jacques Derrida)[1]

Closed, this book is held between two images from Roni Horn's *Bird* series (2008). Opening its pages, you are following these birds without being able to catch up with them. Horn's images open the vexation of before and after, temporally and spatially. They take part in what is called portrait by an artist who has often entered this genre at an oblique angle not necessarily directed towards the supposed essence of the photographed subject, even in *Index Cixous*, Horn's photographs 'of' Hélène Cixous.[2] The *Bird* series comprises pairs of birds all shot from behind, effectively capturing the head and shoulders but letting the face of the birds escape. Before a plain white modernist backdrop all attention is focused upon feathers as their tones describe the shape of these birds, the beginnings of their closed wings. This pair – they all go without a name; they are *Untitled* – have deep, meditative, blue feathers that shine like luxuriant cloth veiling something or someone. As eyes are pairs so Horn arranges the photographs as a series of pairs. No matter how counterintuitively, they seem to regard us, while also drawing us in towards whatever might occupy their point of view. Logically we know Horn has photographed works of taxidermy; these are dead, sightless birds, probably killed at the hands of humans, detached from the kitsch uncanny of a trophy case. These birds no more know their death than do we. Without erasing differences in the networks of power that cast this as death, that as sacrifice, the other as nothing, neither birds nor humans stare death as such in the face.

Today, as literature examining 'the animal question' continues to grow exponentially, we know that the topic of the face lands us squarely within an ethical environment whose inhabitants have not been named in advance, rather than one that explicitly or implicitly confines itself to humankind.[3] You will find this book among many other recent publications that rethink our relation with other animals across disciplinary boundaries from philosophy to the sciences and the arts. However, *The Animal Question in Deconstruction* is not an introduction to a delimited field – what we might call 'critical animal studies', 'eco-criticism' or the 'posthumanities'.[4] It has a specific remit. This is to take Jacques Derrida seriously when he says that he had always been thinking about the company of animals and that deconstruction has never limited itself to language, still less 'human' language.

The massive range and determined focus of Derrida's posthumously published book *The Animal That Therefore I Am* continues to offer pedagogical dynamite for many thinkers, whether already engaged with 'animal rights' or newly awoken to the historical and philosophical depth of the programmatic endorsement of the 'human' at the expense of what is called 'the animal'. The titular chapter of his book (first published in English in 2002) and its third chapter, 'And Say The Animal Responded' (first in published 2003) had already generated a huge literature even before the publication of the first two editions of Derrida's seminars on *The Beast and the Sovereign*.[5] A substantial part of that literature has followed Derrida's lead in asking philosophy to begin again through his encounter with his cat, one morning, quite ordinarily, in the bathroom.[6] Through this encounter, Derrida demands reconsideration of the 'animal question' embedded in our Cartesian legacy.[7] This legacy would not see his cat as anything other than an animal-machine, reacting to the world solely at the prompt of need.[8] Establishing a hard and fast divide between 'human' and 'animal' feeds directly into what Derrida had earlier named the possibility of a 'non-criminal putting to death', which is in counterpoint to the crime called 'murder', taken only to refer to the killing of humans by other humans.[9] Rather than rectify Descartes' denial of the capacity to respond to those beings corralled under the singular misnomer 'the animal' by more equally distributing this capacity among species like a new form of identity politics – they can respond too – Derrida continues the reversals and displacements of deconstruction. He both patiently questions whether humans *can* respond and alters what response might mean, such that it does not remain a capacity that belongs to an intending subject.[10] Rather, response becomes adulterated by repetition and joins with Derrida's postal ethics in which all our 'sendings' are beholden to the other. This means that in dispensing with one single grand dividing Difference, Derrida neither understands all species as the same nor locates them on a more refined taxonomic scale, but rather advocates differences 'that grow'.[11] Moreover, Derrida's very title explicitly rewrites the frame of Descartes' 'I think, therefore I am', insisting that thinking begins *with* the animal and that no spatial or temporal stability can be claimed by a sovereign subject.[12] Playing on the French 'je suis' as the present tense of both 'to be' and 'to follow', subjects after Derrida are never alone.

In the midst of the text that he calls a 'zootobiography' – after which we might say that it is 'the ear of the animal other that signs' – Derrida points beyond this one moment of revelation with his little cat.[13] He remarks how animals 'multiply, lunging more and more wildly in [his] face in proportion as [his] texts seem to become autobiographical' and that, if one should look through his other works, they 'emerge on page after page'.[14] He goes on to remind us of 'the horse of *Spurs* [. . .] Florian's hare and Kant's black swan in *Politics of Friendship* [. . .] *Glas*, where a certain eagle soars over the two columns [. . .]' and many others.[15] Some attentive scholars realised that Derrida's work pointed to the deconstruction of the elevation of 'man' above all others well before the pedagogical 'tipping point' of *The Animal That Therefore I Am*.[16] In a fashion difficult to reconcile with the domestic temptation of the cat – especially for gardeners! – Nicholas Royle even suggested that 'the track or the trace is in a sense as much molluscous as human'.[17] Yet these other animals have largely escaped wider attention. Remarking on such creatures as the hedgehog in 'What is Poetry?', Derrida also affirms that his texts 'welcome' animal differences 'on the threshold of sexual difference[s]'.[18] This suggestive concatenation too has been relatively unremarked.[19]

With these other animals in the 'forest of [Derrida's] own signs' in mind, *The Animal Question in Deconstruction* brings together scholars who were invited to consider how the animal question might emerge in other works both by Derrida and by other major figures closely associated with deconstruction, notably Cixous and Royle, without aiming for or making any claim to a complete taxonomy.[20] Thus while the *Animal* is a common reference point for the authors collected in this volume, it is not the central focus of any one chapter. Indeed, the first chapter of this volume, 'A Refugee', is the first English translation of a text by Cixous herself, and several chapters discuss her works as prominently as those of Derrida.[21] The editor has previously written of a 'Cixousian feline uncanny stalk[ing]' the better known *Animal* of Derrida, tracking through the elliptical poetics in Cixous's text 'The Cat's Arrival' as they seemingly predict the arguments that we now recognise regarding response and reaction, modesty, nudity, autobiography, hospitality and the event.[22] While 'The Cat's Arrival' predates the conference presentation of 'The Animal That Therefore I Am',[23] current scholarship intimately involved with the work of Cixous and Derrida – including their writings *on* each other's work – increasingly discusses the ways in which their thoughts frequently interweave.[24] It is a further task of this volume to bring Cixous's thinking on animals to greater attention.

People involved in the politics of representation can become nervous of allegory and drawn to realism. Allegory is the enemy of animals, or so we think, because it always abuses their figures for qualities we take to be human: it seems indentured to anthropomorphism. Derrida went to great lengths to assure us that his encounter really was with a little cat, only to warn subsequently that we could not be certain whether he was not also talking of Lewis Carroll.[25] It is not in the nature of a text to guarantee certainty. While particular fabulous traditions do indeed depict animals in order to speak only of humans (examined in *The Beast and the Sovereign*), if we maintain a distinction between the fealty of realism and the betrayal of allegory then we only shore up a key problem. It is rather like Jacques Lacan's assumption that 'the animal' may pretend in the exceptional circumstances of seduction and combat, but cannot 'pretend to pretend' as human beings are thought to do in manipulating a notional second order of language.[26] Thinking that animals are best served by realism alone – the style without a style – assumes a firm division between need and desire, the world and language. It assumes that only so-called human language signifies. That assumption loses ground in *The Animal Question in Deconstruction*.

Cixous does not simply run risks with figural language when writing of animals. Even, perhaps especially, in what seems like an autobiographical address such as that of 'A Refugee', she often shifts the first person such that we move between several voices, rather than remain within a strict first-person singular: 'A Refugee' conducts the voices of Cixous and her cat, Cixous and herself as she accuses herself of a 'crime of species'. She runs the two of them together, her cat is 'mycat' [*machatte*]. It is the cut of a decision that divides them, after which she is – she is following – a halfcat [*demichat*]: in the heat of the moment Cixous sides with a bird, the prey of her cat. Saving this bird, she 'kills' this cat. That symbolic death happens once; it does not raise a general law. Each of the 'two actors' – but which two? – thinks of the rhythm of 'life death' in the same way.[27]

The last chapter, 'Mole', was first given as a paper by Royle in 1997 at that same Cerisy-la-Salle conference at which Derrida lectured on the autobiographical animal.[28] Ironically Royle reminds Derrida of his own delayed engagement with the animal in *Spectres of Marx*, even as the question of the animal would, as he there predicted, 'become massively

4. See especially the *Posthumanities* series, edited by Cary Wolfe, from Minnesota University Press.
5. See Jacques Derrida, 'The Animal That Therefore I Am (More to Follow)', trans. David Wills, *Critical Inquiry*, 28, Winter 2002, pp. 369–418, and 'And Say the Animal Responded?', trans. David Wills, in Cary Wolfe, ed., *Zoontologies: The Question of the Animal* (Minneapolis: Minnesota University Press, 2003), pp. 121–46; Derrida, *The Beast and the Sovereign*, trans. Geoffrey Bennington, 2 vols (Chicago and London: University of Chicago Press, 2009, 2011). Commentaries include Tom Tyler, 'Quia Ego Nominor Leo: Barthes, Stereotypes & Aesop's Animals', *Mosaic*, 40.1, 2007, pp. 45–59; Matthew Chrulew, 'Divinanimality: Derrida and the Discourse of Species in Genesis', *The Bible and Critical Theory*, 2.2, 2006, pp. 1–23; David Wood, 'Thinking with Cats', in *Animal Philosophy: Ethics & Identity*, ed. Peter Atterton and Matthew Calarco (London: Continuum, 2004), pp. 129–44.
6. Derrida, *Animal*, pp. 3–11.
7. Ibid. p. 8.
8. See René Descartes, *A Discourse on the Method* [1637], trans. Ian Maclean (Oxford: Oxford University Press, 2008), pp. 47–8.
9. Derrida, 'Eating Well', p. 278.
10. Derrida, *Animal*, p. 8.
11. Ibid. pp. 29–31.
12. Ibid., pp. 3, 29.
13. Ibid., p. 34. See Jacques Derrida, *The Ear of the Other: Otobiography, Transference, Translation*, ed. Christie McDonald, trans. Avital Ronell (Lincoln, NE, and London: University of Nebraska Press, 1988), p. 51.
14. Derrida, *Animal*, p. 35.
15. Ibid., pp. 37–8.
16. Leonard Lawlor treats the question of the animal as intrinsic to Derrida's work in *This Is Not Sufficient: An Essay on Animality and Human Nature in Derrida* (New York: Columbia University Press, 2007).
17. Nicholas Royle, *After Derrida* (Manchester: Manchester University Press, 1995), p. 33.
18. Jacques Derrida, 'Che cos'è la poesia?', in Weber, ed. *Points . . . Interviews*, p. 297; Derrida, *Animal*, pp. 288–99.
19. With the notable exceptions of *Demenageries: Thinking of Animals After Derrida*, ed. Anne Emmanuelle Berger and Marta Segarra (Amsterdam and New York: Rodopi, 2011), and Kelly Oliver, *Animal Lessons: How They Teach Us to Be Human* (New York: Columbia University Press, 2009).
20. Derrida, *Animal*, p. 37.
21. Hélène Cixous, 'Un réfugié', in *L'amour du loup et autres remords* (Paris: Des Femmes, 2003), pp. 53–60.
22. Lynn Turner, 'When Species Kiss: Some Recent Correspondence between *animots*', *Humanimalia*, 2.1, 2010, p. 61.
23. Hélène Cixous, 'The Cat's Arrival', *parallax*, 12.1, 2006, pp. 21–42; Cixous, 'Arrivée du Chat', in *Messie* (Paris: Des Femmes, 1996).
24. For example, Hélène Cixous, *Insister of Jacques Derrida*, trans. Peggy Kamuf (Edinburgh: Edinburgh University Press, 2007); Jacques Derrida,

H. C. for Life, That is to Say, trans. Laurent Milesi and Stefan Herbrechter (Stanford: Stanford University Press, 2006).
25. Derrida, *Animal*, p. 7.
26. The limitations with which Lacan constrains 'the animal' come under fire in Derrida, *Animal*, pp. 119–40.
27. Echoing the modulations of *fort/da* as 'life death' in Jacques Derrida, *The Post Card: From Socrates to Freud and Beyond*, trans. Alan Bass (Chicago: University of Chicago Press, 1987), p. 285.
28. Conference proceedings: Marie-Louise Mallet, ed., *L'Animal autobiographique* (Paris: Des Femmes, 1999).
29. Jacques Derrida, cited in Nicholas Royle, *The Uncanny: An Introduction* (Manchester: Manchester University Press, 2003), p. 245.
30. Nicholas Royle, 'Mole', in *The Uncanny*, pp. 241–55.
31. Jacques Derrida, 'Freud and the Scene of Writing', in *Writing and Difference*, trans. Alan Bass (London: Routledge and Kegan Paul), p. 214. Nicholas Royle subsequently writes precisely on the non-anthropomorphic veer of the environment in *Veering: A Theory of Literature* (Edinburgh: Edinburgh University Press, 2011).
32. Elaborated in my 'Animal Transference: A "mole-like progression" in C. J. Cherryh', *Mosaic*, 44.3, 2010, pp. 163–75.
33. Derrida, 'Che cos'è la poesia?', p. 36.
34. Derrida, *Beast*, I, pp. 16, 60, 98. Hélène Cixous, 'Love of the Wolf', trans. Keith Cohen, in *Stigmata: Escaping Texts* (London and New York: Routledge, 1998), pp. 84–99.
35. Jacques Derrida, 'Tympan', in *Margins of Philosophy*, trans. Alan Bass (Chicago: University of Chicago Press, 1982), pp. ix–xxix.
36. *Verlan* is a form of French slang working through the inversion of syllables (thus, from '*l'envers*' to '*verlan*'). *Vers*, as Kamuf elaborates, means 'worm' as well as 'verse' and 'towards'.
37. Jacques Derrida, 'Signature Event Context', in *Margins of Philosophy*, pp. 307–30; Derrida, *Signéponge / Signsponge*, trans. Richard Rand (New York: Columbia University Press, 1984).
38. Jacques Derrida, *Edmund Husserl's Origin of Geometry: An Introduction*, trans. John P. Leavey Jr (Lincoln, NE, and London: University of Nebraska Press, 1978).
39. Giorgio Agamben, *The Open: Man and Animal*, trans. Kevin Atell (Stanford: Stanford University Press, 2004), p. 37.
40. Derrida, *Animal*, p. 64.

Chapter 1

A Refugee

Hélène Cixous

Brief squawks stitched to the sky's bluish gauze. The birds are pulling from west to east. Short swift black notes fly straight as beetle-planes. The attack is aimed at us. My cat and I have the house's hull for a land; the ceiling is lower this morning. The whole dwelling crouching on its hind side, its face turned motionless eastwards. The house's brow lies open to the sky. We are the inside, the blind alley. The birds have all the rest of the world. This is what they cry, brief, mockful, victory, passing to and fro very far away from us. We do not fly. We lack wings to such an extent that we are suffering quite vividly right now this lack on our shoulders, this stumping, this clumsiness, this disability of the heart which heaves in vain.

Dry tears sear my eyelids. It is the suppressed pain gnawing me. I did what I had sworn in all conscience not to do any more and ever, I did again, the thing, the kind of crime of all crimes of which I had sworn never to be the author, I couldn't do otherwise than do it, it goes extremely fast, one hurries to do the deed fleeing under the black squall which rumbles over the soul, faster than the thought which far behind has not begun, one is borne, lifted by a power, a split so pure in two hostilities, a disapproval so absolute of what one ineluctably gets ready to carry out, the clasp between the two wrestlers so tight that the same null thought has no chance of creeping in. I did against myself what I would have given my right hand which did it not to be led to do it. I had to do it, a contrary duty; who can imagine the rigid destruction that instantly takes hold of the being bound to attack its own beingness. I killed myself, I pierced one of my sides through the other, I took the bread out of my child's mouth, I wrenched the breast from the newly born's limp avid little jaws. I betrayed my love whom I love more dearly than myself, my innocent, hairy daughter with transparent eyes, I did the deed and carved out of my flesh a cut full of tears.

And what for? And for whom? Ah! That's the crime of the crime. Not even for. No for but only some cause. Because of a bird. Of the bird. A bit of bird, almost nothing, then. For almost an almost I betrayed in my heart of hearts the cherished heart of my cat which I pierced, I had to and while trembling I did. No harshness, no. Limp and shivering, blurred, hazy and diluted, I did. I robbed my adored one of her spoils, I stripped her of the joy and enjoyment, leaving her but one single unstolen thing: the illusion that I am still hers, the one who loves her and who can want only within what she wants and live only in step with her life. She doesn't know that I have deceived betrayed robbed her. That I haven't bungled at least. I have taken everything from her but trust. I have deceived myself. To me she comes and shows with the eternal gentleness of innocence the wounds which my own hidden hand has dealt her. That I have managed to pull off: concealment. She hasn't seen me doing the deed. She hasn't seen me furtively, feverishly nabbing the swallow and chucking it over the balcony with a backhand.

(Or else has she seen me? And then – forgiven?) She calls me and leads me to all the places where the thing took place, the joy was lost, the memory collapsed, in blood, in broken feathers. She guides me on the battlefield: here the bird was knocked over by a giant stroke of the paw. Slumped face down against the ground the animal looked like a huge rat split open twice bigger than itself. With a sharp stroke of my right paw I brought it back to life. The bird took shape again and dashed sideways over here. In the corner behind the sofa. Here the bird lay on its back, one wing folded the other twisted. A cushion fallen upright pretended to shelter it. I pushed the cushion several times with my tail. Here I called you. Come! Come! I called out. I wanted to share my great moment of life. A bird! I called out. I have it! O come, come! I have a bird for you!

'I committed a crime.'

'What is it you did? You let her do it?'

'Well, precisely – I didn't. I committed a crime of species: I made a human law for mycat [*machatte*]. As if I had applied the right for me against her. As if my right were mightier than hers, I wronged mycat, I bombarded her right and denied her cat culture.'

I accuse myself.

And in the name of which right? Between cat and bird I took a place, I judged, settled, deprived, decided, granted. I sided with the bird without name and without face against mycat my friend my hairy daughter my sister and my consolation. I forbade death and the life that passes through death. I behaved in everything like a human being with power.

And for mycat whom I love, what did I do? I lied and betrayed, I saved my image of kindness in her favour.

To me she comes and complains: my bird has been taken from me, I had it, I was playing, I was slapping it, I was chasing it, I laid it flat stiff with terror then I shook it awake, it moved again, it was intense, sometimes it played possum, I was establishing a patience. We were lying motionless for hours together, it – lying in flawless motionlessness, except for the warmth except for the warmth, me – sitting in serene equanimity, we stayed together as if dead for one hour. Between our brains fine thoughts observed one another in silence. Tireless we are. Watching each other a long time a long time as if dead is our divine trance. During this long time we respect, we think everything, we are in prayer before the edge of the world we are sacred.

Suddenly war grips us again. We run we let out a scream, we don't know yet whether this instant is the last or the next.

It takes refuge in a corner of the room. It makes itself smaller. Here there is no more exit. It waits. I could kill it. It waits. I wait too. That's what happens. Both with a slow heart.

Now it is there and then that the end began – to separate us.

My bird has been stolen from me. Who when and how I couldn't see. It was there where it no longer is, right here, come, follow me, mycat says, I'll show you. There we are, walking around the whole house according to the precise plan of their mutually finished story, we retrace the oblique paths where not long ago the two of them were living out their hunt, we make a stop where they enjoyed a stop, I follow mycat, she busy surprised robbed clear as spring water, me with my soul thickened by a mire, a lump of shame in my throat, red salt in my eyelids, repeating at each footstep the prolific lie, mycat dashes along, a fine haste gives her wings, me heavy grief-stricken leprous.

Betrayal fast gnaws at me. I betrayed you. And thereupon remorse comes over my eyes, over my lips, over my tongue, over my hands. The whys bark at my heels I have lost the reply. I had to – steal. And there was betrayal.

'I have no justification.'

Next time I shall sacrifice the bird. I shall sacrifice it to me. I shall sacrifice it to you. I shall sacrifice myself better, more lovingly, more courageously, less cautiously.

But I've already said that, it seems to me.

I had already said 'next time'. This will then be the next?

But I've lost confidence, this trust, this time [*cette foi, cette fois*], I can no longer count on myself either.

I did one duty, only one duty, one single duty out of two. And it is not mine. I did it blindly and voluntarily involuntarily *(actually is it me who did it?)*.

I sacrificed the joy of mycat who is my greatest joy. I harmed myself in the utmost possible way and why and why.

But still: a minute yet strong circumstance comes back to my mind:

When I first seized the bird in the corner in my gloved hand while being careful not to injure it more seriously it squeaked – under the effect of a greater terror than the one which prompted it to keep deadly silent. Or else as if it had responded to the call of my hand, or as if it had cried: I am alive still.

It squeaked. And with this cry it became somebody. What if he had not hurled this brief sound?

Would I have carried him away to the balcony with a leap, would I have set him down nimbly in the rose tub? As one sets down a slightly injured bird. Would I have believed returning him to the celestial world? He stays motionless in the tub. Mycat is already all joy and astonishment. I toss him over the balcony.

Cross-examination

How to justify this? How did I justify it? Did I want to save the bird? 'Did you want to save the bird?' 'No. Ah, if only he had been already dead! If only mycat hadn't invited me to share what is joy to her. If she hadn't trusted me.'

'Ah, if only it had been too late.'

'I didn't want to be the witness.'

'I didn't want to see with two sights my cat's and mine. My two sights are out of tune.'

The two actors paused for a moment, one lying on its back did not breathe did not breathe. It was playing possum to perfection. The other was watching kneeling motionless with her eyes plunged in the dream of this forever lasting moment which was to last forever. Suspended in silent communion in the fateful wake they were thinking. Each was thinking: life, death space, life: death space, life death: space. The cat's thought was ambling noiselessly until the end . . . The bird was not surrendering to despair. Stiff as if dead it was struggling with its last strengths.

A. 'You killed it?'

H. 'I killed her. I killed. Not the one you think.'

Demicat that I am, human all too human.

Translated by Laurent Milesi

Chapter 2

Swans of Life (External Provocations and Autobiographical Flights That Teach Us How to Read)

Sarah Wood

We begin to follow in the first hours and days – the 'sensitive' or 'critical' period – on the shore, beside a glimmering lake, not far from a putrid marsh, at the Margins of Philosophy – where the first thing we see, or hear, is a communication on the nature of signatures.[1] It moves off and we follow, moving off from the thought of moving off, before we know what or who we are following, even before we know what or who we are.[2] Onward! Each step is a sign of life; each step follows a sign showing the way Out:

> By definition a written signature implies the actual or empirical nonpresence of the signer. But, it will be said, it also marks and retains his having-been-present in a past now, which will remain a future now, and therefore in a now in general, in the transcendental form of nowness [*maintenance*]. This general *maintenance* is somehow inscribed, stapled to present punctuality, always evident and always singular, in the form of the signature. This is the enigmatic originality of every paraph.[3]

Not-thereness plus nowness: I look for it in the singular strokes and loops of orthography, every last flourish of handwriting reminds me of the movement of living thought, which I follow when I read, dreaming all the while of recognising the 'enigmatic originality' of a writing that would be *someone's* writing, a dream that keeps me here today, lost in a fictive 'now' – for this is a text of many times and hands, where I wait for the countersignature that follows me to find me here, in the first hours and days, like a cygnet (do you see?) a bird of the family Anatidae, newly hatched and catching sight of something moving before me, which I follow, love, seek to become, attach myself to and which provides the model for future attachments in which I seek that contingent First Mover, the Not-Yet-Known.

   You take me just a word away from the word I have been given to give to you, aside into a new scene that holds the word hidden as a hand might hold a tiny feather, a little piece of memorabilia that magically turns pen and writes the world. *Swan*, I said and you wrote: 'My words were: white, lake, grasses. And my passage: The train passes the tall grasses on the lake and out of the window I see the swans amongst them. Many, many swans. But I'm seeing them now from the other side, as the train is passing over there, behind the swans, as I'm walking down by the river.'[4] And you wrote: 'Proust, glide, transformation. *Glide* was the word I settled on. The scene: John Ashbery is writing a poem. And he hands over to Marcel Proust.'[5] And you wrote: 'Proust, white and Queen. The word that I chose was *Queen* and my sentence was: Holding a sword above her crown, Her Majesty attempts to save all the swans. Her attire isn't suited to such adventure.'[6] And you wrote: 'My swan word was *white*. The scene was something along these lines: White wet light / Spain / My bedroom there / Smells of washing powder / Smells of sweat.'[7] Later, you wrote about the swan himself:

> The landscape is a foreign language. The swans are mute. I know that in retrospect, mute swans, a specie. Someone else I know is writing about swans. I imagine the crystalline beauty of the thought she will bring to her words in a piece I will eventually see. I would have liked to have tagged the one I watched three days ago, the preenery of his long neck, his grooming beak. When he undulates his long white neck, it seems an obscenity. His head underwater, pulled out, water dripping from his beak like a strand of saliva. From the bridge above him it is possible to see what he eats from the clear water, the arguments he pulls out, the shape of worms, or weed. From the bench it is possible only to see his absorption, self- I would add before it if I knew Swan had a sense of self. I wanted to strip away all associations, lake, song, Leda, see nothing but bird, feather, S-shaped neck like a stammer or a place where hands can be wrung. I wanted to regard purely the gluttony of his self-regard, his imperturbability. Before the picture-perfect picture was this, the original, circumvented by mallard ducks and smaller cheekier birds, diving like arrows, headfirst. Abandon versus regalia. A parade unto himself.[8]

This desire to strip away all associations, the wish for *nothing but this bird*, the complex desire for the narcissism of the other animal, for pure impure uninterrupted Swan, *this* one, emerges as a movement of writing that necessarily evokes the repeatable (language, thought, specie). Writing harbours a desire to escape its own forms: the desire for the first and only, the one and only, 'an absolute reduction of the text, or even of articulated language, in a quest for something absolutely unrepeatable'.[9] The desire brings with it the recollection of what it would like to forget. To reduce the text to a cry, to see the swan one sees, it is already necessary to be reading and writing. But in Derrida's work, Geoffrey Bennington resumes, the point is not 'to disapprove of or attempt to destroy this type of desire, which we cannot but share [...] for it is desire itself, but to show how this desire is possible only to the extent of the radical impossibility of its accomplishment'.[10]

§

Far off, and departing from us like an ideal taking flight before undeniable reality, a swan. The swan I had hoped to write vanishes from the scene the moment it opens. I'm left with other people's swans to begin with, and one of them, to my mind perhaps the best one, is not even in the form of a swan. It's a crypto-swan, a nothing-like-a-swan, rarer even than that creature Kant says a friend with whom a secret can be trusted is as rare as, a black swan.[11] But it moves like a swan, so I am sticking by it, which is likely to be difficult because as I said just now, a swan departs, leaving me to follow on as best I can.

Before that one, another – it's becoming impossible to count them – direct from Barry MacSweeney: a MacSwan. It arrives via Pearl, his girl, his friend, his pupil and teacher, his poem or cycle *Pearl*, which is not his to begin with, but by the medieval writer we now know as the Pearl-Poet, to whom it, or she, the 'peerless' Pearl, was given, or returned, in a dream.[12] Pearl says – although she can't speak, having a cleft palate and being a dumb poem into the bargain – she says, MacSweeney writes, silently through or up from the paper's depths: 'I am just a common white swan. / Fierce am I when I want . . .'[13]

The common Mute Swan, *Cygnus olor*, has according to *Encylopaedia Brittannica*, a 'pugnacious disposition' and 'poses a threat to other waterfowl'.[14] And MacSweeney's friend Pearl is that kind of swan: she comes back at Kant like a real ordinary unfriendly bird. She is not a brother. For Kant, Derrida points out, the exceptional secret-keeping friend is going to be a brother.[15] She's a complete swan: don't idealise or patronise her, she can break your arm. Worse – she can dream your death, to guard language from despoliation and appropriation by bureaucrats, hacks, politicians, academics and other would-be layers-down-of-the-law. MacSweeney is a guardian of language,[16] and he writes at her dictation in a dream:

> There is so much wickedness.
> They want to tax my ABC, they want to jail my tongue.
> I dream their high-up heather deaths
> Though I do not emit articulate sound.
> I am just a common white swan.[17]

Pearl is a danger to those who, one way or another, would domesticate her speech.

Now follows the swan that does not look like one. It's in the form of a quotation and it concerns the taking flight of the present, its inaugural quality that departs and moves off discontinuously without being accompanied by what had seemed to be its indispensable context. Derrida speaks of this taking flight without script, here and now as if for the first time, in 1974: 'now here [*ici maintenant*] is right away a singularity I would like to insist on, rather than on what I have written and which is a little bit somewhere else, somewhere else for me, somewhere else for others'.[18] They ask Derrida about what he has written and he wants to start from now, from the scratch of now. He improvises the better to follow on.

On. Another scene: Aeschylus's *Agamemnon*, and another feminine swan rebel who sings rather than speaks. Cassandra lies dead in Agamemnon's palace in Argos. Clytemnestra points to her body: 'here is the prisoner and prophet [. . .] Who so recently sang like a swan.'[19] Cassandra's speech before dying is the earliest recorded swan song in Western culture. In it she laments her own death and truthfully describes the tragedy going on around her, including what lies ahead. The Chorus who are there with her don't entirely follow what she says, only believing the part they already know, but it's obvious what she is talking about, once you know the story. She foresees murder and revenge in the house of the Atreidae, but what she announces partly escapes those who are with her in the play. She is alone: the paradoxical condition for the strongest identifications. The Chorus sees her as an animal, 'like a hound, / Sniffing out murders', but they don't want to know what she has found: 'we are not looking for prophecies'.[20] She continues her song but they receive only a vague fear, not the strange knowledge the song might contain. This is not simply the Chorus's failing – Apollo gave Cassandra the gift of genuine prophecy, but when she would not become his lover, he declared that her words would not be believed. She is destined to be impossible to follow, she must carry those she addresses over uncrossable distances, like a poet, or as a parent swan makes room for her young on her back. The Chorus says Cassandra is crazy, too lyrical: 'You cry out for yourself / A tune without tune, like the shrill nightingale's / Insatiable cry.'[21] It's true: 'It is difficult to get the news from poems.'[22] This difficulty is not just to do with cognitive complexity or aesthetic distance but something worse. It involves going without an alibi, in order to speak in a world where speech is jailed. Cassandra's first words in the *Agamemnon* are not words but a strange cry to the absent Apollo: 'ὀτοτοτοῖ πόποι δᾶ. Ὤπολλον Ὤπολλον' or '*otototoi popoi da/ opollon opollon*'.[23] The language is not Greek, nor the language of Troy: it is untranslatable. It is too soon to say that Cassandra's exclamations are not articulate sound: their meaning has not reached us yet. Perhaps she is speaking Swan.

We are following swans. It is difficult to believe: we have to glide, I have to hand over to the other. There was the one we saw last summer behind the gallery, in a dead-end off Regent's Canal. She was fierce, making room for herself and her young. She had no patience with the coots or the moorhens. She spoke to my heart, I became her for a moment, returning to myself with a kind of countersigning surprise at how threateningly swan I might be when I want, but it's still true to say that if I want to follow an animal in deconstruction, I must go on an adventure of reading. The things I read happen to me too. I head somewhere else: into the letter-thicket of a text, across its plains. I suddenly find myself on a lone shore, in a flooded Fen, in an enemy palace, in another language or no language at all – with 'ὀτοτοτοῖ πόποι δᾶ' or Pearl's 'a-a-a-a-a-a-a-', 'a-a-a-a-a', 'a-a-a-a-a-' and 'a-a-a-a-a-'.[24] I circle back, remembering, waiting for signs of life. I am 'thrown out on the roads and in the fields'[25] where poems are found, or *in the outside*, as if I were dreaming. And if what comes to me, comes in this surprising and dreamlike fashion, then it is surely a risk to rely on it in a rational argument. The approach must have changed. Perhaps this is the neighbourhood of *khōra*?

It is difficult to say for certain because Plato tells us that *khōra* comes 'as in a dream' and this way of appearing, Derrida points out, 'could just as well deprive it of lucidity as confer upon it a power of divination'.[26] Plato's text brings thought towards the origin of space and time, the unrepresentable birth of relation and difference. He directly insists that *khōra* must be 'apprehended without the senses by a sort of bastard reasoning [*logismō nothō*] and so is hard to believe in'.[27] Derrida recaps: 'by the *ontological logos* which lays down the law in the *Timaeus*: *khōra* is neither sensible nor intelligible'.[28] In the language of the Saussurean sign-system, which Derrida has done so much to shake up, *khōra* is something other than a signified, because it is not a rationally intelligible concept, and neither is it a referent, because it is not a material reality available to the senses. And if *khōra* is neither of these, the word *khōra* is not a signifier either – because a signifier should be accompanied by its signified, its concept, or should refer to something materially present. Deconstruction reveals again and again that the sign 'has always been thought on the basis of [the] distinction between the sensible and the intelligible, and cannot be thought of otherwise'.[29] And a troubling of the sign affects Plato's text, where according to Derrida, 'the discourse on *khōra*, as it is *presented*, does not proceed from natural or legitimate *logos*, but rather from a hybrid, bastard or even corrupted reasoning'.

And this *khōra* that there is no reasonable way to speak about is the name of what or who makes room, the room that is needed, taken by the unstoppable as it advances.

At the end of the second section of his text 'Khōra', about half-way through, Derrida addresses her by name. (The essay I am writing is to be presented in a book called *The Animal Question in Deconstruction*, but to whom do we imagine this 'animal question' being addressed and how? How do I know that I am not writing, now, to the animal that you also are, using such resources as I can find to do so, without knowing in advance who you are or what old facilitations I might be following?) Poets do not hesitate to address animals, especially birds. Philosophers and scholars would not usually dare. Derrida speaks to *Khōra* using the intimate form *tu*, as if she were someone, perhaps a woman, and as if by addressing her he might find her, find 'its/her [*sa*] place, which is not just a place among others, but perhaps place itself, the irreplaceable place'.[30] He asks 'Who are you, *Khōra*?' and this address is a way of following, seeking or desiring her, in her singularity. He goes on, when other ways of knowing her or describing it are exhausted.

I would like to reason on the dream and on what it gives us to think. But it comes to me in such a strange way that it escapes me: the dream itself does not think, it produces an image of thought, a fake coherence by virtue of the secondary revision that organises it into a narrative, more or less.[31] It has a spurious or bastard quality in relation to thought. Freud insists on the enigmatic originality of dream language and Derrida relaunches the interpretation of dreams as dream-writing. He is the dream reader of Freud, who:

> makes of psychical writing so originary a production that the writing we believe to be designated by a proper sense of the word – a script which is coded and visible "in the world" would only be a metaphor of psychical writing. This writing, for example the kind we find in dreams which "follow old facilitations," a simple moment in a regression towards a "primary" writing, cannot be read in terms of any code. It works, no doubt, with a mass of elements which have been codified in the course of an individual or collective history. But in its operations, lexicon, and syntax a purely idiomatic residue is irreducible and is made to bear the burden or interpretation in the communication between unconsciousnesses. The dreamer invents his own grammar.[32]

This singularity of the dream and psychical writing might just as well mean that it is not a language at all and does not mean much to anyone, as be the sign of its divinatory force. Dream-writing draws on memories of sensory impressions rather than on direct sensory experience to put together its rebus-like sentences. I dream of a swan. But what have I dreamed of? Does it exist? It seems, like the thought of *khōra*, 'somehow necessary', as if it 'must be' that there is a place that provides room for it, that there is space, there is some *khōra* for it, for *khōra*, swan, whatever.[33] Having identified the necessity of place itself Plato's text moves on to describe the beginning of the cosmos in primitive chaos. *Khōra*, the nurse of becoming, moved with a motion transmitted from the elemental forces that were her contents, and also passed her own movement on to them. It was a shaking. Water, fire, earth and air 'were in a constant process of movement and separation, [...] the four basic constituents were shaken by the receptacle, which acted as a kind of shaking implement'.[34] The Greek word for these sieves or riddles is σειόμενα, *seiomena*. Derrida later commented on this movement:

> There is in the *Timaeus* a figural allusion which I do not know how to interpret and which nevertheless seems to me decisive. It refers to the movement, the shaking (*seiesthai, seien, seiomena*), the tremor in the course of which a selection of the forces or seeds take place: a sorting, a filtering in the very place where, nevertheless, the place remains impassable, indeterminate, amorphous, etc.[35]

This shaking recurs in different modes throughout Derrida's work, picked up in various ways: there is the *ébranlement* starting up like an engine in *Writing and Difference*, the little jerks of *Glas*, the differential vibrations of speech and sexuality in 'Dialanguages', and all the implicit–explicit pursuit of resonance and sound-vibration in these texts and others, for example 'Tympan', not forgetting the existential trembling in *The Gift of Death*.

Derrida wanted to put a lyre/sieve in the park at La Villette, because (I think) he knew we are animals who sometimes need to shake, to be shaken from inside, to *sort ourselves out*. We need reminders to sense ourselves in ways both intense and subtle. His practices of reading, thinking, speaking and writing resonate with those of psychotherapists like Peter Levine who remember that we are also animals, and who attend to 'the dynamic balance between the most primitive and most evolved/refined parts of the brain' in order to allow 'trauma to be resolved and difficult emotions to be integrated and transformed'.[36] In traumatic fear one freezes, then shakes it off. If the immobilisation is prolonged and the shaking-off prevented, the freezing becomes associated with dread and helplessness. One begins to fear one's own reactions. Thought needs to avow fear not to be stopped by it. Fear cannot be stopped, no more than love, and least of all by thinking. The part of the brain devoted to these connections between our archaic and sophisticated selves is the insula, which according to Levine 'receives input from the internal structures of the body, including the muscles, joints and viscera. Together, insula and cingulate help us make sense of these primitive sensations by weaving them into nuanced feelings, perceptions and cognitions.' Deconstruction, also, goes deep into the islands of the brain where the body talks to itself. It partakes, we partake, in the shaking and perpetual metamorphosis of *khōra*, which 'has not for its own even that substance for which it came into being, but fleets ever as a phantom of something else'.[37] Plato can't hold it; it launches thought and we're off. Faster and more faithfully, everything moves. In dreams too everything is moving. The dream beguiles the dreamer, who is at the same time everywhere in the dream. You might be anywhere, you might be water, shore, bird, the rhythm of an event, the relation of elements of a scene, a sentence or a word, a word away from a word, or the field of possibility this relation may open. Sign, signature, cygnet? We do not know what is interpretable and what is not, what is psychic machine, what is mere remnant, what is precious. Even 'no' loses itself.[38] Something has befallen signification.

If I am everywhere, I dimly realise, not even half awake, where am I? What am I? Who? An owl answers. The owl and the swan are unclean birds, according to the Bible.[39] Who? There is more than one owl. What mimic hootings come and go across the night lake? I am a boy again, as often happens when I hang out with the poets. In this scene I am all child, anticipation, memory and necessarily somewhat owl. I do not move but stand alone. I quote-hoot, calling and waiting. When I do this, am I reading, or writing? Am I third or first person, what grammar must I invent to let it happen?

> There was a Boy – ye knew him well, ye rocks
> And islands of Winander, and ye green
> Peninsulas of Esthwaite – many a time
> [   ] when the stars began
> To move along the edges of the hills,
> Rising or setting, would he stand alone
> Beneath the trees or by the glimmering lakes
> And through his fingers woven in one close knot
> Blow mimic hootings to the silent owls,
> And bid them answer him. And they would shout
> Across the wat'ry vale, and shout again,
> Responsive to my call, – with tremulous sobs
> And long halloos, and screams, and echoes loud
> Redoubled and redoubled – a wild scene
> Of mirth and jocund din! And, when it chanced
> That pauses of deep silence mocked my skill,
> Then often in that silence, while I hung
> Listening, a sudden shock of mild surprize
> Has carried far into my heart the voice
> Of mountain-torrents; or the visible scene

> Would enter unawares into my mind
> With all its solemn imagery, its rocks,
> Its woods, and that uncertain heaven, received
> Into the bosom of the steady lake.[40]

Listening becomes very important, and poetry, when you realise that perhaps your signal will not be returned, even by yourself, that there is such a thing as silence, and there are such things as space and time, often code-named Separation and the End. But also, here the very rocks and islands are capable of recognition and familiarity. Nothing is simply inanimate. Listening is a receiving and a kind of following and to read is to hang and listen, to hang listening, to hang on the silence in the wild scene of dream, pausing to await the call, words or gestures of another.

Through all this, thought does not stop. But it has to follow something else. Something shakes the signifier, there is a tremor in the course of which a selection of forces or seeds takes place, and thanks to this a reinvention of the signified becomes possible. The articulation of an otherwise inconceivable concept can only be brought about by a work that does not think. This movement is what it takes to dream, to write, to think and we are all capable of it. But who, here among the hierarchies of knowledge and stultifying explanations, will bear witness to the fact that humans, willingly or not, knowingly or not, are capable of augury? Who are the teachers? Where are the prophets – the people we do not already know how to hear?

§

I return to swans and poets. The Poet in *Alastor* is led by a strong impulse to follow and to become a swan – the animal that escapes him on strong wings that he does not have. Like the Boy of Winander he stops a moment by the water:

> upon the lone Chorasmian shore
> He paused, a wide and melancholy waste
> Of putrid marshes. A strong impulse urged
> His steps to the sea-shore. A swan was there,
> Beside a sluggish stream among the reeds.
> It rose as he approached, and with strong wings
> Scaling the upward sky, bent its bright course
> High over the immeasurable main.
> His eyes pursued its flight.[41]

'A swan was there': where is Shelley's 'there'? Where do you go when you read, or write? To what chasm, chaos, orgasm, magic-origami, *khōra*, or Chorasmian shore? The text leaves me behind. It takes off without me, like a bird. Hélène Cixous, mightiest and fastest living thinker of writing, describes how the 'language of writing' arises like a bird from the formation of letters by her hand on paper: 'the text needs the paper. It is in contact with the sheet of paper that sentences emerge. As if coming out with great wing strokes from a nest hidden beneath the paper. Maybe the sheet of paper is Khora?'[42] It is a different kind of brain-work. Cixous writes to Derrida about how he makes French

> capable of every kind of mobility in the world, that of the bird, that of the feline, that of the ant, that of the poem, that of Time, that of the unconscious, you initiated by Gide (J.D.) me at Joyce (James?) that of the Swan, which is to say of the *Cygne*, which is to say of the Sign[43]

whereupon she launches into an unpunctuated reading-writing of Mallarmé's sonnet beginning '*Le vierge, le vivace et le bel aujourd'hui*', making heard in the intoxicated blow of a swan's wing (the *coup d'aile ivre*), the force of reading and writing (*coup des livres*) and the strange *delivery* of a reading-writing which sets free and sets down in the same movement, at the same blow. Derrida moves like this alarming Mallarméan Swan and the movement of his writing somehow also archives all iced-up flights not flown. One line of Cixous's strikes me like a living hand, like a swan manifesto for reading: '*Lire pour délivrer d'un coup d'aile, d'un coup d'elle ivre le transparent glacier des vols qui n'ont pas fui*', which Peggy Kamuf translates as 'To read in order to deliver with a beating of the wings, with a drunken blow by her, *d'un coup d'aile, d'un coup d'elle ivre*, the transparent glacier of the flights that have not flown' – Derrida's reading-writing initiates future breakings-free.[44] As readers of literature, critics and writers of research we do well to think about the custom of the swan, which is to sing joyously and prophesy at the point of departure. Cixous reminds us that deconstruction releases the library, enswans it, fills it with bird: 'Library, archive of stolen flights in flight but always ready should the ice be broken to take again to the air.'[45] We are not identical with our flights, there is more to us than what we are capable of. The poet who watches the swan is beginning to imagine his own end, which frees him of himself. Cixous has written about the writer's desire to live death – not to commit suicide, but to reach the point where curiosity is satisfied, to get to the end of life, and of the leaving of life that writing is.[46] Shelley finds this swan, a swanlike trust in something beyond thought, which cannot be known by the senses. In a trance of reading we recognise the swan as a sign: the iconic figure of a writing that rises up from the melancholy waste, and knows its way. Song, the work of the signifier, is absolutely integral to this kind of knowledge.

Swans are named for music. The word 'swan' comes from sounding and song-making, via an old Germanic agent-noun *swan-*, from the Indo-Germanic *swon-* or *swen-*, represented by Sanskrit *svánati*, meaning '(it) sounds', and the Latin *sonit* '(it) sounds, (*sonĕre*, later *sonāre*)', Irish *sennaim* 'I make music', Old English *geswin* 'melody, song', and *swinsian* 'to make melody' (*OED*). Poets divine and testify to the singing of the swan. Swans don't sing, if you are an ornithologist. They are generally mute, apart from some trumpeting, snorting, hissing, and the evocative beat of their wings. Even more than the lark or the nightingale, who do sing in natural reality, Shelley's soaring migrant knows how to return home. Not to a home like ours. It goes to a place too far, too high or too deep for us to reach. This quality appears in an English lyric swan-tradition where the swan leaves and cannot be followed.[47] Tradition is perhaps too strong a word; it's not as easily followed as the nightingale, but one might mention Sappho, and in her wake poems by Shelley, Tennyson and Yeats. Mortality is a predominant theme. Tennyson's swans, enviably, know how to die.[48] In time we have Yeats's nine-and-fifty with their clamorous wings, reminding the poet of his years. In the 'Wild Swans at Coole' the swans' remaining is also already a scattering and drift. And of course there is Yeats's Leda, the girl caught up and let drop by a swan. In 'Leda and the Swan' the bird never comes together into a whole image. The bird is the signing-power of time and history condensed and displaced: wings, feet, beak, strange heart – no sooner mastering the situation than away, indifferent, leaving her pregnant and guessing. The lonely Poet in *Alastor*, Tennyson's Tithonus, the ageing man by the streams of Coole, and the girl taken by surprise attack are left behind. The swan has sovereign timing that shatters chronology and synchrony, and provokes us to think about our own deaths. Writing has an unpunctual relation to the writer. It does not arrive or leave all at once. For example, it may be possible to write while not writing. Geoffrey Bennington comments that 'there is no real present moment of writing', so that the claim to presence in a signature, say at the end of a manuscript, entails a kind of fiction, when the signature 'pretends to gather up all the moments of the "enunciation" in the text into this single moment of meta-enunciation of the signature which closes the book for the writer and opens it for the reader'.[49] He adds that the writer's signature lags behind: 'does not accompany this text like the enunciation that is the lining of the speech, but follows it'. The other signs, and in his/her/its own time. The swan teaches us nothing but the power of the indifferent beak of the other (even of an other, earlier me-myself) to sign, and interruption as the condition and precondition of tradition and self-identity. The signature is 'in principle perfectly indifferent as to whether the signatory whose careful paraph is being imitated is still alive or not'.[50]

Virgil, Dante, Shakespeare are all called 'Swan'. The poet is a swan, we dimly feel. But to be a poet is to be other than a swan: painfully and desirously so. Everything remains to be read, including animals, especially including swans. This is as hard to believe in as something known in a dream. Addison's account of Sappho's leap from the Leucadian cliffs has a doubtful, madly wishful quality:

> Many who were present related that they saw her fall into the sea, from whence she never rose again; though there were others who affirmed that she never came to the bottom of her leap, but that she was changed into a swan as she fell, and that they saw her hovering in the air under that shape. But whether or no the whiteness and fluttering of her garments might not deceive those who looked upon her, or whether she might not really be metamorphosed into that musical and melancholy bird, is still a doubt among the Lesbians.[51]

Such a disappearance, metamorphosis or miraculous survival concerns place and spacing, which takes me back to what Plato says about *khōra*: 'we look at it indeed in a kind of dream and say that everything that exists must be somewhere and occupy some space, and that what is nowhere in heaven and earth is nothing at all'. *Khōra* is the precondition of somewhere and anywhere else. It is also, as we have seen, hard to believe in. Given this resistance to presence, following is a form of agency that makes absence and departure intelligible and sensible in relation to one's own movement. Following is the reception of a sense or referent that is not there. Any signature, Bennington responds to Derrida by writing, 'is only memory and the promise of a counter-signature', therefore 'no signature is really complete before the (counter) signature of the other, and Plato's signature, for example, is not yet finished'.[52] This following might look like *swanning*, in the post-war military slang sense of a 'swan' as 'an apparently aimless journey; an excursion made for reconnaissance or for pleasure' (OED). One puts oneself in the hands of memory and promise, imprintedness and improvisation.

§

Choreographer Luc Petton and his company Le Guetteur presented 'Swan' at the Theatre National de Chaillot in Paris in June 2012. They used Konrad Lorenz's research into imprinting to establish a relation between human dancers and birds. Michel Saint Jalme, the director of the zoo at the Jardin des Plantes, explained to the *New York Times*: 'if we take the eggs and incubate them artificially, they will bond to the first person they come into contact with'.⁵³ Then the cygnets accept the dancers, who continue to spend time with them and from there eventually swans and humans can improvise together on stage. They follow each other. Petton emphasises the importance of the beginning, the first hour of life, for this improbable relationship. For him 'Dance is life, all life is dance. *Les cygnes m'ont appris à faire attention. Et ils me disent: "Attention, je te vois. Chaque geste que tu fais est un cygne/signe"* (The swans taught me to be careful. And they said to me: "Look out, I see you. Each gesture you make is a swan/sign.")'⁵⁴ We are read by the other swan. To dance on 'the animal question' I have to think and practise writing differently. I rely on what Derrida calls 'the thought of the trace' and consequently on *flair*, his French word for readerly intuition, or more literally, the animal ability to follow a scent.⁵⁵ This kind of following amounts to an *experience*, a word that for Derrida 'evokes a space that is not given in advance but that opens as one advances'.⁵⁶

Following is the counter-movement to holding-on. Derrida's capacity to extend thought is accompanied by an interest in stopping, freezing and clinging. We cling like baby monkeys holding on to their mothers' fur; writing tears us away. Writing means unhooking, hanging-up, discontinuing and separation. It thereby becomes possible to think 'something like an active absence', and to cultivate awareness of 'what is not there and what should have been there'.⁵⁷ It follows that a traumatic decoupling follows every attempt to be 'in deconstruction', to hold fast to deconstruction, to take up the right threads, to perform a work that is in keeping with a disciple's devotion or sense of archaic belonging that exists only as trace. To read is to separate from where we are, to escape by following what escapes us, to hang listening, to give room to active absences.

It could be that we cling to the notion of readability in ourselves and others because of our animality, which is only revealed to us in fictive thinking of the kind performed by poets and psychoanalysts. We cling to the present, looking for confirmation of *maintenance*, but the present never holds us because we are out in it. It doesn't stop for us. Instead we dream ourselves. You 'dream' he says, 'it's unavoidable, about the invention of a language or a song that would be yours, not the attributes of a "self," rather the accentuated paraph, that is the musical signature of your most unreadable history'.⁵⁸ This signature remains a dream. There is no pure idiom, no private language, no return to 'a simian poetics of the reassuring maternal fur'.⁵⁹ You cannot write or speak without risking being a prophet, without announcing unwanted swans, without taking flight. This trauma is a freedom, as well as the beginning of affiliation. Derrida talked about it in 1976 when an interviewer asked a question about his writing and the different forms it had taken up to that point. He resisted retrospective summary and mentioned instead the singularity of the interview itself, 'this tape-recorded surprise', adding:

> Okay, you are going to think I am piling up the protocols in order to run away [*fuir*] from an impossible question. So running away [*fuir*] is a bad thing? And why is that? Does one have to be noble and brave? What if all the questions put to me about what I write came down to fleeing [*fuir*] what I write?[60]

§

Flight and *flair* return in *The Animal That I Therefore Am* where Derrida thinks about following and about what he is doing when he follows. He elaborates the animal movements of hunting or escape:

> What does "to be after" mean? The steps to be consistently followed will indeed have to resemble those of an animal seeking to find or seeking to escape. Do they not resemble the running of an animal that, finding its way on the basis of a scent or a noise [*au flair ou à l'ouïe*], goes back more than once over the same path to pick up the traces, either to sniff the traces of another [*flairer la trace d'un autre*] or to cover its own by adding to it, precisely as though it were that of another, picking up [*flairant*] the scent, therefore, of whatever on this track demonstrates to it that the trace is always that of another, demonstrating also that in following the consequence or direction of this double arrow (it is a matter of the scent [*il y va du flair*], and the scent one smells [*ce qu'on flaire*] is always the trace of another), the animal becomes inevitable, and before it, the *animot*.[61]

Derrida emphasises that the scent thus picked up is 'always that of another'. Just as the 'animal movement' that starts off his own writing 'seeks to appropriate what always comes, always, from an *external* provocation'.[62] There is something strangely animal at work in reading and writing as Derrida knows and practises them. It is alive but it's not here, a writing that breathes, in the original Latinate sense of animation, from *anima*, 'something breathing or blowing'. The etymology of 'animal' does not go back to anything human or animal, just a movement of air.[63] The *animot* is not, or not only, a living thing. It is quick and unreadable before it corresponds to or lines up under any heading, including what we ponder as 'life'. There is no theory of *flair*, no established critical or analytical language of scent and smell. It lets us sense something-other-than-language that is not part of the continuity of the natural. *Flair* depends on the interruption without which signification and meaning could not happen. The caesura, Derrida says, 'makes meaning [*sens*] emerge. It does not do so alone, of course; but without interruption – between letters, words, sentences, books – no signification could be awakened.'⁶⁴

§

The Animal That I Therefore Am puts autobiography under what Derrida calls the 'sign of life, of life in presence, the manifestation of life in presence'.⁶⁵ This passage repeats the phrase 'sign of life [*signe de vie*]' a number of times, and makes a strange invitation for us to imagine the animal Derrida is, or follows 'signing a declaration'. Repetition silently makes the sign *sign* strange, even designifies it a bit. In order to signify, life enters into the mechanics and automaticity of the nonliving.

> The auto-bio-graphical derives from the fact that the simple instance of the 'I' or of the *autos* can be posed as such only to the extent that it is a sign of life [*signe de vie*], even if the what, or who, male or female, that thereby gives this sign of life finds itself to have passed over to the side of death.⁶⁶

Even if 'it were to be already a dead thing [*un mort*] speaking', even if what speaks speaks thanks to a technique of reproduction, the question of the animal is the question of life and the living being. 'We are here analyzing this sign of life [*signe de vie*] within the very structure of the auto-position of the I or of ipseity' and this '*signe*' is of course in French a homonym for the actively absenting bird that interests me here.⁶⁷

In the context of a book like this one, a collection of essays aimed at students and teachers in universities as well as the general reader, we might wonder what happens to signs or swans of life in teaching, and in particular the teaching of texts and reading? They affect the notion of teaching, of teachable methods of reading and of the transmission of knowledge. Sometimes something that cannot be verified is necessarily part of what one wishes to understand or make understood. If I follow what I follow without ever losing track of the responsibilities customarily associated with pedagogy and pedagogic writing, I cannot teach my students to fly, as readers, on their own wings. A teacher should not only be responsible: consciously and conscientiously consistent, systematic, offering proofs, maintaining a unifying logic or an unbroken argument. There is no teaching without what Derrida calls 'the simple appearing of the "I" in general, the trace of this manifestation of self, this auto-representation as living present (thing), this autobiographical guarantee, even if such a tracing can give rise to fantasy and to nonrigorous philosophical interpretations'.⁶⁸ And this appearing of the 'I' in general may be accompanied by the disappearance of the animal, who has run away, flown, hidden itself, signing by declining all responsibility, as Derrida does when he follows himself, sets out to decipher himself and catch up with himself, saying: 'I respond no more, I no more answer for what I am saying. I reply that I am no longer responding.'⁶⁹ That's him gone then, is it?

There is no teaching without a teacher, whom we follow and to whom we are attached. And it is 'in no way contradictory' that the teacher be a dead man, woman or swan. Plato gives us one such scene, before the death of the teacher Socrates in the *Phaedo*. Socrates makes it clear that to follow swans is to follow prophets, and to overcome the mystifying effects of unavowed fear:

> Simmias! I'd certainly find it hard to convince other people that I don't regard my present lot as a misfortune, when I can't convince even you two, but you are afraid I'm more ill-humoured now than in my earlier life; you must, it seems, think I have a poorer power of prophecy than the swans, who when they realise they must die, then sing more fully and sweetly than they've ever sung before, for joy that they are departing into the presence of the god whose servants they are. Though indeed mankind, because of their own fear of death, malign the swans, and say that they sing their farewell song in distress, lamenting their death; they don't reflect that no bird sings when it is hungry or cold or suffering any other distress, not even the nightingale herself, nor the swallow, nor the hoopoe, birds that are reputed to sing lamentations from distress.⁷⁰ But, as I see it, neither they nor the swans sing in distress, but rather, I believe, belonging as they do to Apollo, they are prophetic birds with foreknowledge of the blessings of Hades, and therefore sing and rejoice more greatly on that day than ever before. Now I hold that I myself am a fellow-servant of the swans, consecrated to the same god, that I possess prophetic power from my master no less than theirs, and that I'm departing this life with as good cheer as they do.⁷¹

This cheerful departing can be read in terms of writing, and the going away from life to write, but also in terms of the 'scene of witnessing' Derrida associates with autobiography: 'Discharged of every onus of proof, pure autobiography authorises either veracity or mendacity, but always in accordance with a scene of witnessing, an "I am telling you the truth" without shame, bareback, naked and raw.'⁷² Like his counter-swan Cixous, Derrida witnesses writing: a corollary to Edmond Jabès's remark about him that it is 'Rare, very rare, to live writing with such intensity.'⁷³ And this teaches a certain fearlessness:

> when I write there is a feeling of necessity, something stronger than myself that demands that I must write as write. I have never renounced anything I have written because I have been afraid of certain consequences. Nothing intimidates me when I write.⁷⁴

We are only beginning to find out what that fearlessness makes possible. If you follow animals in deconstruction your research is likely to put you in the position of an *augur*. In ancient Rome augurs were soothsayers and diviners 'who sought knowledge of secret or future things by observing the flight and the cries of birds; [. . .] [L. prob from *avis*, bird]' (*Chambers*). Following animals and sensing signs of life brings reading to the point of guesswork or augury and writing is, according to Derrida, '*inaugural*, in a fresh sense of the word'.[75] Part of this fresh sense of the word 'inaugural' might concern the revival of its ancient reference to birds. I can only dream of proving this. To get to the starting place I had to improvise, flying by the seat of my writing-pants. Inaugural writing involves what already is, what comes to the writer, what they do not invent or decide but become able to read. And what already is, will, if one does not prevent it, rise up as a sign/*cygne*/swan:

> If writing is *inaugural* it is not because it creates, but because of a certain absolute freedom of speech, because of the freedom to bring forth the already-there as sign of the freedom to augur [*de faire surgir le déjà-là en son signe, de prendre ses augures*].[76]

This upsurge makes of language, and of everything that we can and cannot speak about, a prophetic instrument, which it always has been. All signs are free to lift themselves free of the language-system, to be read as signs of a life that is not mine, that is somewhere else, but that because of death, automaticity, repetition, I can also read. Deconstruction teaches us to take signs seriously – with lightness, on writing-wings, in sky-writing that comes from the earth, the engraved mark, the downcast look and the solitude of the poet on the departure of the swan.

Inauguration takes place afterwards and arrives as an experience of the departure of what will have been swans. This is true today. For we are living in an age when, according to Cixous, there is a 'diminishment of [. . .] signs', so that we find, she says:

less and less poetry
less and less angels
less and less birds
less and less women
less and less courage.[77]

To begin to make more of all these things, try thinking of a swan that is a sign or a sign that is a swan, taking to the air . . .

Notes

1. According to the *Dictionary of Animal Behaviour*: 'Many animals have periods of development when they are especially sensitive to particular

stimuli, especially those associated with their parents and siblings. During these sensitive phases of development certain types of learning, especially imprinting, are facilitated. Examples include language learning in humans and song learning in birds. [...] The sexual preferences of many birds are influenced by early experience, a phenomenon called *sexual imprinting*. [...] Hand-reared birds often become sexually imprinted upon people, and hand-reared mammals often develop special relationships with people.' ('Ontogeny', in *A Dictionary of Animal Behaviour*, ed. David McFarland [Oxford: Oxford University Press, 2006], Oxford Reference Online, http://www.oxfordreference.com/views/ENTRY.html?subview=Main&entry=t158.e274, accessed 23 July 2012).

2. A 'following response' is shown by lambs, ducks, goslings, cygnets and 'many precocial species, which can run around soon after birth. The juvenile initially shows a fairly indiscriminate attachment to moving objects. Thus ducklings (Anatidae) separated from their mother will follow a crude model duck, a slowly walking person, or even a cardboard box that is moved slowly away. Some stimuli are more effective than others in eliciting the following response. [...] In general, the more an animal forms an attachment to one object, the less it is interested in others. Attachment can be enhanced by food reward, or the reward of the mother's proximity. One natural function of imprinting is to learn the characteristics of the mother.' ('Imprinting', in McFarland, ed., *A Dictionary of Animal Behaviour*, http://www.oxfordreference.com/views/ENTRY.html?subview=Main&entry=t158.e209, accessed 23 July 2012).
3. Jacques Derrida, 'Signature Event Context', in *Margins of Philosophy*, trans. Alan Bass (Brighton: Harvester Press, 1982), p. 328.
4. Declan Wiffen, personal email 28 May 2012.
5. David Herd, personal email 26 May 2012.
6. Andrew Atherton, personal email 25 May 2012.
7. Ariane Mildenberg, personal email 19 June 2012.
8. Sampurna Chatterjee, 'Seventeenth of May', *A Hundred and One Days: In, Around and Away From Canterbury*, http://ahundredandonedays.wordpress.com, accessed 28 May 2012.
9. Geoffrey Bennington, 'Derridabase', in Geoffrey Bennington and Jacques Derrida, *Jacques Derrida*, trans. Geoffrey Bennington (Chicago: University of Chicago Press, 1993), p. 159.
10. Bennington, 'Derridabase', pp. 159–60.
11. Jacques Derrida, *Politics of Friendship*, trans. George Collins (London: Verso, 1997), pp. 257ff. He is discussing Kant's *Metaphysics of Morals*, trans. Mary Gregor (Cambridge: Cambridge University Press, 1991), pp. 261–4.
12. Jane Draycott, *Pearl: A Translation* (Manchester: Carcanet, 2011), p. 15. For the original, see *The Poems of the Pearl Manuscript*, ed. Malcolm Andrew and Ronald Waldron (Berkeley: University of California Press, 1978), pp. 53–110.
13. Barry MacSweeney, 'Sweet Jesus: Pearl's Prayer', in *Wolf Tongue: Selected Poems 1964–2000* (Tarset: Bloodaxe, 2003), p. 196.
14. 'Swan', *Encyclopaedia Brittanica*, XXI (Chicago and London: William Benton, 1962), p. 630.

15. Derrida, *Politics of Friendship*, p. 259.
16. 'For me, theory does not come before, to inspire, it does not precede, does not dictate, but rather it is a consequence of my text, which is at its origin philosophico-poetical, and it is a consequence in the form of a compromise or urgent necessity.' Hélène Cixous, 'Guardian of Language: Interview with Kathleen O'Grady', trans. Eric Prenowitz, *White Ink: Interviews on Sex, Text and Politics*, ed. Susan Sellers (Stocksfield: Acumen, 2008), p. 81.
17. MacSweeney, 'Sweet Jesus: Pearl's Prayer', p. 196.
18. Jacques Derrida, 'Between Brackets I', trans. Peggy Kamuf, *Points . . . Interviews, 1974–1994*, ed. Elisabeth Weber (Stanford: Stanford University Press, 1995), p. 10.
19. Aeschylus, *Agamemnon*, trans. Philip de May (Cambridge: Cambridge University Press, 2003), p. 107.
20. Aeschylus, *Agamemnon*, p. 85.
21. Aeschylus, *Agamemnon*, p. 87.
22. This line from William Carlos Williams's 'Asphodel, That Greeny Flower' gave the title to a conference at the University of Kent in May 2012, where a version of this essay was the keynote. Thanks to Matthew Carbery, Declan Wiffen and all those whose associations to 'swan' set the scene.
23. Aeschylus, *Agamemnon*, p. 85.
24. Barry MacSweeney, 'Mony Ryal Ray', 'No Buses to Damascus', 'Pearl Alone' and 'Dark Was The Night And Cold Was The Ground', in *Wolf Tongue*, pp. 200, 201, 205, 208.
25. Jacques Derrida, 'Che cos'è la poesia?', trans. Peggy Kamuf, in *A Derrida Reader: Between the Blinds*, ed. Peggy Kamuf (New York: Columbia University Press, 1991), p. 229.
26. Jacques Derrida, '*Khōra*', trans. Ian McLeod, in *On the Name*, ed. Tom Dutoit (Stanford: Stanford University Press, 1995), p. 90. He is quoting Plato, *Timaeus* 52b.
27. Plato, 'Timaeus', in *Timaeus. Critias. Cleitophon. Menexenus. Epistles*, trans. R.G. Bury, Loeb Classical Library (London: Harvard University Press, 2005), p. 123; *Timaeus and Critias*, trans. Desmond Lee (Harmondsworth: Penguin, 1977), p. 71. *Nothōs* when applied to animals means 'cross-breed', like the 'strange animal, half kitten, half lamb' in Kafka's 'A Cross-Breed [A Sport]', trans. Willa and Edwin Muir, in *The Complete Short Stories of Franz Kafka*, ed. Nahum Glatzer (London: Vintage, 1999), p. 426.
28. Derrida, '*Khōra*', p. 96.
29. Bennington, 'Derridabase', p. 27
30. Derrida, '*Khōra*', p. 111.
31. Sigmund Freud, *The Interpretation of Dreams*, trans. James Strachey et al., in *The Standard Edition of the Complete Psychological Works*, V (London: Hogarth Press, 1991), p. 490.
32. Jacques Derrida, 'Freud and the Scene of Writing', in *Writing and Difference*, trans. Alan Bass (London: Routledge, 2001), p. 262.
33. Plato, 'Timaeus', trans. Bury, p. 123; trans. Lee, p. 71.
34. Ibid., trans. Lee, p. 72.
35. Jacques Derrida, 'Why Peter Eisenmann Writes Such Good Books', trans. Sarah Whiting, in *Psyche: Inventions of the Other*, II, ed. Peggy Kamuf and Elizabeth Rottenberg (Stanford: Stanford University Press, 2008), p. 111.

36. Peter A. Levine, *In an Unspoken Voice: How the Body Releases Trauma and Restores Goodness* (Berkeley: North Atlantic Books, 2010), p. 71.
37. Plato, 'Timaeus', trans. Bury, p. 123.
38. See Freud, 'Negation', in *Standard Edition*, XIX, pp. 235–41, and 'Timaeus', trans. Bury, p. 123, where Plato makes it known that the reasonable idea that 'that which is neither on earth nor anywhere in the Heaven is nothing' fails to account for the logic-of-non-contradiction-defying *khōra*.
39. Hebrew *tinshemeth*, an unidentified bird forbidden to be eaten in Deut. 14.16, is translated as 'swan' in the King James Version but is thought unlikely to have been what we would recognise as a swan and could be a horned owl. In Lev. 9.30, KJV translates *tinshemeth* as 'mole'. For an advanced practice of mole-augury, see Nicholas Royle's essay in the present collection.
40. William Wordsworth, 'MS Drafts and Fragments, 1798–1804', in *The Prelude: 1799, 1805, 1850*, ed. Jonathan Wordsworth, M.H. Abrams and Stephen Gill (London: Norton, 1979), p. 492.
41. Percy Bysshe Shelley, 'Alastor; or the Spirit of Solitude', in *Shelley's Poetry and Prose*, ed. Donald Reiman and Neil Freistat (London: Norton, 2002), pp. 80–1, ll. 272–80.
42. Hélène Cixous, 'Writing Blind: Conversation with the Donkey', trans. Eric Prenowitz, in *Stigmata. Escaping Texts* (London: Routledge, 1998), p. 198.
43. Hélène Cixous, *Insister of Jacques Derrida*, trans. Peggy Kamuf (Stanford: Stanford University Press, 2007), pp. 48–9.
44. Hélène Cixous, *Insister á Jacques Derrida* (Paris: Éditions Galilée, 2006), p. 39; *Insister*, p. 48.
45. Ibid., p. 49.
46. Hélène Cixous, *Three Steps on the Ladder of Writing*, trans. Sarah Cornell and Susan Sellers (New York, Columbia University Press, 1993), p. 18.
47. It is also in the papers: 'Swans Disappear from Westgate Gardens', *Kent Messenger Extra*, 22 May 2012, p. 5.
48. See, for example, 'Tithonus' and 'The Dying Swan'. Catherine Maxwell patiently and brilliantly traces lines between Sappho, the first dying-disappearing lyric bird-woman, and her male inheritors in the English lyric tradition in *The Female Sublime from Milton to Swinburne: Bearing Blindness* (Manchester: Manchester University Press, 2001).
49. Bennington, 'Derridabase', pp. 153–4.
50. Ibid., p. 156.
51. Addison, *Spectator*, 27 November 1711, quoted in Maxwell, *Female Sublime*, p. 34.
52. Bennington, 'Derridabase', p. 164.
53. Amy Serafin, 'Humans Share Stage With Birds in "Swan"', *New York Times* supplement in the *Observer* newspaper, 24 June 2012, p. 8.
54. Luc Petton, online video 'Dancing with Swans' http://www.nytimes.com/video/2012/06/01/arts/dance/100000001582070/dancing-with-swans.html (accessed 5 February 2013).
55. Jacques Derrida, *De la grammatologie* (Paris: Minuit, 1967), p. 233; *Of Grammatology*, trans. Gayatri Chakravorty Spivak (Baltimore: Johns Hopkins University Press, 1976), p. 162. According to Imre Hermann, smelling in humans is 'simply a prominent sense-activity of searching',

while searching is an instinct paired with the instinct to cling. See Hermann, 'Clinging, Going-In-Search: A Contrasting Pair of Instincts and their Relation to Sadism and Masochism', trans. Margaret Nunberg and Frank R. Hartman, *Psychoanalytic Quarterly*, 45, 1976, p. 17.
56. Derrida, 'There is No *One* Narcissism', in Weber, ed. *Points . . . Interviews*, p. 207.
57. Derrida, 'Between Brackets I', p. 6.
58. Derrida, 'Unsealing ("the old new language")', in Weber, ed. *Points . . . Interviews*, p. 119.
59. Derrida, 'Between Brackets I', p. 9.
60. Ibid., pp. 10–11, 19.
61. Derrida, *L'Animal que donc je suis* (Paris: Galilée, 2006), p. 83; *The Animal That Therefore I Am*, trans. David Wills (New York: Fordham University Press, 2008), p. 55.
62. Derrida, 'A "Madness" Must Watch Over Thinking', in Weber, ed. *Points . . . Interviews*, p. 352.
63. 'Animal', in *Chambers Dictionary of Etymology*, ed. Robert K. Barnhart (Edinburgh: Chambers, 1988), pp. 35–6.
64. Derrida, 'Edmond Jabès and the Question of the Book', in *Writing and Difference*, p. 87.
65. Derrida, *Animal*, p. 56.
66. Ibid., p. 56.
67. A rich critical literature arises from the *signe/cygne* homophony. Richard E. Goodkin puts it like this: 'the swan's drama is essentially the drama of language itself', in *The Symbolist Home and the Tragic Home: Mallarmé and Oedipus* (Amsterdam and Philadelphia: John Benjamins, 1984), I, p. 85.
68. Derrida, *Animal*, p. 56.
69. Ibid.
70. Socrates distances himself from mythic tradition here, referring to the alleged metamorphoses of Procne, Philomel and Tereus.
71. *Phaedo*, trans. David Gallop (Oxford: Oxford University Press, 1993), p. 37.
72. Derrida, *Animal*, p. 57.
73. Edmond Jabès, 'The Moment After', trans. Rosmarie Waldrop, in *The Book of Margins* (Chicago: University of Chicago Press, 1993), p. 46.
74. *Derrida*, dir. Amy Ziering Kofman and Kirby Dick, Zeitgeist Films, 2002.
75. Derrida, 'Force and Signification', in *Writing and Difference*, p. 11.
76. Derrida, 'Force and Signification', p. 12; 'Force et signification', in *L'écriture et la différence* (Paris: Seuil, 1967), p. 23.
77. Cixous, *Three Steps*, p. 108.

Chapter 3

Love of the *Löwe*

Marie-Dominique Garnier

Man with mane

Lion-like, white-maned: two descriptions of Derrida, briefly sketched – a public image commonly attached to media-based portraits of the lionised philosopher, in the production notes to the 2002 documentary by Kirby Dick and Amy Ziering Kofman, in Natalia Avtonomova's cameo reminiscence of Derrida in Moscow 'defend[ing] Marx like a lion', and in countless press notes.[1]

Yet anyone familiar with the opening pages of *The Animal That Therefore I Am* will think twice before subscribing to a portrait of Derrida as a maned lion, white or not.[2] In the (twice) soundless opening scene of the book, cat-and-philosopher strike a strange acquaintance, in which Derrida's 'who am I?' remains repeatedly unanswered. It takes many quotation marks, and negative statements, to attempt to capture, to no avail, a feline: 'this cat that is perhaps not "my cat" or "my pussycat," does not appear here to represent, like an ambassador, the immense symbolic responsibility with which our culture has always charged the feline race'.[3] Stalking close behind the tail of the 'little' cat raises the question of naming – a name, Derrida adds, being what 'survives it'.[4] As if to protect the animal from the condition of its 'mortal existence', its name remains unsaid.[5]

As debatable as the leonine, value-based profiling of a philosopher might be, the question of precedence, of which animal shows up 'first' in the genealogy of Derrida's published texts, seems out of place. The 'original' 1962 version of Derrida's *Edmund Husserl's Origin of Geometry: An Introduction*[6] ranks first, but literally comes second, as John P. Leavey Jr notes:

> Derrida has an even earlier essay on Husserl, given at a conference in 1959, entitled 'Genèse et structure et la phénomènologie'. It was reprinted

in *L'Ecriture et la différence* in 1967 [...] but first appeared in 1965 in *Entretiens sur les notions de genèse et de structure* [...] This, then, is both before and after the work on the *Origin* [...].⁷

On the face, or faith, of a date, one animal can claim the status of first animal to be spotted in Derrida's corpus: the lion, a member of the 'feline race' as well as its 'ambassador' – or, rather than the lion, the 'word *Löwe*'.⁸ Bilingual, Derrida's 'first' animal-in-writing haunts the corpus as a word-animal, as an early *animot*.⁹

How far does the liminal occurrence of the 'word *Löwe*' stand from the limitrophic apparatus of the *animot*, the animal in relation to the word, to naming and appellation, developed at the other 'end' of the 'corpus', in *The Animal That Therefore I Am*? Limitrophy, to recall Derrida's exploration of 'another logic of the limit', thrives and thickens 'on the edges of a limit': it is 'what feeds the limit, generates it, raises it, and complicates it', its '*trophein*' having something to do with 'thickening, for example, in curdling milk'.¹⁰

In the limitrophic zone of Derrida's *Introduction* to Husserl's *Origin*, the 'word *Löwe*' looks in more than one direction: it is both *rere regardant*, intercepted by Derrida while following Husserl, who 'first' found it in Hegel (I will come back to the leonine concatenation); and yet looks far ahead, leaping more than a hop, skip and a jump forward in the region of the *animot*. As a semi-translated, chimerical assemblage (in which the animal is supposedly only named, mentioned and not 'used'), Derrida's '*mot* Löwe' in French produces a striking moment of non-translation: the occasion for an umlauted beast to rise from a text in translation.¹¹ Italicised, equipped with its hyper-visible diacritical mark, the '*Löwe*' literally stares from the page, gazing both backward and forward, preceding and closely following the opening scene of *The Animal That Therefore I Am* in which 'an animal looks at me'.¹²

At the other 'end' of the 'corpus' (every edge-related term here having to be set on edge, rendered fidgety about its own status and legitimacy), another lion guards the entrance to the second volume of *The Beast and the Sovereign* – a literary beast, excerpted from Defoe's *Robinson Crusoe*.¹³ Thus framed, kept between twin leonine figures, the 'body' of deconstruction would find itself monumentalised, caught in a parergonal articulation of feline effigies.

But on looking twice at each feline occurrence in or about the liminal moments in Derrida's writing, on looking closely, with particular insistence, at the apparent key, strategically positioned lions in Derrida's *Introduction* to Husserl's *Origin of Geometry* and *The Beast and the Sovereign*, one could affirm, contrariwise, that there is, in the 'entire' 'corpus' of Derridean writing, not a single lion: not a 'single' lion. Not a pard to be put apart, but merely 'limitrophic' lions, borderline creatures, always 'on edge', dovetailing with other species and occupying chimeric 'ground'. What follows follows the *Löwe* from a multiplicity of approaches, as a limitrophic creature for which there is no concept, no *Grundbegriff*: an animal which is itself a moment of densification and multiplicity-forming. By 'limitrophy' is understood what cannot be reduced to the linearity of a single limit, but triggers off a '*trophein*': a feeding, a sustenance, a nourishment.

How does a *Löwe* differ from a lion? How many animals find temporary residence in the thick, limitrophic mane of the 'word *Löwe*'? As a 'word', what parasites does it attract? A diverse phonematic fauna lodges in a *Löwe*'s clothing – a *loup*, a quasi-palindromic wolf, as well as, following close on the *Löwe*-as-wolf, a possible *louve*, the Cixousian second cousin of the *Löwe*, knocking at the door and asking wolfishly: what is the distance that separates the '*Löwe*' from 'love'? How do they 'differ'? How close is Cixous's *L'Amour du loup* to forming part of the Derridean 'corpus' – to being part of its anexact animal pack or pride?[14] How germane are the words *Löwe*/Wolf/Love, once reanimated, reani-maned, made to dance on the twofold tip of a German umlaut?

Articulated to the question of the 'word *Löwe*' as proto- or crypto-*animot* is the matter of names and naming, of the relation between the 'proper' name and the 'word' – a question addressed in the opening pages of *The Animal That Therefore I Am*, in which the 'word *word*' is taken to task:

> The letter counts, as does the question of the animal. The question of the animal response often has as its stakes the letter, the literality of a word, sometimes what the word *word* means literally.[15]

Taking the word and the act of 'lionising' to the letter, after its former, 'original' area of meaning and use, one finds that neither monumentalising nor empowering are involved in the (verbal) process. To lionise once meant, merely, to go and see the lions, to visit the places of interest, namely, to revisit the 'word *Löwe*' imported from Husserl, and the 'terrifying lion whose paw [. . .] will be offer[ed] to Robinson', from Defoe's novel.[16]

Faun, phoneme, phonemenology

Derrida's commentary on Husserl's fragment addresses the question of 'ideal objects' and 'ideal objectivity', with an implicit focus on a specific type of object, the literary object, given pride of place in Derrida's 1957 thesis topic. In 'Punctuations', Derrida recalls that it was, for him

> a matter of bending, more or less violently, the techniques of transcendental phenomenology to the needs of establishing a new theory of literature, of that very peculiar type of ideal object that is the literary object, a 'bound' ideality Husserl would have said, bound in so-called natural language [. . .][17]

Following Husserl's strategy, Derrida's commentary proceeds step by step, as a rigorous concatenation of statements threading through a series of reductions, finer degrees of freedom on the ladder of the 'objective'; while opening the door, on the other hand, to a number of disruptive elements, of abrupt, violent, 'bending' gestures, coincident with the 'textual anxiety' (*l'inquiétude du texte*) that Derrida sees operating in *The Origin*.[18] Enter the 'Löwe', in part V of Derrida's analysis, part of an extensive development leading, in the next section, to what Derrida calls a 'turnabout', an about-face in Husserl.[19]

Together with the 'word *Löwe*', what steps in or takes writing in its stride in those pages is a succession of footnotes thickly effervescing or 'curdling' writing, producing a literal, textual mane. In John P. Leavey's summary of the structure of Husserl's questioning emerges a clear account of Derrida's expository, gradual approach:

> In his comments, Derrida elaborates three degrees of ideal objectivity implicit in Husserl's analysis. First, there is the level of the word's ideal objectivity. The word 'lion', for instance, is recognizable within several languages, but is bound to those languages in which the word itself makes sense. Secondly, there is the level of the word's sense. The intended content or *signification* of the word 'lion' is available in many languages, for example, Leo, Löwe, lion, such that the ideality signified thereby is free "from all factual linguistic subjectivity" (71). Thirdly, there is the level of absolute ideal objectivity, such as the free idealities of geometry. The ideality in question here is that of "the object itself". On this level of objectivity, there is no adherence to any *de facto* language, only adherence to the possibility of language in general.[20]

Two facts seem to be played down in this precise rendering: first, the fact that there is no 'word Lion', but a 'word *Löwe*', a slightly different *animot* literally begging to differ. Second, Derrida's analysis of what threatens Husserlian logic becomes the object of a quick, easily dispensable note: 'However, as Derrida points out in a note [. . .], this ideality occurs and is discovered in a factual language, and this occurrence is "the crucial difficulty of all Husserl's philosophy of history [. . .]"'.[21] But what is elaborated in the space of six dense pages and as many lengthy notes is a complex limitrophic apparatus. Presented as a solitary, ideally objective example occurring 'only once',[22] the 'word

Löwe' paradoxically generates a pride of lions in the mixed habitat of Derrida's commentary and notes – with, in tow, the re-emergence of contingencies introduced by terms such as 'bound' and 'flesh'.[23] 'Flesh' occupies a strange middle ground between the two 'ends' of the 'word *Löwe*', between naming and animality, linking '*le lion en chair et en os*', the 'flesh and blood lion',[24] to, on the other hand, Husserl's wrestling with language: 'Ideality comes to its objectivity by means of language, through which it receives, so to speak, its linguistic flesh.'[25] 'Flesh', in turn, operates as a two-headed animal: Husserl always says that the linguistic or graphic body is a flesh, a proper body, or a spiritual corporality (*Geistige Leiblichkeit*).[26]

Husserl's 'linguistic flesh' reappears in what is both a remote corner and, with hindsight, a visible outpost in Derrida's volume – positioned on the margins, the limitrophy of the book, where it has remained out of translation's reach: on the blurb at the back of the book. Derrida's back-born(e) summary is alive with *animots* – slumbering words ready to pounce, once they leave dormancy:

> Condition et modèle d'une historicité infinie de l'Idée, de la Raison, de *l'animal rationale*, la science requiert la possibilité d'un langage univoque – et finalement l'écriture. Car l'analyse semble tourner autour d'une allusion elliptique: il faut inscrire dans l'espace cette chair linguistique sans laquelle il n'est pas d'objectivité idéale, donc pas de communauté rationnelle. Or la chance est une menace.

> Science, as the condition and blueprint of the infinite historicity of the Idea, of Reason, and of the *animal rationale*, requires the possibility of a univocal langage – and in the end of writing. Indeed, Husserl's analysis seems to be turning around the elliptical intimation that the linguistic flesh without which no objectivity, hence no rational community can exist, must be spatially inscribed. Which is felicitous as much as threatening.[27]

Derrida's '*allusion elliptique*' is itself elliptical: how close is it to geometry? To grammatology? Should it be read as an ellipsis or an ellipse? In the context of divided meanings, of a '*chance*' or good fortune that reverses into a 'chance', a threat, both are suitable candidates. As to the verb used to describe Husserl's stride or strategy, his obsessive, soft-footed '*tourner autour*', a *Löwe* seems to haunt it: the term reads both geometrically (to imply following an elliptical, revolving trajectory), and 'faunetically', as a word carrying a predatory charge, a prowling or roaming for prey. In the limitrophic density of that 'linguistic flesh', something can be read, or 'seen in advance', to borrow Husserl's strange forward-looking phrase.[28] In the space of two sentences, words seems to follow a declension pattern, to be set on a catachrestic course –

machined by a language processor set to translate 'science' into *'chance'*, the latter word a phonetic mutation of Husserl's *'chair'*.[29] In other words, the book's blurb takes a forward, blind course in the direction of *Mes Chances*, of its game of (chance) phonetic exchangeability or mis/translatability – in the fast-forward mode.[30] The prowling *animot* that haunts it belongs to the *Löwe* species – a spotted (visible, yet blind) beast whose 'linguistic flesh' or name contains, without containing, a twice-spotted elliptical letter.

The *Löwe* enters Derrida's introduction as a mongrel: chained to a French *'mot'*. Wielded as a verbal example of the distance between 'pure' signifier and mundane referent, the *Löwe* is mentioned (literally mentioned, not used) as Husserl's first ideal linguistic object:

> No doubt language is 'thoroughly made up of ideal objectivities; for example, the word *Löwe* [lion] occurs only once in the German language, it is identical throughout its innumerable utterances by any given persons.[31]

Two turns are taken by Derrida's analysis: first, a critical statement which follows Husserl's own hesitations, his awareness of the 'considerable difficulties' encountered in the search for 'this ultimate science of pure consciousness',[32] for which a univocity of expression remains to be invented. Second, a twofold detour via the notion of 'neutralisation', in which something refuses, twice, to be neutralised (or neutered) in Derrida's writing. Both the translation and the original French need to be quoted:

> Insofar as this ideal object *confronts language as such*, the latter supposes a spontaneous neutralization of the factual existence of the speaking subject, of words, and of the thing designated.
>
> Dans la mesure où c'est cet objet idéal *qui fait toujours face au langage* en tant que tel, celui-ci suppose donc une neutralisation spontanée de l'existence factice du sujet parlant du mot et de la chose désignée.[33]

The lion returns in the footnote:

> In the *Encyclopedia* (one of the few Hegelian works that Husserl seems to have read) the lion already testifies to this neutralization as an exemplary martyr: '*Confronting the name* – Lion – we no longer have any need either of an intuition of such an animal or even an image, but the name (when we understand it) is its simple and imageless representation; in the name we think.
>
> [...] dans l'Encyclopédie (un des rares ouvrages hegeliens que Husserl semble d'ailleurs avoir lus), le lion témoignait déjà, en martyr exemplaire, de

cette neutralisation: '*devant le nom* – Lion – nous n'avons plus besoin ni de l'intuition d'un tel animal, ni même de l'image, mais le nom, quand nous le comprenons, est la représentation simple et sans image, c'est dans le nom que nous pensons.[34]

'To confront', used both to translate Derrida's '*faire face*' and Hegel's '*devant*', somehow levels out or neutralises what could be approached as threatening signs of a 'faunemenology' at work in Derrida's hand. A moment of '*écriture*' or graphic disruption affects Derrida's approach to Husserl in his use of the phrase '*faire face*', which implies as much a facing as a giving-face, an envisaging as much as a 'visaging'. The 'ideal object' that 'faces language' wavers between the discourse of objectivity (based on the proxemics of standing face to face, object versus subject) and the chance, the threat of writing as a 'giving-face', or an 'about-face'. If language is 'faced', given a face, how ideal are its ideal objects? How long can a *Löwe*, once mentioned, keep from being 'used', from imposing the full usage of the double session of its graphic/phonetic energy?

Hegel's belief in the ability of language to neutralise existence is (humorously) given short shrift by Derrida, who compassionately (perhaps only half in jest) calls the lion 'an exemplary martyr' (the prototype of many more martyrs to come). Giving the lie, as it were, to Husserl and Hegel, the 'word *Löwe*' not only recurs much more than once, but increases, multiplies and mutates. One of its cubs or verbal offspring appears to address Husserl's *Ursprung* and to speak back, in what follows:

> Only within a facto-historical language is the noun '*Löwe*' free, and therefore ideal, compared with its sensible, phonetic, or graphic incarnations. But it remains essentially tied, as a German word, to a real spatiotemporality;
>
> C'est à l'intérieur d'une langue facto-historique que le nom '*Löwe*' est libre, donc idéal, au regard de ses incarnations sensibles, phonétiques ou graphiques. Mais il reste essentiellement *lié*, en tant que mot allemand, à une spatio-temporalité réale;[35]

While following close on Husserl, Derrida's reading/writing accomplishes a literal 'binding', inscribing in writing what links the lion-as-ideal object to the lion as impure verb, as faunetic offspring: transcribing a '*lion*' into a verbal liaison, into '*lions/lié*': binding; being bound; but also, bounding, taking a leap. A phonetic overlap operates the juncture, in French, between '*lion*' and '*lié*'.[36] This oblique, parasitic declension in Derrida's writing differs radically from what Husserl implied when promoting as an example 'the translatability of the word *lion*', or, a few paragraphs further, its impossibility:

> The flesh and blood lion, intended through two strata of idealities, is a natural, and therefore contingent, reality; as the perception of the immediately present sensible thing grounds idealities under those circumstances, so the contingency of the lion is going to reverberate in the ideality of the expression and in that of its sense. The translatability of the word lion, then, will not in principle be absolute and universal. It will be empirically conditioned by the contingent encounter in a receptive intuition of something like the lion.[37]

To what improbable species does Derrida's 'something-like-the-lion' belong? As mutations of Husserl's untranslatable *Löwe*, a number of partial, anexact, vague lions cross Derrida's introduction. Something 'like' the lion occurs in writing in the form of a '*lien*', which in English becomes, by a stroke of luck or 'chance', a '*bound* ideality'.[38] The reductive steps of Husserl's logic are rewritten into a series of 'bounds', of sidesteps or '*pas chassés*', releasing, beneath the voice of phenomenology, a strange continuo, the 'low', persistent, undertone of a *Löwe*. In the equivocation of the '*lien*/lion' an anexact tongue forms, a language resting on the type of equivocity Derrida sees encoded in Joyce, Husserl's unlikely double. Derrida's 'translation' of Husserl results in a partial suspension of translation, involving the stubborn return of an untranslated, twice-branded *Löwe*, and the stray production of an outgrowth of trans/lateral forms (lion/*lien*/*lié*, science/chance). Derrida's long digression describes a form of resistance to target/source translation, and the chance that a Joycean, cross-linguistic form of circulation might actualise phenomenology's desire for a shared horizon of 'free' idealities:

> Like Joyce, this endeavour would try to make the structural unity of all empirical culture appear in the generalised equivocation of a writing that, no longer translating one language into another on the basis of their common cores of sense, circulates throughout all languages at once, accumulates their energies, actualises their most secret consonances, discloses their furthermost common horizons, cultivates their associative syntheses instead of avoiding them, and rediscovers the poetic value of passivity [. . .] this writing resolutely settles itself *within* the *labyrinthian* field of culture 'bound' by its own equivocations.[39]

Towards the end of Husserl's fragment, 'binding' changes sides, to become one of the terms used to describe passivity, a key concept both in Husserl and in Derrida's introduction: 'Passivity in general is the realm of things that are bound together and melt into one another associatively.'[40] Derrida's introduction gives pride of place to the term, bringing up both 'the danger' of passivity, the inferior quality of 'the pure passivity of sensible receptivity', and the 'original presentive intuition (that of geometry, for example), which is both an activity and a passivity'.[41] A 'passive' voice is released, beneath the hypervisibility of an umlauted o, from the prolonged digraph of the weak/strong 'oe' in *Loewe*. And just how much of a lion haunts the abbreviated capitals of Husserl's *Logical Investigations*, the countless LI references in Leavey's translation? Whenever the 'question' of the animal surfaces, as Derrida notes, a letter counts.

How far from a 'name' is Derrida's 'word *Löwe*'? What is it, in an *animot*, that seeks to operate restlessly? How can one be sure, when naming a lion, that in the process the 'naming lion' does not respond?

Derrida's Nemean/naming lion

Derrida and Husserl's citational 'word *Löwe*' turns around an ellipsis – comparable to the 'ellipsis' Derrida sees operating, grammatically or geometrically, in 'The Origin of Geometry'. The question of 'naming' is first posed in an infra-paginal note (triggered off by the 'word *Löwe*' quotation), which marks what could be called one of Derrida's first encounters with Husserl. Beneath the surface of a name emerges the violence of a philosophical encounter involving, beyond naming, what could be termed a Nemean moment, if one agrees to hear a Greek place name beneath a name. The moment of naming the *Löwe* incorporates the forces at play in ancient Nemea, the site of Heracles' slaying of a lion whose hide was considered impenetrable to mortal weapons. Heracles' slaying of Nemea's chimeric beast hauntingly recurs in Derrida's own grappling with 'names' – with the snarling, roaring name of Husserl and with its lionised animal double ('*Löwe*'). Derrida's encounter with phenomenology involves a 'Nemean' or 'naming' battle, occurring at the level of an *animot*, a 'name', whose skin, if not penetrable, is amenable to the stroke of deconstruction. It is from 'within' Husserl's animalised name – the *Löwe* – that Derrida taps a non-semiotic, disseminating force, the same force used in Derrida' own signature '*déjà*', found in the footnote adjacent to the leonine quote.

'*Déjà*': Derrida's tmetic signature appears in the first footnote triggered off by the *Löwe*, a note introduced with the purpose of refusing Husserl any inaugural authority regarding language's capacity to neutralise existence. In this note, which occurs as the *Löwe*'s immediate offshoot or by-product, Derrida displaces and antedates the threshold of originarity and authority, back to Mallarmé, Valéry and Hegel. Quoted in support of this are Hegel's *System* of 1803–4 and the *Encyclopedia of The Philosophical Sciences*, both imported from Maurice Blanchot's *La Part du feu* and Jean Hyppolite's *Logique et Existence*. The lion-sprung footnote, in other words, operates as one of deconstruction's early moments, a moment endowed with the momentum of an animal or *animot*. Signed, that moment bears Derrida's abbreviated signature scent '*déjà*'. Both excerpts speculate on the neutralising force at work in nomination: 'In the *Encyclopedia* [...] the lion already testifies to this neutralization as an exemplary martyr.'[42] The originary gesture by which Adam gained mastery over the animals, according to Hegel, was to give them a name. As an early 'martyr', how close does Derrida's 'word *Löwe*' come to responding, to testifying in the name of martyrdom – in other words to finding a form of survival or living on? Martyred, silenced by Hegelian nomination, something in a Derridean *Löwe* resists both neutralisation and 'neutering'. From the refractory angle of this particular footnote emerges what could be approached as Derrida's non-Adamic gesture. Imperfectly named, named in more than one language, only partially translated yet actively and 'faunetically' present, the 'lion' becomes a mentioned-and-used, French-and-German '*mot Löwe*': an anexact animal, something-like-an-animal lying in wait at the outer/utter limits of nomination, on the periphery of naming, paradoxically ill-said, half-unsayable and yet hyper-written: marked with the double stroke of the twice bitten, or of what Hélène Cixous has called '*remords*' (both remorse and re-biting), in the title of *L'Amour du loup et autres remords*.[43]

One of the side-effects of the graphically active, bilingual, capitalised animal is to allow reading to cross the barrier between the common and the proper – to open the door to cross-species stratifications of the *Löwe/Loew* kind. As an early 'martyr', how close is Derrida's 'original' animal to the name of Rabbi Löwe, quoted and commented on by Paul Celan in *Shibboleth*? The Rabbi in Celan's poem '*Einem, der vor der Tür stand*' is a circumciser of 'words', words which, once cut, become 'opened', to quote Derrida's reading of Celan: 'Like a wound, you will say. Yes and no. Opened, first of all, like a door: opened to the stranger, to the other, to the neighbour, to the guest, to whomever.'[44] Out of the wounded, branded, martyr's 'name' of the lion-as-*Löwe* grows a nominal mane: a neighbouring, limitrophic series of 'guest' proper names. A leonine or leomorphic trail can be followed from Derrida's first reference to the name of the translator of Husserl's *Cartesian Meditations*, namely, Emmanuel Levinas, to the addressee of Husserl's letter of 11 March 1935, Lucien Lévy-Bruhl, a letter written shortly after Husserl had read Lévy-Bruhl's *La Mythologie primitive*. A key articulation in Derrida's philosophical positioning and in his institutional reception, Husserl's letter to Lévy-Bruhl has been the object, Derrida argues, of a mis-reading by Merleau-Ponty, whom he quotes at some length:

In a letter to Lévy-Bruhl which has been preserved, Husserl seems to admit that the facts go beyond what we imagine and that this point bears a real significance. It is as if the imagination, left to itself, is unable to represent the possibilities of existence which are realised in different cultures [...] [Husserl] saw that it is perhaps not possible for us, who live in certain historical conditions, to conceive of the historical possibility of these primitive men by a mere variation of the imagination.[45]

Drawing on Husserl's concept of *Einfühlung* or empathy, and on the transcendental horizon of historical humanities it allows for, Derrida dismisses the notion of non-historicity, as well as the alleged necessity to dislodge imagination in favour of a return to raw, primitive facts in order to accommodate 'primitive' mentalities. It is difficult not to sense in Merleau-Ponty's words an effect of supercilious detachment in drawing a line between 'us, who live in certain historical conditions' and 'these primitive men'. The passive voice of a *Löwe* in Derrida's *Introduction*, like the absent voices of Merleau-Ponty's 'primitive men', begs to differ. A mute manifestation of disagreement, somehow, makes itself heard in the very name 'Lévy-Bruhl', a name twice branded by the mark of the *Löwe*. If its first half sounds Hebrew in 'origin', its second half eerily emits the roar of 'something-like-the-lion' in German (*brüllen*: to roar). Derrida's response to Merleau-Ponty, too, roars back:

> We could then be tempted by an interpretation diametrically opposed to that of Merleau-Ponty and maintain that Husserl, far from opening the phenomenological parentheses to historical factuality under all its forms, leaves history more than ever outside them.[46]

Companion pieces to the 'primitive', silenced, martyred Hegelian *Löwe*, two proper names frame Derrida's *Introduction*: the names of Emmanuel Levinas and Lévy-Bruhl, two '*Loewe*' figures attached, by the etymology of a proper yet common Hebrew name, to the Hebrew tribe of Levi (a term which means 'attached', thus beckoning back to the *lion/ lien* liaison). Derrida's untranslated *Löwe* adds a limitrophic lining to the names of two philosophers, a foreign following as well as an animal doubling 'into the bargain'.

How much does phenomenology 'owe' to the lion, to borrow and deliberately mistranslate the phrase Derrida imports from Hegel's *Encyclopedia*, '*devant le lion*' ('confronting the name – Lion')?[47] How much does the (passive) voice of the 'word *Löwe*' resonate across its territory? A pride of lionising names forms in the tracks of Hegel, Husserl and Heidegger, in the trailing list of their commentators and followers' names: Jacob Loewenberg, Karl Löwith or James K. Lyon among others – in whose names 'something-like-the-lion' rather than a Hegelian 'we' ('in the name we think') thinks.⁴⁸ This erring, errant, leonine trail could be extended, perhaps, to include the name of Lacan's psychoanalyst Rudolf Loewenstein.⁴⁹ In writing, Lacan addressed him, for short, as '*mon cher Loew*',⁵⁰ cutting through the sonorous proper name, opening the name, like Rabbi Loew, to retain only its first syllable, to the effect of producing something which, with a marked French accent, might end up sounding like '*mon cher lov*'. Severed, Lacan's endearing form of address doubles a show of affection with a more threatening underside – the risk of a separation to come, foretelling perhaps the way Lacan would later put an abrupt end to his analysis with Loewenstein.

How close does the 'word *Löwe*' come to resembling a place name, the name of a city that was the occasion of Derrida's first travel abroad from Paris? The multilingual city happened to be Löwen, the German name of a Flemish city in Belgium, otherwise known as Leuven (Dutch) and Louvain (French). It was in Leuven–Louvain⁵¹ that Derrida's research on Husserl took place – that Derrida's early writing literally 'took' place, and that the 'word *Löwe*' began to invite itself in a philosophical 'introduction'. The city in which Derrida conducted his research in 1953–54 at the Husserl Archives, in preparation for his higher studies dissertation on 'the problem of genesis in the phenomenology of Husserl', was not only multilingual: it seemed to have been named after a pack of animals belonging to different species. Louvain, as a name, is literally chained to Husserlian studies – being, namely, the place where Herman Leo van Breda founded the Husserl Archives. From a foreign and familiar, uncouth and uncanny place name, something-like-a-lion seems to break loose, to follow escape routes – until it finds, years later, a temporary habitat in an unrelated but (faunetically) near cognate name: the name of the translator of Derrida's first book, John P. Leavey Jr, who signs the last page of his introduction as follows:

Louvain–Leuven John P. Leavey
December 1976.⁵²

Something like-the-lion haunts the name of a city, a name pliant enough to incorporate in its syllables an animal multiplicity – a '*loup*' or '*louve*', a she-wolf as much as a *Löwe*. The *Löwe/louve/wolf* trail leads to Hélène Cixous's 'Love of the Wolf' – in which the animal's limitrophic tongue is bound to and rebounds from the 'word *Löwe*', from its 'chance':

> We love the wolf. We love the love of the wolf. We love the fear of the wolf. We're afraid of the wolf: there is love in our fear. Fear is in love with the wolf. Fear loves. [. . .] We are full of trembling and ready to wolf down.⁵³

From the genetic margins of the two-headed *Löwe* a lion-cum-wolf escapes, to reappear, briefly, in the pages of Derrida's posthumous *The Beast and the Sovereign*, at the other 'end' of a corpus in which the animal 'responds'.

Law's paw

A lion's hunt is introduced in the opening seminar of 11 December 2002 in Volume II of *The Beast and the Sovereign*, after Daniel Defoe's *Robinson Crusoe*, in the context of the establishment of man's sovereignty and mastery 'over oneself, the slaves, the natives, and the animals' on the *tabula rasa* of a desert island. The quotation from Defoe is postponed to near the end of the seminar, after a series of steps through Rousseau, Marx, Joyce and Woolf. The 'archi-preliminary' text Derrida refers to (and refers his audience to) takes place before the arrival on the island: in the excerpt Xury, Robinson's first pledged subject, must kill a lion, Derrida explains, as proof and pledge of his subjection to Robinson:

> One archi-preliminary example: even before arriving at the island, and all the stories about the slave trade, there is the episode of the Moor thrown into the sea and of the young boy Xury [. . .] whom Robinson asks to pledge an oath of fidelity [. . .] This is almost immediately followed – I leave you to go and see – by the episode during which the first proof given by Xury will be to obey Robinson and go kill in dangerous circumstances a terrifying lion whose paw he will offer to Robinson – who skins it and keeps the skin, a huge skin put out to dry in the sun and on which Robinson later sleeps.[54]

Left to go and see the original, one finds a slightly different narrative. It is Robinson, not Xury, who shoots the lion dead after taking two shots, one of which hits only one leg, while the other is fatal.[55] Defoe's narrative insists on Xury's shying away from the act in fear, letting Robinson take control of the situation. Contrary to Derrida's summary, Xury refuses to go and 'kill in dangerous circumstances a terrifying lion', although such was the initial contract established by Robinson:

> 'You shall go on shore and kill him.' Xury looked frighted, and said, 'Me kill! He eat me at one mouth!' – one mouthful he meant. However, I said no more to the boy but bade him be still [. . .] I took the best aim I could with the first piece, to have shot him into the head, but he lay so, with his leg raised a little above his nose, that the slugs hit his leg above the knee and broke the bone. He started up, growling at first, but finding his leg broke, fell down again, and then got up upon three legs, and gave the greatest roar that ever I heard.

I was a little surprised that I had not hit him on the head [. . .]; however, I took the second piece immediately [. . .] and had the pleasure to see him drop, and make but little noise, but lie struggling for life. Then Xury took heart, and would have me let him go on shore and taking a little gun in one hand, swam to shore with the other hand, and coming close to the creature, put the muzzle of the piece to his ear, and shot him into the head again, which dispatched him quite [. . .] Xury said he would have some of him [. . .] However Xury could not cut off his head; but he cut off a foot, and brought it with him, and it was a monstrous great one.[56]

Derrida's variation on Defoe's story (attributing the actual killing, rather than the final touch of 'dispatching', to Xury) is the occasion for two slips of memory or shifts of attention in the act of reading/writing: Xury does not obey his master, but opts out; the master, not the slave, shoots the animal dead. In Derrida's postcolonial account, a subaltern 'boy' becomes fully empowered, made to attain a partial level of momentary sovereignty. In Defoe's writing, boy and beast are placed on a par in the killing scene, leaving the reader wondering, for a fraction of a second, which 'him' gets shot at. The equation between slave and animal also rests on the animalising term used to describe the end of Xury's small firearm or 'muzzle', the 'muzzle' Xury puts close to the dying lion's ear (in what could be replayed as a scene of cross-species 'bonding', a binding exchange, a non-contractual, affective *'lien'*).[57] Once cut off, the lion's 'foot' strangely revives, becoming, as it were, a foot-in-print.

But how dead is the animal, given the fact that the final trophy, the severed, 'monstrous great' foot, rests on exactly the same word assemblage as those enrolled to describe the 'dreadful monster', the 'terrible great lion' first sighted by Xury on shore, two pages earlier? What if a severed lion's paw, in the hand of Derrida–Xury, became the hand, or 'leg', of writing? – not quite dead, the 'monstrous' foot of an animal inviting itself to a seminar, writing back, the fellow of Heidegger's *Begriff* or concept, endowed with the grieving force of a separated, severed *'griffe'*.[58] Proof, as it were, that a *Löwe* is never quite dead, that the striking effect of its double punctuation is never quite put out, its 'monstrous' foot writes itself large, at large, in Derrida's seminar, in the double session of a slip of memory/reading.

Of the implicit academic contract behind the subject of the seminar, Derrida comments, in the opening words to the second session of 18 December 2002, that the 'rule of this game', no doubt 'a bit crazy', involves reading Heidegger's *Die Grundbegriffe der Metaphysik* along with Defoe. He recalls, too, in words similar to those used at the end of Volume I,[59] that the seminar's key words loom as a 'coat of arms', therefore bringing up, twice, the following heraldic metaphor: 'the beast and the sovereign are like the coat of arms of the seminar'.[60]

How metaphorical is Derrida's 'coat of arms'? In what attitude, in the heraldic sense, can a Derridean, modified lion's foot be emblazoned? The seminar's blazon, like Husserl's *Löwe*, is bound-to – both bound to 'life', to the facticity of contingencies, and bound to break free, to retract from the weight of metaphor – if only partially, in a clawing, cloying, cleaving way.

DeRRIda's RIS

Passing by, driving back and forth between hometown and workplace, Derrida's 'waking' hours must have brought him as close as one can imagine to an impossible event: sharing a coat of arms, donning a coat, or hide, capable of covering heterogeneous data, of projecting far enough to include a seminal, metaphorical 'coat of arms', a (mangled) lion's foot from *Robinson Crusoe*, and the actual city arms of Ris. Escutcheoned on the arms of Ris-Orangis (a city whose name is ready to release an audible, if partial, 'R-oR'), a totemic lion's foot sallies forth against a red field, a trophy torn off, as if smuggled from Defoe's book by Derrida–Xury (or the other way round). The beast once attached to that foot was without doubt a rampant one: standing erect with a forepaw raised against a blood-red background. Or, might one imagine that it once belonged to a lion *passant guardant*, or to a lion *sejant* erect? In heraldry, a lion's paw (or *gamb*) when cut off from a lion's body, as is the case in *Robinson Crusoe* and on the city arms of Ris-Orangis, is more correctly termed a *gamb* erased. When positioned crosswise, it is known as a *gamb* erect. On the city arms of Ris-Orangis, both erased and erect, a *Löwe* strikes twice. Both erect and erased, its protective shield officiates as an 'escutcheon', a term etymologically harking back to what is skinned, '*écorché*', torn apart.

Such is the force, too, of another semi-erased, raised *animot*: the '-ris'. A limitrophic 'ris', or '-ris', forms within/without the names of Derrida and Ris-Orangis, as it does in the latter half of one of the totemic animals found in Derrida/Cixous (a *sou-ris*, or mouse, to which I shall return briefly). The severed syllable is able to race, to run so fast that it can run to death and back, suspended, like a paw against a red field on a coat of arms, between what is erased and what is erect. Escaping from the tail end of a *souris*, a mouse found scampering across the shared landscapes and dreamscapes of Derrida and Cixous,[61] the 'Ris' of Derrida's hometown can give birth to various phonetic games. But round the corner of a

Figure 1 Coat of Arms of Ris-Orangis (Essone, France). Drawn by Wiki User Spedona for the Blazon Project of French-speaking Wikipedia

partial '-ris' an *animot* lies in wait, the same *animot* as that found hiding at the tail end of Derrida's posthumous line, and the sinister homecoming it implies: '*je vous souris d'où que je sois*'.[62] Neither the laugh of a Löwe nor the 'ris' of a *souris* can withhold from leaving their totemic traces on the exits and entrances of a corpus – from cutting their mobile, erased/erect leg or foot loose, free from the burden of legacy.

Detached from the Hegelian–Husserlian body of the 'word *Löwe*', or salvaged by Xury from the 'monstrous' creature on Robinson's island, the severed lion's paw has probably had more than a 'hand' in the writing of the body of deconstruction. That paw, or foot, came to the rescue of Derrida's other two, as he adds in a note to '*Geschlecht* II, Heidegger's Hand':

> One can write on the typewriter, as I have done, with three hands among three tongues.[63]

Notes

1. *Derrida*, dir. Kirby Dick and Amy Ziering Kofman, Zeitgeist Films, 2002; in the press kit, the production notes mention 'this incredible mane of hair': http://www.derridathemovie.com/ (accessed 5 February 2013); 'Tanned, white-maned, high-cheekboned, open-shirted': the words appear in Charles Trueheart's online article 'Paris: The Death of Derrida', http://theamericanscholar.org/paris-the-death-of-derrida/ (accessed 5 February 2013). See also http://www.ruedescartes.org/articles/2005-2-natalia-avtonomova/ (accessed 5 February 2013). Together with the process of lionisation must be brought up equally numerous mediatic and academic attempts at ignoring, misrepresenting and silencing.
2. Jacques Derrida, *The Animal That Therefore I Am*, ed. Marie-Louise Mallet, trans. David Wills (New York: Fordham University Press, 2008), esp. pp. 3–4.
3. Derrida, *Animal*, p. 9.
4. Ibid., p. 9.
5. Ibid., p. 9.
6. Jacques Derrida, *Edmund Husserl's Origin of Geometry: An Introduction*, trans. John P. Leavey Jr (Lincoln, NE, and London: University of Nebraska Press, 1978).
7. Leavey, 'Undecidables and Old Names', Preface to *Edmund Husserl's Origin*, p. 7, n. 2.
8. *Edmund Husserl's Origin*, p. 67 of Derrida's *Introduction*, p. 161 in Husserl's text.
9. Derrida, *Animal*, p. 23: 'The animal, what a word! The animal is a word.' See also: 'This portmanteau neologism [. . .] is pronounced, in the singular or the plural, the same way as the plural of 'animal', p. 165, n. 35.
10. Derrida, *Animal*, p. 29.
11. Jacques Derrida, *Introduction à l'Origine de la Géométrie de Husserl* (Paris: PUF, 1961), pp. 57–8.
12. Derrida, *Animal*, p. 6.
13. Jacques Derrida, *The Beast and the Sovereign*, Vol. II, trans. Geoffrey Bennington (Chicago: University of Chicago Press, 2011).
14. Hélène Cixous, *L'Amour du loup et autres remords* (Paris: Galilée, 2003); 'Love of the Wolf', trans. Keith Cohen, in *Stigmata: Escaping Texts* (New York and London: Routledge, 1998), pp. 70–83.
15. Derrida, *Animal*, pp. 8–9.
16. Derrida, *Beast*, II, p. 28.
17. Jacques Derrida, 'Punctuations: The Time of a Thesis', in *Eyes of the*

University, *Right to Philosophy 2*, ed. Werner Hamacher and David E. Wellbery (Stanford: Stanford University Press, 2004), p. 116.
18. Derrida, *Introduction à l'Origine*, p. 69.
19. Derrida, *Edmund Husserl's Origin*, p. 76 ('it has the style of a turnabout which can be surprising').
20. Leavey, 'Undecidables', pp. 13, 14.
21. Ibid., p. 14, n. 38.
22. Derrida, *Edmund Husserl's Origin*, pp. 67 (*Introduction*), 161.
23. Ibid. 'Bound' occurs over 17 times, with a maximum distribution following page 67 (pp. 76–97).
24. Derrida, *Edmund Husserl's Origin*, p. 71; *Introduction à l'Origine*, p. 63.
25. Derrida, *Edmund Husserl's Origin*, p. 161 [modified].
26. Derrida, *Edmund Husserl's Origin*, p. 88. Derrida quotes Husserl's phrase from *Formal and Transcendental Logic*, trans. Dorion Cairns (The Hague: Martinus Nijhoff, 1969), § 2, p. 21.
27. Derrida, *Introduction à l'Origine* (quatrième de couverture), translation mine.
28. Derrida emphasises Husserl's own addition or afterthought: 'we see this in advance', *Edmund Husserl's Origin*, p. 76. The English translation gives Husserl's remark greater foreseeing power than is implied in the original, the expression '*nous le voyons par avance*' being equivalent to saying 'this is obvious, it is a no-brainer'. With 'hindsight', however, something literally 'sees' in advance in Husserl – blindly looking ahead towards Derrida. Hindsight, or the sight of a ... deer.
29. For a follow-up on Derrida's catachrestic/*chat*/cat-achrestic effects in writing in *The Animal That Therefore I Am*, see my 'Animal Writes', in *Demenageries: Thinking (of) Animals after Derrida*, ed. Anne Emmanuelle Berger and Marta Segarra (Amsterdam and New York: Rodopi, 2011), pp. 23–40.
30. Jacques Derrida, 'My Chances / Mes Chances: A Rendezvous with Some Epicurean Stereophonies', in *Taking Chances: Derrida, Psychoanalysis, and Literature*, ed. Joseph H. Smith and William Kerrigan (Baltimore: Johns Hopkins University Press, 1984).
31. Derrida, *Edmund Husserl's Origin*, p. 161.
32. Ibid., p. 68, n. 63.
33. Ibid., p. 67, my emphasis; *Introduction à l'Origine*, p. 58.
34. Ibid., p. 67, n. 62, my emphasis.
35. Ibid., p. 6, my emphasis; *Introduction à l'Origine*, p. 70.
36. Although the effect disappears in translation, the inscription of the terms '*lien*' and '*lié*' occurs more than once in the French original, with strange effects of juxtaposition: 'désigner le *lion*. Dans ce cas, le *lien* à une généralité', *Introduction à l'Origine*, p. 63. For further readings on the term '*lié*' and its recurrence both as '*bouc lié*' (bound, ligatured ram) and as '*bouclier*' (buckler, scutcheon), see Hélène Cixous, 'Le Bouc lié', *Rue Descartes*, 48, 2005, pp. 15–26. The syllable '*lié*' and the imperative force of '*lions*' (with its animal counterpart, one or several lions) dwells in the open field of deconstruction.
37. Derrida, *Edmund Husserl's Origin*, p. 71.
38. Ibid., p. 71.

39. Ibid., p. 102.
40. Ibid., p. 169. On the importance of the concept of passivity, see Nathalie Dépraz, 'Commentaire de la *Cinquième Méditation*', in J.-F. Lavigne (ed.), *Les Méditations cartésiennes de Husserl* (Paris: Vrin, 2008).
41. Derrida, *Edmund Husserl's Origin*, pp. 99, 71, 100.
42. Ibid., p. 67, n. 62. '*Déjà*' occurs 104 times in the introduction.
43. Keith Cohen's translation gives free rein to a 'bound' in Cixous's epigraph: 'This is a bo(u)nd for a wolf', in *Stigmata*, p. 71.
44. Jacques Derrida, 'Shibboleth: For Paul Celan', in *Word Traces: Readings of Paul Celan*, trans. Joshua Wilner (Baltimore: Johns Hopkins University Press, 1994), p. 61.
45. Derrida, *Edmund Husserl's Origin*, p. 111, n. 122; Maurice Merleau-Ponty, 'Phenomenology and the Sciences of Man', in *The Primacy of Perception and Other Essays on Phenomenological Psychology* (Evanston: Northwestern University Press, 1964), pp. 90–1. The same interpretation, Derrida's note adds, 'is presented in Merleau-Ponty's article "The Philosopher and Sociology"', in *Signs* (Evanston: Northwestern University Press, 1964), pp. 98–113.
46. Derrida, *Edmund Husserl's Origin*, p. 116.
47. Ibid., p. 67, n. 62 ('confronting the name'). Hegel's '*devant*', once dislodged from its confrontational sense, can be translated as imply an 'owing'.
48. Jacob Loewenberg was an eminent professor of philosophy and Hegel scholar, Karl Löwith is the author of *De Hegel à Nietzsche*, 1969, among other texts, and James K. Lyon devoted a book to *Paul Celan and Martin Heidegger: An Unresolved Conversation 1951–1970*. Such a 'partial' gathering of names belongs to the more 'threatening' aspects of this reading of the *Löwe*.
49. I owe this addition of yet another leonine connection to Laurent Milesi. There is no space, here, to expand on the complex relationship between Rudolph Loewenstein and Lacan, but one should add that the name of Lacan's analyst belonged to the category (if there is one) of restless names: 'the misfortune is that I regularly forget his name). There it is: Loewenstein'; Jacques Derrida, *The Post Card: From Socrates to Freud and Beyond*, trans. Alan Bass (Chicago: University of Chicago Press, 1987), pp. 519ff. At work in the economy of a *Löwe* is a ongoing movement of 'owing'.
50. Letter from Jacques Lacan, January 1953, 'La scission de 1953', *Supplément à Ornicar*, 7, pp. 52–3, http://www.lutecium.org/wordpress/en/1953/05/jacques-lacan-ornicar-supplement-no-7-3/ (accessed 4 March 2013). See also Jacques Derrida, 'For the Love of Lacan', *Journal of European Psychoanalysis*, 2, Fall–Winter 1996.
51. The city also happens to be a Lacanian haunt; Lacan gave conferences in Louvain at least twice, in 1957 and October 1972. http://parolesdesjours.free.fr/lacan.htm (accessed 5 February 2013).
52. Leavey, 'Undecidables', p. 21.
53. Cixous, *Stigmata*, p. 73.
54. Derrida, *The Beast and the Sovereign*, Vol. II, trans. Geoffrey Bennington (Chicago: University of Chicago Press, 2009), p. 54.
55. The circumstances of the killing resemble, incidentally, several accounts of the killing of the Nemean lion by Herakles.

56. Daniel Defoe, *The Adventures of Robinson Crusoe* (Harmondsworth: Penguin, 1998), p. 24.
57. See Lynn Turner, 'When Species Kiss: Some Recent Correspondences between *animots*', *Humanimalia*, 2.1, Fall 2010, pp. 60–85, for a reading of border-crossings between species: 'kissing is of the edges', p. 80.
58. Derrida repeatedly quotes the German title of Heidegger's *Grundbegriffe Der Metaphysik* in *The Beast and the Sovereign*. Sarah Kofman's *Autobiogriffures: Du Chat Murr d'Hoffman* (Paris: Galilée, 1984), also stalk, and are stalked by, those *Grundbegriffe*.
59. Derrida, *Beast*, I, p. 341.
60. Derrida, *Beast*, II, p. 45.
61. See Ginette Michaud, '*Comme en rêve*', in *Lire Jacques Derrida et Hélène Cixous*, II (Paris: Hermann, 2010); see also the dream on which Hélène Cixous opens *Insister: Of Jacques Derrida*, trans. Peggy Kamuf (Stanford: Stanford University Press, 2008), p. 3: 'you and I are two mice in sports clothes. And we are playing with a ball. My mouse is stage right. Yours is a hefty little male and you're getting ready to shoot stage left. My little girl mouse is the goalkeeper. She goes back and forth in front of the goal. She's guarding, but at the same time she's very frightened of the shot. She lets go sharp little yelps of apprehension [. . .]. Dream, April 2005'.
62. Quoted in Jean-Luc Nancy and Valerio Adami, *A plus d'un titre, Jacques Derrida* (Paris: Galilée, 2003), pp. 19, 37. 'I smile at you, I bless you, I love you, wherever I am', trans. Charles Truehart, http://theamericanscholar.org/paris-the-death-of-derrida/ (accessed 5 February 2013).
63. Jacques Derrida, '*Geschlecht* II: Heidegger's Hand', trans. John P. Leavey, in *Deconstruction and Philosophy: The Texts of Jacques Derrida*, ed. John Sallis (Chicago: University of Chicago Press, 1987), p. 196, n. 38.

Chapter 4

Insect Asides

Lynn Turner

> Insects: we were born with them. [...] Between us, insects make words, words insect and insexion each other.
> (Hélène Cixous)[1]

The imprint of 'limitrophic violence' marks deconstruction, is the mark of deconstruction, its ragged autograph. Many readers have been drawn in to the moments in *The Animal That Therefore I Am* in which Jacques Derrida displaces the all-time divide between the twin fictions of man and animal with indefinite 'differences that grow'.[2] Rather than a new but fixed number of lines of differentiation, this organic figure of growth and of ingestion maintains the challenge of deconstruction to think difference otherwise. Fleshing out this counter-intuitive, impossible to grasp, movement of difference, Derrida took the geographical term 'limitrophy' – already in communication with the shores of the future in the figure of the *arrivant* – and emphasised its investment in nourishment.[3] He writes, 'Let's allow [limitrophy] to have both a general and a strict sense: what abuts onto limits but also what feeds, is fed, is cared for, raised and trained, what is cultivated on the edges of a limit.'[4] This oral sense of a limit with a bite is the reprint of Derrida's early attention to our inheritance of a dialectical theory of difference as one that problematically cleans up its own operation (the mixed metaphors of organic bite with technical print are not accidental).[5] Limitrophy is as much Derrida's 'subject' in this book as is 'the animal'.[6]

In this chapter I track around the edges of texts touched almost incidentally by insects to ask after their indentations. Primarily, I return to 'Tympan' – the entry point to *Margins of Philosophy*, paginated in roman numerals continuous with the 'Translator's Note' and the pages identifying the publication details, but discontinuous with the remaining chapters, setting a complicated relation between them.[7] Set before the much more widely remarked essays such as 'Différance' and 'Signature

Event Context', 'Tympan' functions as a kind of introduction intimating and enacting Derrida's broader concerns. Bearing in mind what is for me a second key touchstone in *The Animal That Therefore I Am*, namely that animal and sexual differences traverse the same horizon, I look back at 'Tympan' to investigate its practice of '[g]nawing away at the border', of 'eat[ing] the margins' of philosophy.[8] Munching on philosophy, Derrida insists that deconstruction departs from phallogocentrism while, at the same time, an earwig crawls through the dividing columns of this early text. If, much later in his work, Derrida is to demonstrate how 'phallogocentrism' expands to the even greater mouthful 'carno-phallogocentrism', this enquiry considers how that special case of carnivorousness may already be under fire.[9] Starting from 'Tympan's' early deconstruction of what we might call the 'tympanic attacks' of philosophy (after Nicholas Royle), I inch towards the differing infractions of 'committing insect', recalled amid Derrida's account of the archives of *Confessions* in 'Typewriter Ribbon' and then succeeding the exchange of the word '*fourmi*' between Hélène Cixous and Derrida by telephone, that is to say, in the passage of the word from mouth to ear.[10] In such transitions, these 'insect asides' expand our understanding of eating – and/or as hearing – well.

Earrings

> When I begin to 'write', I do not write, I snuggle up, I become an ear, I follow a rhythm.
> (Hélène Cixous)[11]

The question of the limit is sounded in numerous interwoven ways in 'Tympan'. Starting with its oddities in appearance, I have indicated its pagination, but its columns also mark it out from more orthodox typographic conventions and systems of reference, including those of the succeeding chapters. Further, they dramatise the space of the page as a battleground of centres and margins. The left-hand column issues Derrida's text, footnotes supplying both his and his translator's annotations – sometimes at length. But the narrower right-hand column infringing the length of 'Tympan' is a long citation from Michel Leiris's text *Biffures* (translated as *Scratches*) not otherwise referenced.[12] Both columns are 'justified' thus producing another noticeable space as each page proliferates the margins. Again setting it out from the rest of *Margins of Philosophy*, 'Tympan' includes three citations on its title page, all from Hegel, arranged triadically with one centred above two others (rather than one underneath the next) thereby evoking – as well as naming – the process of thesis, antithesis and synthesis. Derrida's type starts on the reverse side of the title page, rather than leaving a blank page and more elegantly, conventionally, taking up its place on the right.[13] While Derrida takes the place of the antithesis, his work is not strictly *antithetical* to Hegelian thesis – 'Tympan' insists upon another type of movement.

'Tympan' strikes at once, with the archaic (transliterated) verb 'To tympanise' directed at philosophy itself. Alan Bass, Derrida's translator, tells us this means 'to ridicule publicly'.[14] Needling the 'need for philosophy' which his epigraphs name, Derrida directs our attention to the delimitation of the limit within the dialectical tradition.[15] The '*relevance*' of the limit turns on the annulling of difference within this frame (Derrida plays on '*relever*' as the French translation of *aufheben*).[16] It is a method for philosophy to absorb 'the margin of its own volume', to overcome the other, to domesticate it.[17] The outside *of* philosophy already belongs to it, grounding any further syntheses. A particular story of the ear supports this fantastical operation. This story is echoed, from the top, in the other column whence Leiris suggests that the 'floral and subterranean name of *Persephone*' signs a proliferating association of spiralled forms including 'the helix inscribed on the shell of a snail, the meanders of the small and the large intestine, the sandy serpentine excreted by an earthworm, [. . .] the concha of the ear'.[18]

Derrida quickly moves to locate philosophy's erasure of difference by the sounding of the same with an otographic figure. Reason, he suggests, in desiring to hear itself speak, 'amortises' all others, making them resound within itself.[19] At first the possibility of interrupting the continuity of the circle of auto-affection takes the form of an exterior violence – and one with a sexual tone – visited upon the ear of reason: how can one 'puncture the tympanum of a philosopher' to be heard and understood without being appropriated?[20] As the essay unfurls, this antagonism between the autonomous sealed ear and the penetrating voice of the other loses its oppositional ground, not least through the spirals coiled in the right-hand column.

The 'philosophical tympanum' deadens the sound of the other. Taking another chance, writing obliquely to catch philosophy by surprise requires not the defloration but certainly the 'deformation' of this drum.[21] This deformation, however, takes account of the biological relations that inhere in the ear, displacing the implicit idealisation performed by philosophy.[22] Derrida does not distil a *figure* of the oblique. He notes the eardrum's oblique stretch – that which maximises its capacity to vibrate – and consequently turns away from 'frontal and symmetrical protest'.²³ Echoing the beginning of his text in the place of the antithesis but without asserting that oppositional position, Derrida seeks ways to 'ambush' the logos (punning on the homonymic Greek *lokhos*, meaning both 'ambush' and 'childbirth').²⁴ Repeatedly describing his practice as one of 'luxating' the tympanum, Derrida's seemingly esoteric choice of verb positively avoids one that begins with a negative prefix such as '*de-*' or '*dis-*' (as in 'dislocate'), again remarking his side-stepping of antithesis. Ambushing the logos, he sets the '*loxōs*' [Gk. oblique] to work within it, licensed by the indirect angle of the tympanum.²⁵

Replying to a philosophical history that can hear no other – other than the one that it sublates and makes resonate in line with itself – Derrida does not think up a better answer. Rather he insists on this work of luxation, of transforming the question, perhaps even disbanding the question insofar as the question/answer couplet already holds fast to an immobilising accord. If the tympanum is imagined as a limit, then it is that concept of limit that must be multiplied, limitrophied. Derrida's tympanum is of another genre. He attends to 'the stereographic activity of an entirely other ear' – one whose graphic divides rather than unifies the sounds of the other.²⁶ This, however, does not leave the philosophical ear intact but rather shows how philosophy has never been able to maintain its idealised tympanum (has never been able to keep it in the undivided presence of the now).

Indexing the interlinked tympanums of a printing press, as well as the hammer, membranes, bones, stones and canals of the ear, Derrida implicates a physiology and a technology without absolute distinction. More than that, in loosening the grip of a fantasy of autonomy cut off in kind from being offset by any other through the annihilation of the outside (as discussed above), difference emerges within the would-be subject of reason. The line of thought that links Hegel with psychoanalysis is affected by this move in ways still scarcely addressed. Introducing difference into psychoanalysis must here be understood as a *différance* that does not divide evenly into discrete elements but rather fosters divisibility without end. Thus, castration is not that primary division that might threaten or befall a subject, symbolically or otherwise. As Derrida writes it: 'a tympanum, punctures itself or grafts itself. And *this*, however one writes it, resists the concepts of machine or of nature, of break or of body, resists the metaphysics of castration [. . .]'.²⁷ 'Puncture' carries the greater association with a wound, but 'graft' also carries the sense of the force of the instability of context, already 'there' at work in the ruination of self-presence. Indeed, Derrida was later to remark that 'the question of the graft in general has always been – and thematically so from the beginning – essential to the deconstruction of phallogocentrism'.²⁸

Ruining this fiction, however, is at the same time a process invoking the traversal of animal and sexual differences (the subject of reason is implicitly a virile, masculine figure, named as such in the interview 'Eating Well').[29] Leiris's text is grafted from the chapter named 'Persephone' in the first volume of his autobiography, *Scratches* (itself evoking the traces of animals as well as humans and troubling the signifying capacity of both). Redistributed in a narrow column, Leiris's experiences gathered under the name 'Persephone' follow the first three pages of Derrida's column, where he is most emphatic about the cooptation of frontal opposition. That name opens a further association with the insect known in French as a *'perce-oreille'*, an earwig in English.[30] Leiris identifies Persephone and *perce-oreille* with piercing, while acknowledging that the former's sibilant syllables modify, even disperse this sense. Yet the latter, the earwig, founders in its curiously persistent yet unfounded association with human ears (Leiris acknowledges that this association is fabulous, in the sense of a fable). Indeed, in her 'modern bestiary' May Berenbaum notes that among the arthropods in fact cited as requiring medical removal from ears, earwigs do not feature.[31] She also notes that the English 'earwig' may sound less invasive than the *perce-oreille* but that it still carries the sense of wiggling into ears through its etymological – not entomological – root in the Old English *wicga*.[32] Piercing is, however, associated with *phone*. The mythic earwig was deployed as a spectral threat to the ear by Leiris's mother when he was too noisy as a child (perhaps imperilling his own vocal cords); the implication is that she will allow an earwig to puncture his eardrum, a threat that is easily reminiscent of an archetypal threat to masculine genitals (*if you don't stop playing with that, mummy will take it away . . .*). This threat is typographically close to Derrida's lengthy footnote invoking various types of thought that etymologically and conceptually link the vestibule of the ear with that of the vulva.[33] Continuing his earlier suggestion of dismantling the opposition between the tympanum as a membrane sealing off the subject from the penetrations of the sound of a definitively exterior other, and here making complex play with the spirals of snails, shells and the form of the human ear, Derrida suggests that the spiral of this other tympanum is both 'closed in on itself *and* open to the sea's path'.[34] Auto-affection, including that of 'the voice that keeps silent', is always affected by the other.[35] In spite of this heteroaffective mechanism, a metaphorics of the 'bloodiness of a disseminated writing' nevertheless continues to lean on the violence of an encounter with the other (here *not* moderated by negation) as one resonant with defloration. Would that Derrida had been able to turn to Berenbaum's bestiary: he would have found that earwig males of the Anisolabididae family have a spare penis. While females have only one genital opening 'male anisolabidids have a pair of organs, one of which points in what would seem to be the wrong direction'.[36]

Leiris identifies both *perce-oreille* and Persephone with dark, cavernous places: the non-fabulous earwig gnaws into the stones of fruit; the goddess occupies the underworld – 'the deep country of hearing'.[37] Hearing, then, opens Leiris's musings on the geologics of caverns, grottoes and other hollows in the earth that become sounding chambers.[38] He refers to the difference between a singing and a speaking voice as a mystery whose margins are described by a fringe, echoing Derrida's attention to limitrophy. He suggests that the singing voice – the influx, perhaps we should also say the 'exflux', of rhythm – particularly foxes the differences between human voices and those of other fauna and flora and 'even' minerals.[39] Adjacent to this species of confusion, Derrida names '*limitrophic* violence' as that which is 'imprinted according to new *types*' to the detriment of the ability of the philosophical tympanum to negate the other.[40] The typography of 'types' bridges the organic (representative kinds of species) and the technological. Limitrophy bites (chemicals used in print-making also impress a surface with their 'bite'). From organically generated voices, Leiris moves to mechanically produced ones.[41] 'His' column tracks that of Derrida, at this point explicating the tympanic technology of the printing press (the ear again joining with his expanded sense of writing through sonic impressions).

Nibbling the ear of the other

> But *we* are never *ourselves*, and between us, identical to us, a "self" is never in itself or identical to itself.
> (Jacques Derrida)[42]

As indicated above, Derrida aligns phallogocentrism with dialectical philosophy from which he distances his preferred 'rhythm without measure' on numerous occasions in 'Tympan'.[43] It is not until the interview with Jean Luc Nancy entitled '"Eating Well" or the Calculation of the Subject' that Derrida augments this concatenation with a further prefix – 'carno-'.[44]

The meat course of this segmented word 'carno-phallogocentrism' remains unclean.[45] It should not be. It should be drawn by centrifugal force into strictest equivalence with the phallus made symbol made word (for that matter phallus should also fall down here, and so – even

– should logos). Remembering that cleanliness is intimately related to the proper should open some leeway. In the 'Eating Well' interview, meat names sacrifice, or rather the failure to sacrifice sacrifice.[46] While Derrida raises serious problems with the consequences of this failure especially for non-human animals here and in *The Animal That Therefore I Am*, he does not move to thoroughly eliminate sacrifice.

On the one hand, this failure arises within a familiar discourse of the subject (Derrida names that of Emmanuel Levinas) for whom ethical relations arise through the command 'Thou shalt not kill' in distinction from a possible 'Thou shalt not kill the living in general'.[47] That is to say the performative address from the other implicitly shapes a human institution, a human 'face'. It allows for a 'non-criminal putting to death' of others, typically animals and those humans instrumentally convened under the trope of the animal for this purpose.[48] It is the title of the journal issue, in light of which frame the interview takes place, that prompts Derrida's line of enquiry here: 'Who Comes After the Subject?'[49] While the topic of the subject is nominally in question, Derrida finds it reinstalled in the maintenance of the 'who' and thus he refuses 'to see the "who" restricted to the grammar of what we call Western language, nor even limited by what we believe to be the very humanity of language'.[50] Rather than erect a new law such that 'Thou shalt not kill the living in general' (a command facing a truly unwieldy category, potentially including everything from elephants to viruses), Derrida's affirmative ethical injunction proposes that 'One must eat well.'[51]

On the other, the failure to sacrifice sacrifice speaks to a more specifically psychoanalytic engagement, even though the work of Nicolas Abraham and Maria Torok is not named as such in 'Eating Well'.[52] While their work participates in the 'linguisticistic' operation of psychoanalysis that cleanly exchanges thing for word in the becoming of the human subject, in Derrida's hands it enables a more radical array of metonymies.[53] In 'Eating Well' the 'executions of ingestion, incorporation, or introjection of the corpse' are named immediately following the identification of a 'non-criminal putting to death' as at issue.[54] Two analytic names for different types of identification are joined with ingestion. A couple of pages later eating is named as a 'metonymy for introjection' and thus Derrida redoubles the stakes for just how one should eat well.[55] Unlike Abraham and Torok's privileging of the mouth as just such a metonymy (since, in the legends of psychoanalysis, this is the orifice that anticipates speech in the autotelic image of the human), Derrida radically opens the body. He writes that for '*everything* that happens at the edge of the orifices (of orality, but also of the ear, the eye-and all the "senses" in general) the metonymy of "eating well" [*bien manger*] would always be the rule'.⁵⁶ It is not just the mouth, then, that displaces the face of the other.⁵⁷ The ear is implicated in eating the other. With the ear too 'One must eat well.'

In the tympanic attack suffered by the subject of dialectics, the other is blanked out. Any different note is neutralised, brought into line, quashed. But the implication of the other type of tympanum at stake for Derrida is not the opposing number which would command that one must silently listen to the other and respect their terms, their limits, *completely*. That would fall into the same logic: the question determines the answer. Likewise, the implications of 'Eating Well' are not simply to refuse to eat the other and as a consequence to properly respect that other. What becomes clearer with Derrida's critical engagement with Abraham and Torok is the way that the metonymy of ingestion and processes of identification trouble how we decide to eat. One must eat not just because there are basic needs to be met such as the need for nutrition, but rather because one must identify with others in order to form any self of one's 'own'. Through identification, or in Abraham and Torok's specific term introjection, we all 'eat meat'. Thus the distinction between symbolic and actual anthropophagy cannot be maintained. Thanks to this unclean fault line, even when we refuse to eat meat or consume animal products more widely, we nevertheless 'eat meat' through ingestion as identification. The pincers of these quotation marks should neither ring alarm bells, mock the activism of vegetarians or vegans, nor be taken as a dilution of what is at stake.⁵⁸ The philosophical ear deconstructed in 'Tympan' professes to determine whom it takes in and how much – everything: this ear would aurally digest the other without remainder, without margin for error. The path of the concept, or indeed the signifier, is construed to be perfect.

Derrida's less rigidly orchestrated understanding of eating as a metonymy of introjection does not, cannot, decide how much of the other we digest, nor which other remains 'with' us through variously introjective or incorporative processes.⁵⁹ For Abraham and Torok, the latter organise two opposing processes that produce either the sociality of language (in which the introjected other is recirculated) or the silence of the crypt (the loss of the other is denied by incorporation, secreting that other away in a 'crypt').⁶⁰ For Derrida, this opposition cannot hold and it is not determined that identifications will only manifest in strictly linguistic terms. Introducing this undecidability alters the properties of the carno-phallogocentric subject. Yet violence remains. A 'limitrophic violence imprint[s] according to new *types*'.⁶¹ Luxating the philosophical tympanum fosters this limitrophy, it eats the margins. Kelly Oliver has indicated that there always remains the chance that the *trophos* of limitrophy as nourishment will flip over into a triumphant trophy, since deconstruction never provides a quick and infallible fix.[62] So, while we may yet fail to sacrifice sacrifice since we must 'eat', the operations of the animal trope as that which allows for a 'non-criminal putting to death' are diminished and an ethics of 'infinite hospitality' take their place.[63]

Typo

> I am about to sacrifice: I cut, I write, I sacrifice.
> (Jacques Derrida)[64]

Subsequently writing about another set of types, the imprint on a certain 'typewriter ribbon' in relation to the performativity of confession and its impact on the very possibility of an archive, Derrida recasts the infringement of the organic and the technological found in 'Tympan' with the hyphenated notion of the 'machine-event'.[65] There too, in the peripheries, insects emerge. The broader direction of 'Typewriter Ribbon: Limited Ink (2)' opens up a new type of thought through this awkward hyphenation of two concepts ordinarily (conceptually) separated (reminiscent of Derrida's insistence that 'what we call "thinking"' is rethought in the encounter with the animal).[66] Perhaps we can say that limitrophy characterises this hyphen as the margins of spontaneity and mechanical repetition are eaten. Indeed the 'machine-event' of 'Typewriter Ribbon', first given only a few years after Derrida's address at the Cerisy-la-Salle colloquium *L'Animal autobiographique*, becomes kin to the core deconstruction of response and reaction in *The Animal That Therefore I Am*, wherein response characterises human life and reaction dooms the mechanical – and the animal cast as 'animal-machine' – to be categorically less significant.

There are several insects in 'Typewriter Ribbon'. Towards the end of this long address they appear almost out of the blue; even Derrida says at first that he 'does not know' why he is telling his audience about them.[67] He has been troubling the most proper form of the archive – autobiography – in light of the machinations of repetition between and within the *Confessions* of Rousseau and of Augustine, as discussed and as curiously managed and/or effaced in the work of Paul de Man. Repetition is, of course, exactly what the discourse of confession should not entertain if it is not to call the normative view of performativity into question (which is precisely what Derrida aims to do). But Derrida pauses and recalls two instances of insects preserved in amber. The first case names

> the cadaver of an insect surprised by death, in an instant, by a geological or geothermal catastrophe, at the moment at which it was sucking the blood of another insect, some fifty-four million years before humans appeared on earth.[68]

After this surprise by death Derrida mentions that of another pair, this time two midges, 'immobilised in amber the color of honey when they were surprised by death as they made love'.[69] Having shaken up the organic, spontaneous and assumed-to-be-human event with the mechanical, repetitive animal-machine, Derrida mulls over the curiosity of these midges archived in amber as a kind of natural print technology in commemoration of a singular event. Held in amber, if not frozen in time, the singular event of their sudden death that happened just once, continues to happen for Derrida as we contemplate their trace. This event 'happened to some living being, affecting a kind of organised individual, already endowed with a kind of memory, with project, need, desire, pleasure, and aptitude to retain traces'.[70] These midges too may constitute 'autobiographical animals' – writing, in spite of themselves on the natural technology of amber.

Just as the wretched discourse of 'the animal' performs a specific kind of idealisation when animal and machine are made equivalent – the machine repeats perfectly; the animal is adapted perfectly and thus has no need of technology or language – so Derrida's realignment of machine and organism throws a spanner in the works, so to speak. In 'Typewriter Ribbon' the inclusion of the mechanical is not a naive return to the *concept* of perfect self-authoring that otherwise goes by the name of God, likewise divorced absolutely from the 'human'.[71] In his later locution, this machine is '*quasi*-machinelike'.[72] Reminiscent of the other tympanum that 'grafts itself', '[t]he machine is *cut* as well as *cutting* with regard to the living present of life or of the living body'.[73] We inheritors of Descartes must learn to think again.

Rousseau and his dramatic ambition to set forth through and as his *Confessions* 'an enterprise that has no precedent and [...] will have no imitator' trips Derrida's memory.[74] He recalls a typographic error performed by a compositor who anagrammatically substituted 'insect' for 'incest' and so set an epigraph in *Of Grammatology* citing Rousseau from the *Confessions* to say 'I was as if I had committed an insect'.[75] Correcting the typo, Derrida returns Rousseau to the Oedipal terror of incest, a machine for producing the law (and law as a machine that repeats).

Committing insect

> We know less than ever where to cut [. . .].
> (Jacques Derrida)[76]

Derrida had previously recalled this typo of committing insect and his temptation not to correct it during his paper named 'Ants' presented at a colloquium on 'Readings of Sexual Difference' following that of Hélène Cixous (Centre d'Etudes Féminines, Université de Paris 8, 1990). At that moment, Derrida himself wonders whether, in talking of a telephone conversation in which Cixous tells him of an ant, he had committed it too.[77] This time, we assume, he means 'insect'.

'Ants' is an essay in which the question of divisibility, rather than one grand cut of castration, or one grand divide between man and animal – or man and machine – comes to the fore along with sexual difference through the segmented figure-body of its titular insect.[78] Less peripheral than the earwig of 'Tympan' and this time given without the force of an Oedipal threat to organs that may be categorically damaged, this insect is transmitted by telephone. Cixous names the ungrammatically masculine '*un fourmi*' – rather than '*une*' –when recounting a dream to Derrida (a practice, both oneiric and telephonic that we know to be a familiar one) and Derrida subsequently takes this gift of a word as the *topos* of his discussion in 'Ants'.[79] This word is passed from mouth to ear, but it does not arrive intact. It is also foreshadowed in the text by sexual difference described as 'formidable', in English meaning fearsome, redoubtable, which, while not a strict translation, is at the same time the more colloquial French word meaning tremendous, great stuff.[80] The first two syllables form a near homophone for '*fourmi*' and presage the many turns of the text in which Derrida finds this '*fourmi*'; already swarming ('*fourmille*'), providing ('*fournit*') food and drink ('*la fourme*').[81] Thus this ant infiltrates while itself succumbing to alterations.

While the word '*fourmi*' arrives through a dream, Derrida is clear that his antics in 'Ants' do not amount to a 'mere' fable of the animal that would always only allegorise the human. Like Cixous he does not pose a strict choice between the fable *or* the real animal – this zone is akin to that presented by eating as a metonymy of introjection. Limitrophy traffics between these ostensibly different orders. Common to his interweaving of the sexual and the animal is their non-availability to an empirical determination by sight exacerbated by their telephonic donation as well as their embrace of divisibility. This divisibility differs from the logic of a major divide and thus runs counter to the most considered psychoanalytic responses to the pressing question of the animal, which typically respond through revising the trauma of the real *as* that of the animal (from which signifying humans thus remain barred).[82] In the dialectical logic of psychoanalysis the animal is always anterior to the human. Yet like the machine that detaches from a concept of self-maintenance in 'Typewriter Ribbon' in order to be cutting *and* cut, this ant, this '*fourmi*' comes biting and bitten. Derrida remarks that the Latin for insect, 'this plural neutral, *insecta*, does not mean un-sectile [*inseccable*], indivisible, atomic'.[83] Rather '*insecta* comes from *inseco*, which means to cut, to dissect, at times to tear apart with the teeth'.[84]

Eating well in the guise of hearing well, Derrida takes this ant, given without predication by Cixous, that surfaces in this relatively spontaneous lecture and repeats it some ten years later as an aside in 'Typewriter Ribbon'.[85] Although Derrida again does not mount a frontal attack on the position of psychoanalysis, the differences he lets loose implicitly affect its emphasis on *the* cut, that of castration. The cuts of the insect – as 'cut/not-cut' as 'separated/not-separated' at the same time – do not *oppose* the 'un-cut'.[86] These cuts are both of the name and of the body, 'strictured by an annular multiplicity of *rings*'.[87] Divisibility deters calculation: *insecta* is a figure of the miniscule and of innumerable teeming.[88] Like the eating of the other that cannot eradicate the eating of 'meat' and so does not entirely eliminate sacrifice, the cutting or biting of the insect – especially in light of the Greek *entomos* – opens a relation to sacrifice.[89] Derrida names writing, cutting and sacrifice as substitutable – but after having modified all these terms. The inscription of writing obliges incision in the form of decision. Scission without premeditation; different each time, there is no special case determined as the 'what' that can be put to death without penalty. This filigree of the cut, this contamination puts Derrida in mind of 'a sort of incest (*incestus* which means what we call incest, in every sense, but also adultery and stain, contamination in general)'.[90] He is put especially in mind of that typo, of Rousseau committing insect. Derrida may leave the thought here, mid-essay, but he 'leave[s] it to multiply', to limitrophise.[91] He cannot arrest this insect, even if there is the '*temptation* not to touch it'.[92]. Touching this insect in 'Ants' and 'Typewriter Ribbon', it gets away. Committing insect, Derrida takes the taboo held to be *the* foundation of human culture, and commits it to the wider case of contamination. Limitrophy becomes the law.

Notes

1. Hélène Cixous, *Insister of Jacques Derrida*, trans. Peggy Kamuf (Edinburgh: Edinburgh University Press, 2007), p. 130.

2. Jacques Derrida, *The Animal That Therefore I Am*, trans. David Wills (New York: Fordham University Press, 2008), pp. 29–31.
3. The figure of a shore both conjures the sense of an ever-changing geo-psychic coastline and engages the pun that Derrida makes when speaking of the 'to-come': the shore or '*la rive*' rhymes with the present tense of the verb '*arriver*' meaning 'to happen' or 'arrive'. See Jacques Derrida, *Aporias*, trans. Thomas Dutoit (Stanford: Stanford University Press, 1993), p. 35.
4. Derrida, *Animal*, p. 29. He goes on to unravel the implication with nourishment through the routes of *trephō, trophē* and *trophos*.
5. Indeed today's 'bytes' induce another overlap between ostensibly separate categories.
6. David Wills, the translator, remarks on the echoes with the 'Woman will be my subject' of Derrida's previous Cerisy-la-Salle address on Nietzsche in 1972 (*Animal*, p. 166, n. 38).
7. Jacques Derrida, 'Tympan', in *Margins of Philosophy*, trans. Alan Bass (Chicago: University of Chicago Press, 1982), pp. ix-xxix. Elsewhere I have focused on the phonic aspects of this text in relation to the feminine and the posthuman; see my 'Tympan Alley: Posthuman Performatives in *Dancer in the Dark*', *Derrida Today*, 6.2, 2013.
8. Derrida, 'Tympan', pp. xxiii, xxv.
9. Jacques Derrida, '"Eating Well" or the Calculation of the Subject' [1988], trans. Peter Connor and Avital Ronell, in *Points . . . Interviews, 1974–1994*, ed. Elizabeth Weber (Stanford: Stanford University Press, 1995), p. 280.
10. Nicholas Royle punned on 'tympanic attacks' during his paper 'Gulls' given at the conference 'Cosmopolitan Animals', University of Kent, 2012. See Jacques Derrida, 'Typewriter Ribbon: Limited Ink (2)', in *Without Alibi*, trans. Peggy Kamuf (Stanford: Stanford University Press, 2002), p. 132 (first given as a keynote address at the 'Material Events: Paul de Man and the AfterLife of Theory' conference at the University of California, 2000) and Derrida, 'Ants', trans. Eric Prenowitz, *Oxford Literary Review*, 24, 2002, p. 34.
11. Hélène Cixous, 'Tales of Sexual Difference', trans. Eric Prenowitz, in *The Portable Cixous*, ed. Marta Segarra (New York: Columbia University Press, 2010), p. 59.
12. The English edition consulted here is Michel Leiris [1948], *Scratches: Rules of the Game Volume 1*, trans. Lydia Davis (Baltimore: Johns Hopkins University Press, 1991).
13. The French original did not use this textual comment of starting Derrida's chapter on the reverse side of the epigraphs from Hegel. Through the use of a slightly larger font it did match up the columns of Derrida and Leiris. See Jacques Derrida, *Marges de la Philosophie* (Paris: Les Éditions de Minuit, 1972). See also Johnny Golding's lucid account of Hegel in her 'Fractal Philosophy', in *Deleuze and Contemporary Art*, ed. Simon O'Sullivan and Stephen Zepke (Edinburgh: Edinburgh University Press, 2010), pp. 150–1, nn. 3, 4.
14. Derrida, 'Tympan', p. x, n. 1.
15. Other thinkers of Derrida's generation devised different routes into coun-

tering the dialectical tradition, most obviously Michel Foucault, Gilles Deleuze and Félix Guattari, and Jean-François Lyotard.
16. Derrida, 'Tympan', p. xi. Usefully glossing the implication of Derrida's critique of this central Hegelian movement, Bass notes 'there is nothing from which the *Aufhebung* cannot profit'; *'Différance'*, in *Margins of Philosophy*, p. 20, n. 23.
17. Derrida, 'Tympan', p. x.
18. Ibid., pp. x–xii.
19. Ibid., p. xii.
20. Ibid., p. xii. Footnote 6 indicates the prolific sexual investments that 'constrain the *discourse of the ear*' (p. xiv, italics original).
21. Ibid., p. xiv.
22. Ibid., p. xvii.
23. Ibid., p. xv.
24. Ibid.
25. Ibid.
26. Ibid., p. xxiii.
27. Ibid., p. xxviii.
28. Derrida, 'Eating Well', p. 283.
29. Ibid., pp. 280–1.
30. Robert Magiola notes the play Derrida obtains from the homophony of '*oreille*' and the present conditional '*aurait*', what 'would have', in 'Derridean Gaming and Buddhist Utpada/Bhanga (Rising/Falling): How a Philosophical Style Can Devoid Substantive Field', *International Journal for Field-Being*, 1.1, 2001, p. 24.
31. May R. Berenbaum, *The Earwig's Tail: A Modern Bestiary of Multi-Legged Legends* (Cambridge, MA: Harvard University Press, 2009). She cites data from Johns Hopkins emergency department reporting that, in fact, it is cockroaches that are commonly removed from human ears!
32. Berenbaum, *Earwig's Tail*, p. 10.
33. Derrida, 'Tympan', pp. xvii–xviii, n. 9.
34. Ibid., p. xviii, n. 9, my emphasis
35. See Jacques Derrida, 'The Voice that Keeps Silent', in *Voice and Phenomenon*, trans. Leonard Lawlor (Evanston: Northwestern University Press, 2011), pp. 60–74.
36. Berenbaum, *Earwig's Tail*, p. 14.
37. Derrida, 'Tympan', p. xvi.
38. Ibid., p. xxv. The ellipsis in the Leiris citation here edits out further specific examples – a dentist with a *basse taille*, Arab or Andalusian singers. See Leiris, *Scratches*, pp. 74–5.
39. Bass's translation misses out the sounds attributed to 'even those' of minerals. See Leiris, *Scratches*, p. 75.
40. Derrida, 'Tympan', p. xxv, italics original.
41. Two more ellipses in the citation follow – Derrida edits out Leiris's association of phonographs with his familial home. This may be to make sure the citation ends at a particular point, level with his own text and/or to excise possible over-association of acoustic economies with fathers and sons. See Leiris, *Scratches*, p. 76.

42. Jacques Derrida, 'Mnemosyne', trans. Cecile Lindsay, in *Memoires for Paul de Man*, rev. edn (New York: Columbia University Press, 1989), p. 28.
43. Derrida, 'Tympan', p. xxviii.
44. Derrida, 'Eating Well', p. 280.
45. Ibid., p. 280.
46. Ibid., p. 279
47. Ibid.
48. Ibid., p. 278. This violent trope 'the animal' also convenes animals under its sacrificial logic.
49. 'Who Comes After the Subject?' was the title of the special issue of *Topoi* (7.2, 1988) for which 'Eating Well' took place. Judith Still surmises a certain irritation on Nancy's part at the direction in which Derrida proceeds in her *Derrida and Hospitality* (Edinburgh: Edinburgh University Press, 2010), p. 227.
50. Derrida, 'Eating Well', p. 277.
51. Ibid., p. 282.
52. Derrida had already previously published 'Foreword: *Fors*: The Anglish Words of Nicolas Abraham and Maria Torok', in *The Wolf Man's Magic Word: A Cryptonomy* [1976], trans. Nicholas Rand (Minneapolis: Minnesota University Press, 1986), pp. xi–xlviii.
53. See Derrida, *'Fors'*, p. xxxvii.
54. Derrida, 'Eating Well', p. 278.
55. Ibid., p. 282.
56. Ibid., p. 282, italics original.
57. I develop the nasal ingestion of the other in my 'Animal Melancholia: On the Scent of *Dean Spanley*', in *Animality and the Moving Image*, ed. Michael Lawrence and Laura Macmahon (New York: Columbia University Press, 2014).
58. Kelly Oliver deftly discusses the key arguments voiced regarding possible compatibility between vegetarianism and deconstruction (by David Wood, Matthew Calarco and Leonard Lawlor), in *Animal Lessons: How They Teach Us to Be Human* (New York: Columbia University Press, 2009), pp. 106–7.
59. For an insightful discussion of how we might eat insect others, see Stephen Loo and Undine Sellbach, 'Eating (with) Insects: Insect Gastronomies and Upside-down Ethics', *parallax*, 19.1, 2013, pp. 12–28.
60. Indicated in the very title of their 'Mourning *or* Melancholia: Introjection *versus* Incorporation' [1972], in *The Shell and The Kernel*, trans. Nicholas Rand (Chicago: University of Chicago Press, 1994), pp. 125–38.
61. Derrida, 'Tympan', p. xxv, italics original.
62. Oliver, *Animal Lessons*, p. 126.
63. Derrida, 'Eating Well', p. 282.
64. Derrida, 'Ants', p. 33. 'Ants' gleans some inventive attention in Michael O'Rourke's essay 'David Wojnarowicz's *Fourmis*'. See http://www.academia.edu/479288/David_Wojnarowiczs_Fourmis (accessed 5 February 2013).
65. See Derrida, 'Typewriter Ribbon', pp. 71–3.
66. Derrida, *Animal*, 29.
67. Derrida, 'Typewriter Ribbon', p. 131.

68. Ibid., p. 130.
69. Ibid. In the only reference to the insects in 'Typewriter Ribbon' that I have yet found, Caroline Rooney manages to mix up these two successive sets of insects. Her guarded antipathy towards Derrida's insistent interweaving of machine and event ('techno-performativity' as she calls it, as if nothing is altered or displaced in this new relation) leads her to confuse the murderous bloodsucker with the mating midges and so accuse Derrida, when he talks of their *jouissance*, of both a machinic fervour and simple sexism. See Caroline Rooney, *Decolonising Gender: Literature and a Poetics of the Real* (New York and London: Routledge, 2007), p. 157.
70. Derrida, 'Typewriter Ribbon', p. 131.
71. Rooney appears to think that Derrida is making just such a return. I take his use of the term 'concept' in relation to *causa sui* to indicate the reverse. See Rooney, *Decolonising Gender*, p. 157.
72. Derrida, 'Typewriter Ribbon', p. 133
73. Ibid.
74. Rousseau, cited in 'Typewriter Ribbon', p. 132.
75. Ibid. My 'Corrected Edition' has further 'corrected' Rousseau's odd locution of 'J'étois comme si j'avais commis un inceste' as 'I felt as if I had been guilty of incest' (Rousseau avoids both the verb 'to feel' and naming 'guilt' as such). See Jacques Derrida, *Of Grammatology*, trans. Gayatri Chakravorty Spivak (Baltimore: Johns Hopkins University Press, 1997), p. 95.
76. Derrida, 'Eating Well', p. 285.
77. Derrida, 'Ants', p. 34.
78. The question of the divisibility of the letter is central to Derrida's critique of Jacques Lacan, in his 'Le Facteur de la Verité', in *The Post Card: From Socrates to Freud and Beyond*, trans. Alan Bass (Chicago: University of Chicago Press, 1987), pp. 411–96, and echoed in his discussion of Paul de Man's framing of the purloined ribbon in 'Typewriter Ribbon', p. 115.
79. See Cixous, *Insister*, p. 130, among numerous references to such exchanges.
80. Derrida, 'Ants', p. 18.
81. Ibid., pp. 18–19.
82. For example, John Mowitt, 'Like A Whisper', *differences: a journal of feminist cultural studies*, 22.2–3, 2011, pp. 168–89.
83. Derrida, 'Ants', p. 21
84. Ibid.
85. Uncannily doubling Rousseau's confession of the 'same' event in writings ten years apart ('Typewriter Ribbon', p. 100).
86. Ibid., p. 22.
87. Ibid., p. 21, italics original.
88. Ibid., p. 20.
89. Ibid., p. 33.
90. Ibid., p. 34.
91. Ibid., p. 35.
92. Ibid., p. 34, emphasis mine.

Chapter 5

Sponge Inc

Laurent Milesi

What if deconstruction were a sponge, an animal tissue or texture capable, when wet, of soaking up traces – the trace being for Derrida a more appropriate, more generalisable substitute for the sign since it can include its animal and technological nature?[1] But also of sponging off the lexicon of the bodies of texts with which it grapples by contagious proximity or paradox, like the parasite it has often been dismissively assimilated to, whose signature could anticipate a recent cartoon hero: not Deconstructo[2] but SpongeBob.[3] SpongeJack...

To take the plunge and take up the sponge faster, I will allow myself a summary quotation, a parasitic self-quotation from an earlier study, 'Dry Ink: Arguing (to) the Limits', whose own beginning, on the allegedly parasitic nature of deconstruction, can be read in retrospect as my prelude to the present essay:

> With its sustained interest in the logic of supplementarity, parergonal (framing) effects, the iterability (i.e. repeatability *and* alterability) of structurally counterfeitable signatures, and conceptual de-limitations etc. [...] deconstruction has very early been accused by its detractors of being a parasitic activity sponging off not only the primary matter of literary, philosophical (etc.) texts but also their normative interpretations.[4]

Sparked off by Wayne Booth's assertion, echoed by M.H. Abrams, that the deconstructionist reading of a given work 'is plainly and simply parasitical' on 'the obvious or univocal reading', the accusation of parasitism was re-staged citationally by Hillis Miller in his rejoinder to the latter one year later, in Spring 1977, and uncannily dovetailed with the more bitter, if not unrelated feud that ensued from the publication of the English translation of Derrida's 'Signature Event Context', followed by Searle's surly 'Reply', then Derrida's unusually polemical retort as 'Limited Inc abc . . .', in the first two issues of the newly founded critical journal *Glyph* that same year.[5]

Framed between the original French version of 'Sec' (Derrida's own 'dry' acronym for his essay's title), which appeared in 1972, and its fraught English dissemination, Derrida's lecture on French poet Francis Ponge, *Signéponge*, first given in 1975 and subsequently excerpted for French publication in 1976 and 1977, reminds us beyond its uproarious verbal capers of the continuous engagement with Austin's theory of performativity and speech acts which had provided the touchstone for his deconstruction of the 'signature' in 'Signature Event Context'. Like a so-far hidden genealogy, *Signéponge*, or *Signsponge*, is in fact one uncannily premonitory missing link in the evolutionary chain of texts and contexts which were to lead to the controversy with Searle, starting as it does on an 'attack' with a 'scratch': the 'remark' on Ponge's 'self-remark', an utterance which Derrida also remarks can itself be grafted, cited, suspended between quotation marks:

> Francis Ponge will have been self-remarked [*se sera remarqué*].
> I just pronounced a sentence. It can be repeated, by me or by you if you cited it some day. Nothing will keep you from putting it into quotation marks [. . .]. You can put it out to dry [*sécher*] – it's still very fresh – with the kind of clothespins [*épingles à linge*] that are used now and then by photographers to develop a print [*cliché*]. Why clothespins, you will ask. We don't know as yet; they also form, like quotation marks, a part of the negative that is being developed.
> In any case, I assume the risk of this attack
> [. . .]
> In the rhetorical code, an attack, the first piece, designates, in French, the first piece of a text, of a theatrical scene or an act, the intrusive intervention of a preliminary speech act which no longer leaves you in peace [. . .]
> I am betting today that this gripping force of an attack never occurs without a scratch [*griffe*]; never, in other words, without some scene of signature.[6]

Some three years after concluding his very dry ('Sec') discussion of the overlap between parasitism and normality in citational speech acts,[7] Derrida begins *Signéponge* by inviting us to 'put out to dry' a citation we might wish to make of his inaugural remark or attack. And unlike 'Sec', which ends on the mimetic 'counterfeiting' (photocopied rather than photographed) of his own handwritten signature,[8] *Signéponge* will fail to display, thus somehow erase, the trace of Ponge's autograph on the black-and-white reproduction of the 'BANDE A FAIRE SAUTER'.[9]

This attack, then, hinges on the thorny, evasive question of mimesis – since 'Francis Ponge will have been self-remarked' was mimicking (or already pretending to mime)[10] a remark from Ponge's poem 'Le Carnet du bois de pin' – which Derrida proposes to sidestep rather than approach frontally, and reduce to a 'minuscule vanishing point at the already sunlit abyssal depths of the mimosa', whose root *mimo-* is used for those so-called 'mimic plants' 'which contract when touched'.[11] Miming mimesis 'itself', chameleon-like, apotropaically: for an *exposé* which will turn out to abound in facetious quirks of language and argumentation, the inaugural tone is decidedly also very (self-)protective, as if, its signatory already on his guard, it had uncannily anticipated and attempted to ward off the spikiness of the double debate in 1976–77 (Booth–Abrams vs. Hillis Miller; Searle vs. Derrida), parasiting – not to say 'para-citing' – it and sponging off it in advance, as it were.[12]

Derrida thus attacks a signature, but the attack, rather than making the attacked fall into pieces, monumentalises it.[13] From this monument or 'colossal corpus', in the circuitous exchanges between signature, text and thing, he will draw out only 'a very light, aerolithic, or spongy stone [...] perhaps a pumice stone [*pierre ponce*]'.[14] And Derrida's own object or thing, 'that which is going to prescribe a rhetoric proper to this event', is 'Francis Ponge' who,

> without effacing his name, [...] has nonetheless effaced it by showing that the stony monumentalization of the name was a way [...] of sponging his signature. And, of course, this is the twist of the signature, *vice versa*.[15]

The event of a signature, the structure of its taking place, then of its countersigning, raises the question of the relationship between the author and his so-called 'proper' name, 'whether his proper name is truly his name and truly proper'.[16] It is in this interrogation of the porous interstitial space between the common and the proper, the proper and the non-proper, 'the abyss of the proper [in which] we are going to try to recognise the impossible idiom of a signature',[17] that 'Francis Ponge' enters and *signsponge*. And, in his eponymous text, Derrida himself as SpongeJack, like a mimic plant, may also contract when touched, hiding a more ancient, 'drier' (*plus sèche*), more protective creature . . .

Wet cleaning: SpongeJack

J'éponge, donc je suis

So what *is* a sponge? According to the OED, from which I shall extract the first and third definitions, the contained and the container, it is

> The soft, light, porous, and easily compressible framework which remains after the living matter has been removed from various species of porifers

> [. . .], characterised by readily absorbing fluids and yielding them on pressure [. . .]
>
> One or other of various species of aquatic (chiefly marine) animals [. . .] of a low order belonging to the group *Porifera*, characterised by a tough elastic skeleton of interlaced fibres.

Thus it is an animal which is no longer a living animal, about whom Derrida could therefore venture later, in 'Force of Law', that

> [a]n animal can be made to suffer, but one would never say, in a sense said to be proper, that it is a wronged subject, the victim of a crime, of a murder, of a rape or a theft, of a perjury – and this is true *a fortiori*, one thinks, for what one calls vegetable or mineral or intermediate species like the sponge.[18]

This concession to the impropriety of the sponge should be tacitly contrasted with his admission of his own *souffrance* in *Signsponge*,[19] in the difficulty of citing any text of Ponge's as an exemplary demonstration since every poem bears the hallmark of a unique signature and rhetoric. This also anticipates the more crucial point, echoing Bentham, about animals being capable of suffering and being made to suffer in *The Animal That Therefore I Am*,[20] which subsequently imbibes in passing earlier instances of Derrida's attention to the sponge in his own zoopoetics or bestiary:

> well before Ponge's zooliterature in *Signsponge* (the swallow, the shrimp, the oyster); well before the sponge itself, that marine zoophyte that is wrongly held to be a plant [. . .] which had passed through my work earlier, again in 'White Mythology', in relation to what Bachelard identified by the name of the 'metaphysics of the sponge'.[21]

Lower than an animal (*OED*: 'of a low order'), then, the sponge would further attest to its deconstructive lowliness by not preserving the difference between the two senses of the 'proper', and even by contaminating the possibility of separating the proper from the improper or common, the *nom propre* from the *non-propre*. Retaining the dirt which it sucks up until it expunges it when (ex)pressed in clear or fresh [*fraîche*] water, the sponge promiscuously mixes the common and the proper. No one else than somebody named Ponge could have been more alert to this 'essence' or 'nature', self-deconstructive or paradoxical rather than dialectical, since, for him as for Derrida (for instance in *Glas*), Hegel 'is not very proper,[22] and after reading him, you have to wash up [*se laver*], to wash your hands of him',[23] using *savon* (soap) against the Absolute Knowledge of a regal *nous savons*:

He will have speculated as no one else on the proper, the proper way to write and the proper way to sign. No longer separating, within the proper, the two stems of *propriety* and *property*.[24]

In the linen (of the body), its tissue, its text, *proper* envelops both propriety and property.[25]

On the one hand, the sponge expunges [*l'éponge éponge*] the proper name, puts it outside of itself, effaces and loses it, soils it as well in order to make it into a common noun, it contaminates the proper name on contact with the most pitiful, the most unqualifiable object, which is made to retain every sort of dirt. We gather together here a group of negative values that could cause us to reject the sponge for being dirty, and for sponging away the proper. But simultaneously, the sponge can also retain the name, absorb it, shelter it, and keep it within itself. Then, too, it holds clean and proper water as well as dirty water, insatiably. [. . .] the sponge remains undecided and *undecidable*. Not because it holds what is dirty and improper, but because it is sufficiently equivocal to hold the dirty *as well as* the clean, the non-proper as well as the proper. This is why it is not noble, not frank [*franche*]: *ignoble*, rather.[26]

the sponge [. . .] is 'ignoble' in that it lends itself to all contraries, both the proper and the non-proper. [. . .] The sponge is only a muscle filled with wind, with clean water or dirty water, as may be: this gymnastic is ignoble.[27]

But, and this is its redeeming paradox, the one that allows 'Ponge' to mobilise it via the *froufrou* of his first name 'Francis',[28] for Ponge is ultimately obsessed with cleanliness:

Ignoble as it may be, and lacking in natural nobility; poor in its genealogical extraction, and unable to choose between the proper and the improper, the economy of the sponge is nonetheless better able to resist the oppressor – *its ignoble labor enfranchises it* [*l'affranchit*].[29]

Through its dual act of 'impressionable aspiration and expression',[30] the sponge can thus ward off oppression 'since it [. . .] always recovers its countenance [. . .], on account of which it is a free and frank object, a subject which knows how to enfranchise itself'.[31] Like that of deconstruction, its 'economy' is thus not one according to which things merely and simply 'come back to the same', despite its returning to its earlier form or countenance and thus resisting disfiguration, but rather one that in this process of 'purification' palimpsestically erases the traces of what 'is'[32] in the tempor(al)ising *différance* between the improper and the proper. This work or 'toil' of deconstruction, also Ponge's preoccupation, is registered in the articulation between the *sale* and the *sali(e)* – whose '+ i' formula we shall return to later – the 'soiled' and the 'moiled':

> I shall now bring out the resoluteness with which he will have taken sides with the proper against the dirty [*sale*], or rather against the soiled [*sali*], the sullied, a distinction which reveals a whole story, one that takes time and decomposes itself: there is no dirty thing, only a soiled thing, a proper thing which is made dirty. Which is moiled, since impurity [...] often comes about through liquid means, and so should be absorbed by a cloth which is appropriate. Appropriating. The proper is moiled. That which is soiled [*souillé*] is moiled [*mouillé*].[33]

But unlike the deconstructive logic of the exappropriative nature of the signature,[34] the 'text(ile)' operation or scene of Ponge's writing, like a washing machine (his poem 'La lessiveuse'), attempts a purificatory reappropriation as the (s)Ponge still relentlessly hopes to clean(se) the improper from the proper.[35] Just like the soap that also figures the subject, 'that *sort-of-stone-but* – which polishes (*ponce*) like the pumice stone – "washing and washed" (*qui lave et se lave*)',[36] where the reflexive recalls Derrida's gloss '*ça se déconstruit*', in which the *se* 'is not the reflexivity of an ego' or egological subjectivity but a mark of auto-affection, and reminds us of the essentially figurative activity of clean(s)ing.[37]

One form of contamination in which the poetry signed (s)Ponge and Derridean deconstruction intersect can be located in 'the fabulous story and the rich possibilities of syntactical articulation': Derrida's (at least) 'double syntax', which he repeatedly stated is more than its more publicised lexical coinages, the deconstructive operation and strategy *par excellence*.[38] It is instanced in the all-absorbing, (self-)copulative work of the name Francis Ponge, which 'spins' parts of speech like the indiscriminate sponge: 'Francis est Ponge, Francis et Ponge' (the 'harmonious heterosexual couple' or 'lucky coupling' – what Greek *syn-tax* also meant),[39] and, since *Francis (s')éponge/c'est Ponge* (Francis sponges himself/is Ponge), the (s)Ponge porously absorbs all possible morpho-syntactical positions: 'Eponge éponge, l'éponge éponge, l'éponge est Ponge'.[40] In their leaky, overflowing abundance,[41] the sponge, the syntagm *signéponge*, but also the *tissu-* or *serviette-éponge* 'on either side of the hyphen or the incessant copulation',[42] mediate between subject and attribute, substance and accident, noun and adjective: 'Affecting itself with everything, the sponge is sponged [*l'éponge s'éponge*]. Itself, himself.'[43] And since the porous sign 'sponges the signature', like a reversible garment or an item of clothing turned inside out to dry better, 'l'éponge est un signe. Puis le signe est Ponge',[44] which can then be hacked into 'le signe hait Ponge' ('the sign hisses Ponge'),[45] counterfeited as 'signé Ponge', given as an order to you ('signez Ponge') or, with a *virgule*, to him ('signez, Ponge').[46]

Such a rhythmic oscillation playing on homophony and syntax can be heard (but was infelicitously left out of the translation) in one of the most hilarious climaxes of Derrida's text – which should be understood in the distant wake of his attempt to force Ponge not to wash his hands of what Derrida is saying about him as Ponge feels like doing with any unclean philosophy,[47] as well as in anticipation of the figure of *Ponce* (Pontius) Pilate who, after Christ's crucifixion, washed his hands (of the whole thing):

> Car Francis se fout de l'éponge.[48]

> A chaque coup [*de mots*], il se fout de l'éponge. [. . .] Il exprime son nom, c'est tout. A travers tout le corpus.[49]

> Il se fout de l'éponge, éperdument, partout. Un peu partout, sur le corps.[50]

True, Francis 'tient à l'éponge' ('sticks by the sponge'),[51] since he is so obsessed with clean(s)ing and the 'proper'; then, in moments when the discouraging sponge will never have had enough, 'jette l'éponge' ('throws away the sponge'), takes it up and drops it;[52] but the idiomatic *se foutre de*, iterated in three progressive stages to ensure we register the *double entendre*, here means not only 'not to give a damn' or 'fig' (since the sponge 'will not have been his thing' and he 'reserv[es] all rights for himself – the right to make fun of it, to raise it or lower it')[53] but also 'to stick something all over' – one's *corpus* (of texts) or one's *corps* (body, covered by the linen washed clean), the words squeezed out or 'expressed' being also 'bodies, pieces of his body, extremities where his grasping body takes him'.[54]

Derrida mops up and gathers all the spongisms secreted by Francis Ponge, traces or remarks attesting to the dirty that will have been: 'The *spongismos* is a scraping, a piece of dirt removed from the sponge, set apart, chosen, said and read, collected with a sponge (*spoggizô, spoggologueô*).'[55] More generally, Derridean deconstruction is imbued with the verbal ink spillings from earlier texts, which it dissolves and 'analyses' (from *ana-luein*: to break down) in such relentless operations that, to its detractors, it becomes 'imbued with itself' and *imbuvable* ('intolerable').[56] Sponge-like and sponging off like mad, deconstruction *se fout de tout*. Here, there and everywhere . . .

The absorptive sponge-text of poetry

For Ponge, poetry, in order to remain an event, had to forever reinvent not only its language, style, tone or rhetoric but also its objects, and not shy away from 'the thing of low extraction', such as the sponge-towel or the washing machine.[57] And indeed, stretching texts and tissues a little, one could venture that poetry, its 'putting into work' or *en-ergeia*, involves a process of con*ver*sion, from impression to expression,[58] not unlike the sponge when it washes and is rinsed.

Such defamiliarisation against the ready-to-wear metaphysics of 'classical' poetry is also the aim of the deconstructionist poetics of the Language (or L=A=N=G=U=A=G=E) poets, whose major conceptual manifesto, Charles Bernstein's 'Artifice of Absorption', written out in verse, sets up the poem as a sponge of sorts:

> A poetic *reading* can be given to any
> piece of writing; a 'poem' may be understood as
> writing specifically designed to absorb, or inflate
> with, proactive – rather than reactive – styles of
> reading.[59]

Thus, to echo Derrida's renegotiation of the traditional boundary between human response and animal reaction in 'And Say the Animal Responded? to Jacques Lacan',[60] if reading is already a response to a piece of writing from the other side or *esponde/sponda*,[61] 'proper' poetry for Bernstein would grow with more proactive, rather than simply reactive, reading. Poetry would be truly expressive, 're-sponsive', when absorbing automatically, spontaneously (*sponte sua*); its *spongistikè tekhnè*[62] would consist already in being a response to what it sponges up and expunges or expresses, according to Derrida's laws of automaticity and 'living spontaneity'.[63]

Paralleling at a distance his earlier adoption of Steve McCaffery's Derrida-inspired interdependency between a 'general' (non-utilitarian, disseminative) and a 'restricted' (recuperable) economy,[64] Bernstein elaborates on his anti-traditional 'dialectic' between absorptive and anti-absorptive poetic language, underscoring once again the spongy texture of the textual tissue:

> Insofar as I make a distinction between the
> absorptive & antiabsorptive, these terms
> should not be understood as mutually exclusive,
> morally coded, or even conceptually separable.
>   [...]
> From a compositional point of view
> the question is, What can a poem absorb?
> Here, think
> of a text as a spongy substance, absorbing
> vocabulary, syntax, & reference.[65]

While the absorptive and the antiabsorptive works both require artifice, 'the former may hide / this while the latter may flaunt / it';[66] Bernstein's (and, more generally, language poets') inclination is to 'frequently use opaque & nonabsorbable / elements, digressions & / interruptions, as part of a technological / arsenal to create a more powerful / ("souped-up") / absorption than possible with traditional, / & blander, absorptive techniques.'[67]

Although deconstructive writing does not feature in Bernstein's elliptical catalogue of nonabsorptive poetics in the twentieth century,[68] it would legitimately qualify among those 'recent antiabsorptive techniques [that] have tended / to use syntactic and graphemic rather than lexical / invention',[69] as I recalled earlier, alongside Ponge, whose emblematic 'Fable', starting 'Par le mot *par* commence donc ce texte', flaunts a type of syntactical self-consciousness not unlike the opening line of Bernstein's 'Wait' (though without the same kind of 'internal twist'): 'This is the way to start a sentence about startling [sic] a sentence.'[70]

Ponge's celebrated 'Fable', discussed in *Signsponge*,[71] so arrested Derrida that he squeezed some more substance out of it in a sub-section of the titular introductory essay of *Psyche: Inventions of the Other*, in order to reiterate, long after the verbal sparring with Searle had abated (though well before the near-final 'Toward An Ethic of Discussion'),[72] how fables are 'beyond speech acts', since Ponge's poem, 'owing to a turn of syntax, is a sort of poetic performative that simultaneously *describes* and *carries out*, on the same line, its own generation'.[73] Its 'invention' consists in conflating, through citational effects, the two poles – for speech-act theory, 'two absolutely heterogeneous functions' – of the constative and the performative,[74] use and mention:

> The constative statement is the performative itself [...]. Its performance consists in the 'constation' [*constat*] of the constative – and nothing else. [...]
>
> The infinitely rapid oscillation between the performative and the constative, [...] calls for a new theory and for the constitution of new statutes and conventions that [...] would be able to account for them. I am not sure that speech-act theory, in its present state and dominant form, is capable of this.[75]

But each fable has more than one animal at least and our ubiquitous sponge which, no matter how much it absorbs, never loses countenance and is never dis-figured, may not be the only animal of this tale ...[76]

Dry cleaning, or *le nettoyage à seiche*

J'éponge, donc j'essuie

Among the many rhetorical and argumentative flourishes deployed by Derrida to counter Searle – aliased as SARL, French for 'Ltd' or 'Inc[orporated]' – in 'Limited Inc abc . . .', one may pick up in transit but also in translation this teasing observation, soon after Derrida has taken great pains to quote the passage in 'Signature Event Context' where, in conclusion, he had abbreviated the title of his essay as 'Sec':

> *Sec* is set there – in a manner which, you may take my word for it, was hardly fortuitous – in italics. Three points follow, which lead to the apparent simulacrum of 'my' signatures, of my seal in bits and pieces, divided, multiplied. [. . .] why does that absorb [*passionne*] and irritate Sarl to such a degree? [. . .]
> The 'very dry discussion' conducting *continuously* to the multiple signature of *Sec*, *Sec* will henceforth designate the whole of *Sec* plus (including) its multiple, presumed, divided, and associated signatories. Which signals [. . .] that *Signature Event Context* might also lend credence to the parasite of a 'true' dependent proposition: 'signature event that one texts' [*signature événement qu'on texte*].[77]

'Absorb' will have been unwittingly 'absorbed' and 'remarked' into this all-inclusive signal remark-in-translation, which tantalisingly overlaps with Bernstein's observation that, in 'political' contexts, the mechanism and threat of absorption can be infinitely self-replicating, 'down to the individual divided against itself'.[78] And since the all-absorbing *Signsponge* as a sequel of sorts to 'Sec' conceals a whole 'zooliterature', one should not be surprised to extract or express from it, unbeknownst to it perhaps, what is called in French *une seiche*, a cuttlefish sounding homophonously and originally spelled like the feminine form of '*sec*' (*sèche*), that animal which protects itself with(in) its own *ink*, and which could even be hiding in an epitaph behind a certain 'dried fig' (*La Figue* [*sèche*]) culled from one of Ponge's figural poetic leaves.[79]

Sponging up more zooliterature and, after Derrida's own invitation, putting it out to dry within quotation marks compared to tweezers (*pincettes*),[80] one could conjure up the ironic description of Casaubon's coat of arms in *Middlemarch*: 'As to his blood, I suppose the family quarterings are three cuttle-fish sable, and a commentator rampant.'[81] And by linguistic cross-breeding, one might wish to hijack or sponge-Jack this 'sable', or the black ink exuded or 'spilt' by the cuttlefish to conceal itself[82] into the French for 'sand', that substance, ground from stone (*pierre*), in which the proverbial *autruche* (ostrich) buries its head, conflated with the intrusive 'i' of *Autriche* (Austria) in Lacan's 'Seminar on "The Purloined Letter"', whose pun on *politique de l'autruiche* was used to castigate the self-deceptive protectiveness of those who do not want to (be) see(n).[83] While the signsponge, the sponge-as-signature, 'also regards me',[84] in both senses of 'it concerns me' and 'it looks at me' since it exchanges between the inside (impression, absorption) and the outside (expression, expunging), the self-absorbed cuttlefish, hidden away within the text of *Signsponge*, withdraws from our gaze.[85]

Sèche and *seiche*: this incremental swelling '+ i' (with or without diacritic), reminiscent of other such supplementary formulas in the Derridean corpus,[86] should not be construed as the telltale sign of an unconscious drive towards capitalisation, overbid or surplus value, so often called into question since the essay against Hegel's restricted economy. Rather, it is the hallmark of a difference that divides the proper between property and propriety – but which is also at work, as we foresaw, between the *sale* and the *sali(e)* – and after stating Ponge's obsessional 'speculation' on the duality of the proper,[87] *Signsponge* recapitulates some instances of what it calls Ponge's 'treatment' of the I:

> The only difference, after all, between the one and the other [*propreté, propriété*], is an I out of which we can always make some dead wood. He has treated the I in every way, in every language, in upper case ([. . .] one, simple, single, singularity [. . .]); in lower case, taking it off [*le faisant sauter*] in order to write, in the *Pre*, 'a verdant verity' [*une vérité qui soit verte*]; playing with its frail or fresh erection in *the Making of the pre*: 'Difference between the liquid drop or accent (acute here) dot on the i and the virgule of the grass. Virgule, verge [*vergette*]'.[88]

Here the French does say 'Il a traité le I de toutes les manières', rather than *traité du*; that is, perhaps not merely 'dealt with it' but also 'treated it' in all possible ways, proper or improper, in upper or lower case.[89] The virile, erectile I – which could also be the one the *verge* would discreetly insert *in absentia* in a *vierge* – is there to remind us that a 'subject' may be 'maltreated' and therefore, when under attack, protect itself in its own ink (like the *seiche*). Or even – to use a cliché or *poncif*,[90] parsing it as *Cif* (Jif) on *(pierre) ponce* (pumice) or Ponge – scratch back if the deconstructive sponge is rubbed the wrong way and, no longer wishing to absorb blows or sponge off the slate,[91] turns abrasive.[92] In which case Derrida, unlike his citations held by Ponge's tweezers, *n'est pas à prendre avec des pincettes* (is 'like a bear with a sore head').

If one signatory can inc(orporate) another, for instance a corporate SARL within a not-so-singular Searle, a *seiche* can conceal a *sec* in its ink (but also 'tamarisk' a 'tamis' and 'mimosa' a 'mima'),[93] and here one should carefully analyse all the idiomatic turns in *sec*, such as *aussi sec* or *à sec* (*ça rapplique à-Sec*), enlisted by Derrida in 'Limited Inc a b c ...' in order to expose S(e)ARL(e)'s sneakily absorptive gesture 'which recurs regularly in the reply and consists in taking arguments borrowed *from Sec [à Sec]*', parasitically reapplying and replying supposed objections lifted from *Sec* which Derrida himself will therefore have signed and countersigned in advance.[94] 'Sec' will have 'absorbed' sponge Searle, who unwittingly expunges back to Derrida his own 'dry' words.

Unlike the cuttlefish, which rather unambiguously endeavours to protect itself and secure its own immunity, the all-absorbing, retentive sponge keeps (*garde*) as well as expunges.[95] Its ambivalent double gesture can be recast in the light of two of deconstruction's most versatile, reversible formulas: *l'Un se garde de l'autre pour se faire violence* in *Archive Fever*,[96] and the problematic of 'auto-immune supplementarity', *save by itself*, contaminating the immunitary in 'Faith and Knowledge'.[97] *Signsponge* is that auto-immune sign(ature) which keeps (away from) or guards (against) the other within itself – 'the self-otherness or self-difference (the difference from within oneself)'[98] of the 'sign(s)Ponge'. It keeps and erases the movement of *différance* within the self and, in so doing, 'abrases': raising or erecting itself into abrasive violence, including to itself, 'between a certain *effacing* of the signature [. . .] and a stubborn [*acharné*] *redoubling* of the signature',[99] between *Francis et Ponge*, the virile principle of frankness with its erect i's, aitches and hatchets, '[t]he hard kernel of Francity' (*franchise, hache*,[100] Greek *spoggios*), and the feminine sponge as limitlessly passive all-absorbing receptacle as well as *subjectile*[101] for writing (also Greek *spoggia*):

> The common name loses, but then again, by canceling the debt, it seals and keeps [*garde*] the proper name, and Francis will have been a kind of *spongoteras*: the Greeks gave this name to the animal that guards [*animal gardien*] the sponge, that goes on guard [*monte la garde*] before it, but also lets itself be sheltered by it.[102]

> Thanks to what condemns him in advance, he also preserves himself [*se garde*]: against any aggression, against infection by a foreign body [. . .] against the other in general. For the sponge will have let him sign in advance – the absolute antidote – almost the entire body [*corpus*] of the French language.[103]

Unlike Plato's *Sophist*, where the difficult separation between best and worst is called a 'diacritical' process of purification, one of whose two methods of argumentation is spongistics, sponge-deconstruction remains 'on its guard' by being 'pre-critical', on this side of the separation between the two 'stems' of the proper, or between the proper and the improper as *sale, sali* and so on.[104] Unlike the animal as it is envisaged by philosophical tradition, it is equally capable of leaving tracks/traces (*tracer*) and of effacing them (*effacer ses traces*),[105] its own animal signatures as much as others', proper or improper, in an oscillation which ultimately redraws the lines between 'what is' and what remains, in the syntactical double bind of a '*reste à disparaître*'.[106]

What if, after all, deconstruction could also on occasion mimic a cuttlefish, spread and concealed across 'two sessions'?[107] A cuttlefish almost invisible behind the 'sweet illusion' of a mimosa ('from *mimus*, because those plants, when contracting, seem to represent the grimaces of a mime'),[108] like 'the necessarily invisible quotation marks surrounding the proper name',[109] whose signature would be *Jacques sec/seiche*, rather than the *j'accepte/ Jacques sept* of *The Post Card*?[110] Sepia ... From the sponge to the *seiche*, from wetness (back) to *sec*: this chapter's trajectory will thus have revealed and dramatised how, when under attack, Derrida's generously all-absorptive sponge – whose more abrasive scratch-pad should, however, not be forgotten and which in any case is far from the sponge Zarathustra advises us to understand if we 'want to be loved by overflowing hearts'[111] – can metamorphose into an ingeniously defensive cuttlefish with a dry or wry tone.

Notes

1. See Laurent Milesi, 'Semiology and Deconstruction: From Sign to Trace', in *Transmodernity: Managing Global Communication*, proceedings of the Second ROASS Conference, ed. Doina Cmeciu and Traian D. Stănciulescu (Bacău: Alma Mater, 2009), pp. 135–46, whose introduction refers to my earlier companion pieces '*Saint-Je* Derrida', *Oxford Literary Review*, 29, 'Derridanimals', ed. Neil Badmington, 2007, pp. 55–75, and 'Almost Nothing at the Beginning: The Technicity of the Trace in Deconstruction', in *Language System After Prague Structuralism*, ed. Louis Armand with Pavel Černovský (Prague: Litteraria Pragensia, 2007), pp. 22–31 – which can also be taken as more distant points of departure for this essay. Hélène Cixous also commented on the animality of the Derridean trace in 'Jacques Derrida: Co-Responding Voix You', in *Derrida and the Time of the Political*, ed. Pheng Cheah and Suzanne Guerlac (Durham, NC: Duke University Press, 2009), pp. 41–53.
2. See Gerard Jones, Ron Randall and Randy Elliott, 'Justice League Europe', nos. 37–9 (DC Comics, 1992).
3. See the Spongebob Squarepants cartoon created by Stephen Hillenburg, © 2013 Viacom International Inc.
4. Laurent Milesi, 'Dry Ink: Arguing (to) the Limits', *Word and Text. A Journal of Literary Studies and Linguistics*, 1.2, 'Limits of Criticism/ Critique of the Limits', ed. Laurent Milesi and Ivan Callus, December 2011, p. 8.
5. The double chronological sequence of essays is as follows: 1. Wayne C.

Booth, 'M.H. Abrams: Historian as Critic, Critic as Pluralist', *Critical Inquiry*, 2.3, Spring 1976, pp. 411–45; M.H. Abrams, 'Rationality and Imagination in Cultural History: A Reply to Wayne Booth', *Critical Inquiry*, 2.3, Spring 1976, pp. 447–64; J. Hillis Miller, 'The Critic as Host', *Critical Inquiry*, 3.3, Spring 1977, pp. 439–47. 2. Jacques Derrida, 'Signature Event Context', trans. Samuel Weber and Jeffrey Mehlman, *Glyph*, 1, 1977, pp. 172–97; John R. Searle, 'Reiterating the Differences: A Reply to Derrida', *Glyph*, 1, 1977, pp. 198–208; Jacques Derrida, 'Limited Inc abc . . .', trans. Samuel Weber, *Glyph*, 2, 1977, pp. 162–254.
6. Jacques Derrida, *Signéponge / Signsponge*, trans. Richard Rand (New York: Columbia University Press, 1984), pp. 2, 4. In his foreword or 'Greenwood', Rand remarks that '"Signature Event Context" anticipates the cosigning of the (fantastic) contract between poet and thing' (p. x). Implicit in this passage is the analogy between *griffe* and *greffe*, either as 'graft' (feminine in French) or, if masculine, related to the act of transcribing a (legal) document, from Greek *graphein*: to write, already brought together in the 'coup de griffe et de greffe' of *Le Monolinguisme de l'autre, ou la prothèse d'origine* (Paris: Galilée, 1996), p. 124 (left untranslated in the English version). See *Demenageries: Thinking (of) Animals after Derrida*, ed. Anne Emmanuelle Berger and Marta Segarra (Amsterdam and New York: Rodopi, 2011), p. 10 (in their introductory 'Thoughtprints').
7. Jacques Derrida, 'Signature Event Context', in *Margins of Philosophy*, trans. Alan Bass (Brighton: Harvester, 1982), p. 329. All citations from this essay refer to this version rather than to the original English publication referenced in note 4.
8. Derrida, 'Signature Event Context', p. 330.
9. Derrida, *Signsponge*, p. 155.
10. Ibid., p. 10
11. Ibid., pp. 4, 6, 138.
12. Ibid., p. 6.
13. Ibid., p 4.
14. Ibid., p. 20; also p. 108.
15. Ibid., p. 26. See also Jacques Derrida, 'Counter-Signatures', in *Points . . . Interviews, 1974–1994*, ed. Elisabeth Weber, trans. Peggy Kamuf et al. (Stanford: Stanford University Press, 1995), pp. 365–8, in response to the first question about Derrida's discovery of the revelatory force of Ponge's poetry when he wrote *Signéponge*, especially p. 366: 'by inscribing the name in the thing, from one angle, I lose the signature, but, from another angle, I monumentalise the name, I transform the name into a thing; like a stone, like a monument'. This extract, originally published in *Fig. 5* (1991) from a radio interview broadcast earlier, should not be confused with 'Countersignature', a lecture given at a conference on the poetics of Jean Genet in 2000, trans. Mairéad Hanrahan, *Paragraph*, 27.2, July 2004, pp. 7–42, which also evokes the problematic of Ponge and countersignature (especially pp. 27–8).
16. Derrida, *Signsponge*, pp. 24, 26.
17. Ibid., p. 28.
18. Jacques Derrida, 'Force of Law: The "Mystical Foundation of Authority"',

trans. Mary Quaintance, in *Acts of Religion*, ed. Gil Anidjar (New York and London: Routledge, 2002), p. 246.
19. Derrida, *Signsponge*, p. 21; mistranslated as 'problem' rather than 'suffering'.
20. Jacques Derrida, *The Animal That Therefore I Am*, ed. Marie-Louise Mallet, trans. David Wills (New York: Fordham University Press, 2008), esp. pp. 81, 103, 108.
21. Derrida, *Animal*, p. 406. See 'White Mythology', in *Margins of Philosophy*, p. 259, n. 66, citing Bachelard's description of Descartes' metaphysics of space in the context of a citation on the relationship between the proper (literal), the metaphorical and truth or reason. *Signsponge* had already recalled the definition from *Littré*, 'neither proper nor improper, neither simply a thing, nor simply vegetal, nor simply animal. They call this thing either a *zoophyte*, an animal plant, or else the substance "deriving from a marine zoophyte" (*Littré*)' as well as Bachelard's 'metaphysics of the sponge' used to dismiss Descartes (*Signsponge*, pp. 70, 98).
22. Since, like other philosophers, he does not interrupt his texts with the act of signing with the idiom of his name and language, and instead speaks in necessarily improper concepts and generalities (*Signsponge*, p. 32).
23. Derrida, *Signsponge*, pp. 30, 32.
24. Ibid., p. 28.
25. Ibid., p. 46.
26. Ibid., p. 64.
27. Ibid., p. 66.
28. See ibid., p. 42 for 'all the words beginning in *fr-*, like freshness, describ[ing] a certain way of handling linen', and p. 62 for Derrida's development of the singular signature of Ponge's forename with *franc*, *franchise* and *Francité*.
29. Ibid., p. 66.
30. Ibid., p. 64.
31. Ibid., p. 66.
32. For example, ibid., p. 72.
33. Ibid., p. 36.
34. Ibid., p. 132.
35. Ibid., pp. 36, 38.
36. Ibid., pp. 40, 41; also p. 110. Pierre/*pierre*: Derrida never explicitly underlines how this French word does not differentiate between the common and the proper, as in *Tu es Petrus et super hanc petram aedificabo ecclesiam meam* from Matthew's Gospel (Matt. 16.18: 'You are "Rock" and on this rock I will build my church').
37. Jacques Derrida, 'Letter to a Japanese Friend', trans. David Wood and Andrew Benjamin, in *Psyche: Inventions of the Other*, ed. Peggy Kamuf and Elizabeth Rottenberg, II (Stanford: Stanford University Press, 2008), p. 4.
38. Derrida, *Signsponge*, p. 118. Derrida himself has commented on this crucial aspect of deconstruction on numerous occasions, ever since he explicitly focused on it as a poetic operation, not reducible to semantics, in his reading of Mallarmé in 'The Double Session', in *Dissemination*, trans. Barbara Johnson (London: Athlone, 1981), pp. 173–286. See also,

for example, Rodolphe Gasché, *The Tain of the Mirror: Derrida and the Philosophy of Reflection* (Cambridge, MA, and London: Harvard University Press, 1986), esp. pp. 244–5, 249–50 on its syncategorematic nature.
39. Derrida, *Signsponge*, pp. 67, 68
40. See ibid., p. 73; also pp. 84, 85 on *tissu-éponge* and *serviette-éponge*.
41. Ibid., pp. 72, 80.
42. Ibid., p. 84.
43. Ibid., p. 74.
44. Ibid., p. 101.
45. Ibid., p. 100.
46. Another instance is the near-final 'BANDE A FAIRE SAUTER' (*Signsponge*, pp. 148, 150: 'BOUND TO TAKE OFF'), where the *bande* or wrapper (band) can be perversely read as a sexual imperative for 'have a hard on', since *se faire sauter* can also be slang for 'to get laid'. The development of this 'Afterpiece' (*Après Coup*) is in line with the frequent recalls, in *Signsponge*, of the problematic of the (counter)signature as a double band or contraband in *Glas* (pp. 56, 128), which first introduced the recurrent motif of *bander* (usually rendered as 'band erect'). See Jacques Derrida, *Glas*, trans. John P. Leavey, Jr, and Richard Rand (Lincoln, NE, and London: University of Nebraska Press, 1986).
47. Derrida, *Signsponge*, p. 32; also pp. 126, 110
48. Ibid., p. 69.
49. Ibid., p. 71.
50. Ibid., p. 71.
51. Ibid., p. 68.
52. Ibid., p. 68.
53. Ibid., p. 68.
54. Ibid., p. 70.
55. Ibid., p. 74.
56. Ibid., p. 80.
57. Ibid., p. 88.
58. One famous instance of such a kinesis, which can also be viewed as a transition from impressionism to expressionism, is Ezra Pound's Vorticist conception of the haiku's conversion of 'a thing outward and objective' into 'a thing inward and subjective' as a basis for the poetic 'image'; see his *Gaudier-Brzeska: A Memoir* (New York: New Directions, 1970 [1916]), p. 89.
59. Charles Bernstein, 'Artifice of Absorption', in *A Poetics* (Cambridge, MA, and London: Harvard University Press, 1992), p. 9. Bernstein refers to Brecht's *Verfremdungseffekt* (alienated into a burlesque '*verfrem*dum-dum*den* effect') as either 'Unfamiliarization' (p. 66) or 'Defamiliarization (p. 83).
60. Derrida, *Animal*, pp. 119–40.
61. Derrida, *Signsponge*, p. 120
62. Ibid., p. 74.
63. Jacques Derrida, 'Faith and Knowledge: the Two Sources of "Religion" at the Limits of Reason Alone', trans. Samuel Weber, *Religion*, ed. Jacques Derrida and Gianni Vattimo (Cambridge: Polity Press, 1998), p. 47 (also

pp. 19, 46; and pp. 32, 57 for the link between *spondeo* and *re-spondeo*). The essay indirectly uncovers the etymological nexus between 'reading' and 'religion', via Latin *legere*: to harvest, gather (French *lier*; but also read: French *lire*), hence *re-legere* (pp. 34, 71, n. 20).
64. Bernstein, 'Artifice of Absorption', pp. 16–17. Pitting Bataille against the Master of Absolute Knowledge, the opposition was first introduced in 'From Restricted to General Economy; A Hegelianism without Reserve'. See Jacques Derrida, *Writing and Difference*, trans. Alan Bass (London: Routledge, 2001), pp. 317–50.
65. Bernstein, 'Artifice of Absorption', p. 22. In one of the epigraphs to this central section on 'Absorption and Impermeability', Bernstein had quoted from Voloshinov's *Marxism and the Philosophy of Language*: 'The entire reality of the word is wholly absorbed in its function of being a sign' ('Artifice of Absorption', p. 19).
66. Ibid., p. 30.
67. Ibid., p. 53.
68. Ibid., pp. 55–6.
69. Ibid., p. 57.
70. Charles Bernstein, 'Wait', in *Rough Trades* (Los Angeles: Sun and Moon, 1991), p. 44.
71. Derrida, *Signsponge*, p. 102.
72. Derrida's 'Psyché: Invention de l'autre' is dated 1983–84 and, in its 'uncanny' footnote recalling the seminar he taught on 'The Thing', focusing on Ponge in 1975, at Yale at Paul de Man's invitation, harks back to the development on 'Fable' in *Signsponge* promising a 'Remark to follow' (Derrida, 'Psyche: Invention of the Other', in *Psyche: Inventions of the Other*, ed. Peggy Kamuf and Elizabeth Rottenberg, I [Stanford: Stanford University Press, 2007], pp. 1–47). Replying to Gerald Graff's questions some eleven years after the raging polemic, 'Toward An Ethic of Discussion' was published as an 'Afterword', in *Limited Inc*, ed. Gerald Graff (Evanston: Northwestern University Press, 1988), pp. 111–54.
73. Derrida, 'Psyche', p. 11.
74. Ibid., pp. 11–12.
75. Ibid., pp. 12–13.
76. Derrida, *Signsponge*, p. 66.
77. Derrida, *Limited Inc*, p. 108, n. 1.
78. Bernstein, 'Artifice of Absorption', p. 20.
79. Derrida, *Signsponge*, pp. 62–3.
80. Ibid., p. 44.
81. George Eliot, *Middlemarch*, ed. W.J. Harvey (Harmondsworth: Penguin, 1965), p. 80.
82. A note about Austin's posthumous 'Three Ways of Spilling Ink' was to feature in the last of Derrida's serial involvements with speech-act theory. For a discussion, see Milesi, 'Dry Ink', p. 16.
83. Jacques Lacan, 'Seminar on "The Purloined Letter"', in *Écrits. The First Complete Edition in English*, trans. Bruce Fink in collaboration with Héloïse Fink and Russell Grigg (New York and London: Norton, 2002), p. 10.
84. Derrida, *Signsponge*, p. 22.

85. In *The Animal That Therefore I Am,* Derrida accuses philosophers of regarding the animal as 'something seen and not seeing' (p. 14). I discussed the issue of this unilateral gaze, in connection with his essay on Camilla Adami's giant portraits of apes ('Tête-à-tête', *Camilla Adami* [Milan: Gabriele Mazzotta, 2001], pp. 5–15) and the idiomatic phrase *ça me regarde*, in '*Saint-Je* Derrida', pp. 66–7. See also Berger and Segarra, eds, *Demenageries*, pp. 6–7.
86. For instance, the '+ R (Into the Bargain)' section of *The Truth in Painting,* trans. Geoff Bennington and Ian McLeod (Chicago and London: University of Chicago Press, 1987), pp. 149–82, or the supplementary incalculability of a *plus d'un(e)* (more than one, no more of one), as in the 'n + One' or 'One + n' of 'Faith and Knowledge', pp. 28, 65–6.
87. Derrida, *Signsponge*, p. 28.
88. Ibid., p. 28.
89. Ibid., pp. 28–9.
90. Ibid., p. 13.
91. Ibid., pp. 96, 126.
92. This could be contrasted with the fragile hedgehog of poetry in 'Che Cos'è la poesia?' (Weber, ed. *Points . . . Interviews*, pp. 288–99), in spite of its spikes, which had helped Derrida oppose 'poetic thinking' to the *ti esti* of 'philosophical knowledge' (*Animal*, p. 7).
93. Derrida, *Signsponge*, p. 136.
94. Derrida, *Limited Inc*, p. 47. I have developed Derrida's exposure of Searle's reappropriative 'economy' in 'Dry Ink', pp. 11–12, 14.
95. Derrida, *Signsponge*, pp. 64–5.
96. Jacques Derrida, *Archive Fever: A Freudian Impression,* trans. Eric Prenowitz (Chicago and London: University of Chicago Press, 1996), p. 78.
97. Derrida, 'Faith and Knowledge', pp. 56, 25 (also p. 55 about the 'gesture that attacks the blood of its own body'). See also '*Sauf le nom (Post-Scriptum)*', trans. John P. Leavey, Jr, in *On the Name*, ed. Thomas Dutoit (Stanford: Stanford University Press, 1995), pp. 35–85. Both *se garder* and *sauf* had been combined in an earlier formula – whose double syntax has not been kept in Nicholas Rand's translation – to designate the inside/outside *fors*; see Jacques Derrida, 'Fors. Les mots anglés de Nicolas Abraham et Maria Torok', in *Cryptonymie. Le verbier de l'Homme aux loups* (Paris: Aubier Flammarion, 1976), p. 13.
98. Derrida, *Archive Fever*, p. 78.
99. Derrida, *Signsponge*, p. 32.
100. Ibid., p. 62.
101. Ibid., p. 66. Added to the later French edition; see Jacques Derrida, *Signéponge* (Paris: Seuil, 1988), p. 56.
102. Derrida, *Signsponge*, p. 72.
103. Ibid., p. 82.
104. Ibid., p. 74.
105. Derrida, *Animal*, p. 135.
106. Derrida, *Signsponge*, pp. 56, 57.
107. Ibid., p. 74.
108. Ibid., pp. 6, 138. Derrida's essay 'The Double Session' coincidentally

opens with a discussion of Mallarmé's short sketch 'Mimique', featuring a Pierrot (*Dissemination*, pp. 175ff. – p. 176: 'two sessions'). In his introduction to *Signsponge*, Rand adduces the contemporaneity of Genette's 1976 study *Mimologiques* as a possible source of inspiration (p. 10).
109. Derrida, *Signsponge*, p. 8.
110. Jacques Derrida, *The Post Card: From Socrates to Freud and Beyond*, trans. Alan Bass (Chicago: University of Chicago Press, 1987); cf. Translator's Introduction, p. xiv. Marian Hobson chooses to read the polymorphous title also as 'Signe est Ponge', therefore as a variant on 'S is P' (*Jacques Derrida: Opening Lines* [London and New York: Routledge, 1998], p. 126).
111. Friedrich Nietzsche, cited in *The Politics of Friendship*, trans. George Collins (London and New York: Verso, 2005), p. 286.

Chapter 6

Elephant Eulogy:
The Exorbitant Orb of an Elephant
Kelly Oliver

> One thinks of this elephenomenelephant that was no longer looking at them but could have seen them, with its own eyes seen the king see it in its own autopsy [. . .]
> (Jacques Derrida)[1]

Like the fables of La Fontaine that he cites, Derrida asks us to read (hear) his seminar *The Beast and the Sovereign* as a fable. Just as La Fontaine's fables often employ two (or more) characters – animals – to teach us lessons about political power, this is the story of two characters – two animals – the beast and the sovereign, engaged in a life-and-death struggle, in which the sovereign turns out to be the most beastly of the two. If Derrida's *The Beast and the Sovereign* is also a fable, we might ask what is its moral? What lessons are we to learn from it? In a word, we could say it is a lesson about the workings of sovereignty, but of course it is also much more. Indeed, it is a sort of counter-fable set as counterweight to the fable of sovereignty, particularly the fable of human sovereignty over animals. Although various animals show up in this text (and in Derrida's work more generally), one story that illustrates some of the stakes of his counter-fable about sovereignty is that of a big elephant and a little king. Derrida asks us to imagine the doctors, 'or other armed butchers', 'trembling with lust for autopsy', impatient to sink their axes and knifes into 'the great defenseless body', while the diminutive king, Louis le Grand (Louis XIV), makes a grand entrance in great pomp and ceremony to inspect the 'enormous, heavy, poor beast'.[2] Unlike the fables of La Fontaine, however, the 'moral' of this story is not obvious. Indeed, the circulation of the gaze required to prop up His Majesty the little king on the back, so to speak, of this great animal, this *elephenomenelephant*, is head spinning.

Like La Fontaine's fable of *The Wolf and the Lamb* with which Derrida begins the seminar, and *The Heifer, the Goat and the Ewe in*

Society with the Lion that shows up later, this too is a story of might makes right. But, unlike those stories in which the Wolf and the Lion are clearly the stronger of the animals (the Lion threatens to devour the others and the Wolf makes good on the threat), here the giant elephant, which could crush the little king with one footfall, is lying at the foot of the strutting sovereign. There is no conversation, no debate, no outwitting or intimidating, as with La Fontaine's animals. Rather, there is a dead elephant centre-stage surrounded by the king and his court performing sovereignty in the autopsy chamber. Perhaps Derrida seeks to provide the kind of fabulous conversation that might lead to this scene with a mighty beast fallen before a puny man, the backstory of why and how this dead giant is needed in both the fable of the king's sovereignty over his subjects and the fable of man's sovereignty over other animals.

Although he claims that he too is engaging in fables, Derrida also insists on exposing the fable of sovereign political power as a fable (exposure is a complicated gesture in the Derridean corpus), and avoiding fables that involve the fabulisation of animals in 'an anthropomorphic taming, a moralizing subjection, a domestication', which is part and parcel of the discourse of man's sovereignty over them.[3] As a start, then, we could say that the moral of Derrida's counter-fable of the elephant autopsy is that man's sovereignty comes at the price of animal lives. That man lives through killing animals. Moreover, the political animal in particular requires necropsy in order to sustain its political power. Furthermore, we could say that a certain sovereignty as necropsy erects itself through this autopsic model of power: 'we are dealing with a political organization of the field of knowledge, in the form of the anatomy lesson or the lesson of the natural sciences', that is to say, the autopsy.[4] Like the fabled elephant who never forgets, Derrida does not let us forget that sovereign power is erected on death, particularly the death of animals, both the animals with which we share the planet and the animals within us.

In this essay, I take up what Derrida calls 'the globalization of the autopsic model' of sovereignty in relation to the counter-fable of the elephant autopsy.[5] I consider the mechanism of the 'sovereignty effect' of both the king and of man, and the sovereign power of both to lord over others, which requires a unique witness, and witnesses to that witness, in a circulation of the gaze that ends in autopsy. Sovereignty requires the spectacle or performance of sovereignty and the testimony of an intermediary both uniquely present at this performance and yet necessarily absent from the 'official aesthetic' of sovereign rhetoric. Yet, as we will see, there is a blind spot in this sovereign gaze that again is both necessary and unsettling to it, namely the dead eyes of the elephant. The eyes of this *elephenomenelephant*, with their exorbitant orbs in excess of what is proper to the limits of man, necessarily exceed the boundaries of the autopsic model of sovereignty; and, like the return of the repressed body, the body become corpse, they look back at the living even in death; not by yielding their secrets to the light, but rather by refusing the light with their opaqueness, these dead elephantine eyes. The secrets of this elephant, the secrets of life itself, do not yield to the autopsic gaze. Rather, there is always something beyond the limits of human seeing, something exorbitant, beyond the limits of human understanding.

Derrida challenges us that, even as we define ourselves as human against the animal and against the machine, we cannot ever know with certainty who we are or what they are; or that we can tell a who from a what. He is not taking the all-too-simple line that we are animals or that we are machines; or that animals or robots are people too. He rejects that view as asinine. Rather, he is challenging the limits, the borders and the border-police, who insist on fixed categorical oppositions between 'us and them' in order to justify building fences and walls, and worse to justify building zoos, slaughter-houses, asylums, prisons, gas-chambers and other beastly technologies of death. He is reminding us that there is always something exorbitant, something that exceeds the limits and borders that we erect, most particularly the border between 'us and them'.

The elephant autopsy points to one of the ways in which we justify our beastly treatment of them. In the name of knowledge and science, we perform our lust for autopsy. Derrida's invocation of the elephant, however, also operates as a kind of eulogy to the exorbitant grandeur of the elephant that escapes the elephantine spectacle surrounding it through which the diminutive king asserts his power. Derrida asks us to imagine the scene and to remember this grand nameless beast, to see the scene from its perspective. He follows the trace of the life's breath of this real big elephant, the invisible revenant beyond autopsy, the secrets of its life and death that remain unseen, beyond the scope or scale of humanity and its assertions of self-sovereignty. In a way, he asks us to mourn this grandest of animals, an animal also known for its capacity to mourn. Following Derrida, I suggest that mourning, particularly elephant mourning, is what resists autopsy, or at least is what never fully yields or avails itself of autopsy; there is always an other elephant, the real big elephant, the elephant revenant, that denies the satisfaction of autopsy and refuses to give up its secrets, whether it is the secret of what it is to be an elephant, or the secret of what it is to be an animal, or the secret of what it is to be a living being. This is the elephant that looks back from its dead eyes to haunt the fable of the living sovereign. This is the backstory of Derrida's counter-fable of the big elephant and the little king. This is the counter-fable of how an elephant eye puts out the 'I' of sovereignty; it is another story of an eye for an I; another story of how one nail takes out another.

With the fable of the elephant and the king, Derrida shows how the quest for knowledge is driven by lust for autopsy, the desire to dissect the mysteries of life (and death) under a laboratory spotlight. It is a violent operation of subjecting everything to the tools of dissection under glaring lights focused beneath the gaze of one who establishes himself as sovereign precisely through this gaze and the supposed mastery or knowledge it produces, and that he supposedly possesses through it.[6] The autopsic model of knowing is one of prying things open, exposing them to tools, light and scientific gaze, in order to determine the cause-and-effect relationships that supposedly explain our own existence. Today, autopsies are performed (note this turn of phrase) in cases, especially criminal and medical settings, where the causes of death are unknown or uncertain. Forensic autopsies in particular are performed in order to solve the mystery of 'who dunnit' and how. Autopsies are never performed for the sake of the dead, who can no longer benefit from them, but always for the sake of the living, for the sake of revenge or justice as revenge or for scientific knowledge that might benefit the living.

This could not be more obvious than in the case of the elephant autopsy, performed not for that nameless beast or even for his or her kind, but rather presumably to learn something about the functioning of the human body and more especially to entertain the king. More importantly, Derrida argues that the elephant autopsy performs the king's sovereignty over man and beast. The royal scientists and doctors are there at his behest, the spectators too, bowing before him, and the elephant is the carnage, literally, of this spectacle of sovereignty. Laid out in the theatre of autopsy, the giant animal is a testament to the power of the king over the entire world, even the world of nature. Derrida contends that this scene is an emblem of the intimate connection between theory and theatre, between speculation and spectacle:

> this optical, autoptical scene [...] makes use of an absolute power over the beast with a view to seeing and knowledge, in the name, at bottom, of Enlightenment, but of light, always that of the Sun King, light that in the end never dissociates theoretical observation in the service of knowledge, here for example the optics of autopsy – [never dissociates it] from spectacle, theater, ceremony as representation, and representation as representation of the king (a double genitive again), both the spectacular representation given by the king, ordered by him, organized by him in view of himself, and the representation *of* the king that represents the king, that presents him, shows him in his portrait, or recounts him in action.[7]

The etymological connection between theory and theatre is played out in the scene of autopsy. First, as Derrida reminds us, the word *autopsy* is from the Latin *autopsia*, from *autos* (self) and *optos* (seen), to see with one's own eyes, while the word 'theory' is from the Greek *theoria*, which means contemplation or speculation, from *theoros*, which means spectator, to see with the mind's eye. And speculation and spectacle both have the same Latin root, *specere*, which means to look. Indeed, speculation comes from *specula*, the word for a watchtower as a vantage point high above from which to look down and see not only the lie of the land, but also approaching enemies. Speculation as a means of defence. Both theoretical observation and philosophical speculation, then, have their roots in looking, observing from on high, from the vantage point of the king, or at least the king's watchman. Theory, speculation and autopsy are modes of seeing either as eyewitness or with the mind's eye. The spectacle of death, now transferred to the theatre of autopsy, plays out the morbid curiosities of all those present to it, all those interested in seeing, and who can resist? Judging by the popularity of spectacles of death and autopsy scenes in popular television and film, no one. And yet, as we will see (so to speak), the exorbitant eyes of the dead elephant have a look beyond the limits of our vision, of our looking, of our autopsic gaze.

Returning to the relation between theory and theatre, sovereignty is not only a performance in the linguistic sense of saying as doing, but also in the theatrical sense of putting on a show for an audience. The sovereign is nothing without his subjects; his glory must be witnessed. This creates the paradox of sovereignty: the king must be seen seeing and yet not be seen (for what he really is, a mortal man, especially a mortal animal among others). His subjects must not look at him directly, which is why he can be seen only through an intermediary, a representation, a portrait, narrative or otherwise. Even the ceremonial scene of the elephant autopsy is staged so that the king can be seen seeing and the deadly power of his seeing can be witnessed. This is why the role of the historian or the portrait artist is essential to the operations of sovereignty. (Today photography, television and the Internet supplement the historian and portraiture.) The king needs an intermediary to represent his sovereignty, to witness him proclaiming it, to witness to it 'directly'. This witness, however, must efface himself in the process so that his portrait is seen as if it were the king himself. In this way, the king's person, his body, is also disregarded for the sake of his eternal royal body as both sovereign monarch and sacred representative of God on earth.

Derrida invokes an ancient form of the word *autopsy* as the demand that the narrative of past events be authenticated by an eyewitness, in this case the king's narrator whose serves as a 'witness' or even a 'martyr' (originally the same thing).[8] In the sense that the narrator must make himself absent for the sake of making the king's presence absolute through his narrative, he does martyr himself. This sense of the word autopsy is a literal sense of seeing with one's own eyes. But Derrida points out there are two other meanings, one rarer and one current. Autopsy also means participation in the omnipotence of the gods, which Derrida argues is what authorises all narratives of absolute sovereignty. And it has come to mean the dissection of a cadaver or necropsy.

All three of these meanings converge on the sovereignty of the king symbolised by the elephant autopsy with its big animal and little king. The mortal body is there in the dead elephant: 'This dead elephant [. . .] the denied averted, vaguely totemic representation of the dead king, the mortal king, the king dead from a death [. . .] that every subject projects into the autopsy or the necropsy of sovereignty.'[9] The resplendent story of the scene of the autopsy, with its great pomp and ceremony, create the autopsy as participation in the eternal power of god. And, that, in turn, authorises the witness to tell the story as the truth of His Majesty's greatness and thereby produce the sovereign effect through the representation itself. The omnipotence of gods is reflected and deflected through the narrative that both divides and produces its power. The sovereignty effect is the effect of death, both in the real body of the once-majestic animal lying on the operating table in pieces and in the symbolic body that replaces the mortal body of the king. The king's mortality, then, is doubly displaced in this scene of autopsy – perhaps infinitely divisible and displaced in the circulation of representation that produces sovereignty and the sovereign-effect.

The king's body and its displacement on to the elephant point to the dynamic at the heart of the opposition between the beast and the sovereign, between animal and man. For if, within the official aesthetic, the king has three bodies (sacred, soul and body), we could say that the ordinary man has two (soul and body), while animals have only one (body). Indeed, the mortal body of the king, his earthly finite body, is his animal body; and this body is always the animal that must be sacrificed for society and humanity. Recall that in the story of Freud's primal horde, the animal body sacrificed for the sake of the body is memorialised through symbols, particularly the totem; this is how *homo sapiens* became civilised social humans. The body has always been associated with the animal, and it has been sacrificed to gods, to science and to culture. Within the fable of human sovereignty, the sacrifice of the elephant in the spectacle of the elephant autopsy is a necessary part of the process of turning the animal *homo sapiens* into a man and turning a man into a king. In the case of the king, it also requires the third body, the one witnessed and thereby authorised by eternity through the portrait that turns the performance of sovereignty into history. It all begins with the metaphorical death of his animal body – and the literal death of other animal bodies, which are seen as merely bodies and nothing more – for the sake of his eternal soul.

Indeed, these animal bodies killed so that we might become human are not only sacrificed to God in our stead (Freud's totemic animal and the stories of Genesis), or used by us for food and clothing, but also subjected to scientific research in laboratories. The scientific study of animals, which has a history dating back at least to Ancient Greece, not only provides us with shampoos that don't irritate our eyes and helps us find cures for our diseases, but also feeds our hunger for knowledge. The lust for autopsy as the lust for knowledge is supposedly one characteristic that separates us from other animals. We are burning with longing to know, to understand, to unlock the secrets of life. Other animals are presumed to be content to live it rather than understand it or imagine it otherwise. We, on the other hand, require another life beyond our animal mortality to make it worthwhile. This is the driving force behind both science and religion, namely the demand for an explanation beyond this life itself, a life beyond life. For science this means dissecting everything, exposing it to the 'violence of light' in order to satisfy our curiosity about how the universe works – 'just to see' as Derrida repeatedly says in *The Animal That Therefore I Am*.[10] For religion this means belief in a transcendent God greater than us, an absolute sovereign, whose mysteries we cannot know but must accept on faith. In either case, we look for a life beyond life, beyond our mere mortal animal bodies. Derrida maintains in 'Faith and Knowledge' that there is a double mechanics at work here, a machine that reproduces death for the sake of life: 'I refer to it as mechanics because it reproduces, with the regularity of a technique, the instance of the non-living or, if you prefer, of the dead in the living.'[11] It is the deadly machine of life. This mechanism of reproducing death at the heart of life is the motor of the killing machine of both science and religion insofar as both require the death of the earthly body: science in the name of autopsy, dissection and knowledge, and religion in the name of heaven, an afterlife and God.

As we have seen, sovereignty and the circulation of the gaze that supports it requires the death of the mortal animal body and the fantasy of a dead king who becomes more powerful through this imagined death than he is as a living person, which recalls the power of Freud's absent totemic father to be greater than the real father, to be more powerful as a symbol than he was as a living animal. In both cases, mourning is what intensifies the power of the image or representation that both makes die and makes live forever. The performance of sovereignty, which necessitates this infinite mourning of the always already dead sovereign through his sacred image, shares with the religious desire for another life and the scientific desire for absolute knowledge a lust for autopsy that requires the death and dissection of the earthly animal body for the sake of human sovereignty, whether that sovereignty is evidenced by man's dominion over other animals, his immortal soul, or his capacity for knowledge. Indeed, religion and science both rely on the sacrifice of animal bodies for the sake of propping up human exceptionalism and our right to use animals. Traditionally, our dominion over them has been so absolute that killing animals was not seen as true killing, and certainly not as murder or warfare, because animals as bodies are always already merely corpses anyway or, as Descartes imagines them, mere soulless machines. We might ask, however, can animals have corpses? Or are they rather mere carcasses, the term corpse being reserved for humans? Heidegger, for example, maintains that animals do not die but rather merely perish because they have no knowledge of death, no being towards death, which is the special privilege or burden of *Dasein*.[12] He also privileges human hands equipped with opposable thumbs as both literal and metaphorical tools for grasping what other animals cannot.[13] *Dasein* is out of their reach. And, as such (which for Heidegger is precisely what is at stake – the 'as such' and animals' inability to grasp life or death 'as such'), for Heidegger, animals have no relation to death and therefore no possibility of mourning. They are absolutely excluded from the possibility of the infinite mourning necessary for the performance of sovereignty, and thereby excluded from any possibility of representation or culture.

Derrida challenges this traditional belief, shared by Heidegger, that only humans die, only we are capable of mourning, and only we perform rituals of mourning and bury our dead.[14] Reading Heidegger in one hand and *Robinson Crusoe* in the other (as he says in the second volume of *La bête et le souverain*), Derrida quotes Leopold Bloom in James Joyce's *Ulysses*: 'We all do. Only man buries. No ants do. First thing strikes anybody'; and then he comments, 'erreur de Joyce qui croit, comme tout le monde, que les bêtes ne meurent pas au sens propre, ne portent pas le deuil et n'enterrent pas'.[15] Derrida is clear that he thinks it is an error to deny animals death properly speaking, mourning or burial. When it comes to animals, Derrida's deconstructive strategy is to question both whether humans are properly capable of being towards death as such (in Heidegger's sense), mourning or burying, and whether animals are not capable of death, mourning or burying, as such. He refuses the absolute limit between human death, mourning and burial and animal perishing without mourning or rituals around death. This is not to say that animals are people too, but rather, as Derrida repeatedly reminds us, to multiply the limits and borders between the overly general category 'animal' and the overly exclusive category 'human'. Derrida leaves open the possibility that animals know death, mourn their dead and engage in burial rituals.

Was the fabled elephant laid out on the autopsy table before Louis le Grand mourned by his family and friends? Did they protest against the lack of a proper burial for their kin –like a group of zoo elephants supposedly did until the bones of their dead companion were brought back into their enclosure so they could properly mourn?[16] Did the elephant's friends give eulogies for their now forever absent colleague? After all, elephants too are known to mourn their dead with elaborate rituals that go on for years. One elephant researcher concludes 'perhaps more than any other quality, the elephant is thought of as having understanding of death. Grieving and mourning rituals are an integral part of elephant culture.'[17] And, discussing research on elephants, a reporter concludes,

> When an elephant dies, its family members engage in intense mourning and burial rituals, conducting weeklong vigils over the body, carefully covering it with earth and brush, revisiting the bones for years afterward, caressing the bones with their trunks, often taking turns rubbing their trunks along the teeth of a skull's lower jaw, the way living elephants do in greeting.[18]

According to another elephant expert, 'they have a memory that far surpasses ours and spans a lifetime [seventy years]. They grieve deeply for lost loved ones, even shedding tears and suffering depression.'[19] Elephants mourn their dead using their trunks, an appendage so utterly unfamiliar to us, so uncanny in its ability to grasp without those privileged opposable thumbs, without hands or arms. What is a trunk? And how would we measure up on the scale of the trunk? On the scale of the elephant, we are small enough to be crushed with one footfall. And even the grandest of human hands are unable to fully grasp the trunk, at least not without cutting it into pieces through dissection or ripping those magnificent ivory tusks from it.

Indeed, much recent research on elephants suggests that elephants possess many of the characteristics traditionally reserved for humans, including memory, mirror self-recognition, self-awareness, emotions, attachment, social bonds, mourning, stress, trauma, communication, humour, and other complex behaviours and social structures.[20] Neuroscientists have established changes in elephants' brains after trauma; and they have discovered that elephants have an 'extremely large and convoluted hippocampus that is responsible for mediating long-term social memory'.[21] Some of these studies suggest that elephants have even better long-term memories, particularly social memories, than humans. It has become a cliché that 'elephants never forget', suggesting something like an animal archive, the perfect animal-memory-machine, a mammoth memory, or the fable of the elephant. This fabulous elephant memory, bigger than life, is exorbitant insofar as we cannot comprehend another mammal with a life-long memory, perhaps even better than our own. At the same time (or perhaps as a way of burying our own lack of understanding), the elephant becomes the fabular emblem of memory, the fabled animal against which Derrida works his counter-fable, exemplified in his dissection of the fabled elephant autopsy.

This elephant subjected to the autopsic gaze of both science and sovereignty is cut apart for the sake of human knowledge and power. It performs an anatomy lesson in the theatre of science as a body so large that it feeds not only our desire to see the size of its parts but also our desire for trophies of our triumph over the animal kingdom. Through this performance, as we have seen, man becomes the king of the beasts while diminutive Louis becomes the king of men. This fabled elephant becomes part of the symbolic exchange that produces sovereign power.

But what about the 'real' elephant that died, or was killed, and somehow hauled into the autopsy chamber? Can we mourn the nameless elephant on the autopsy table even as he or she represents all elephants, all brains and muscles, and even Louis the Grand himself?[22] What would it mean to mourn a symbol? Or, is all mourning – or what we take to be mourning – for symbols rather than for the singular bodies of individual living beings? How can we mourn that singular 'real big elephant' lying before Louis XIV? Who can mourn this nameless elephant? This question raises the larger question of whether or not we can mourn for animals. Certainly human grief over the loss of an animal companion can be as profound as the mourning for the loss of any other loved one. Yet mourning our animal loves is often seen as excessive or even unacceptable. There is little room for such mourning in the institutions of our culture. Perhaps, then, we are not as capable of mourning and grieving as we think we are.

Did the fabled elephant – or any of the other elephants killed for ivory or for human purposes – receive a proper burial? Elephants are known to bury the dead of other species, particularly humans, especially when they kill them. They have been seen burying dead humans and performing mourning and burial rituals for them.[23] Do we do the same for them? Elephants have even been called in to resolve human–elephant conflict as special Elephant Response Units.[24] Human–elephant conflict is becoming more common as elephant habitats are taken over for human use and poachers continue to ravage elephant populations, particularly older elephants with bigger tusks. One elephant researcher describes a 'war' against elephants 'because humans just throw hand grenades at the elephants, bring whole families down and cut out the ivory. I call that mass destruction.'[25] Various studies show that when the elders of a group are murdered, the young, especially the orphans, develop post-traumatic stress disorders and can become very aggressive against each other and other species, especially other pachyderms and humans.[26] *The New York Times Magazine* article entitled 'An Elephant Crack-Up?' that brought this phenomenon to public attention a few years ago opened with a close-up photograph of a long-lashed welling amber elephant eye, black pupil staring right into the camera, tears rolling down over its wrinkled scaly pachyderm skin. Did our fabled elephant shed tears facing its death? Did its elephant friends cry for it? Can we? Can we shed tears for this elephant or others, so different from us, without reducing them to fables that embody qualities we value in ourselves? Can we look at elephants with compassion instead of the lust for autopsy or the lust for ivory? What do we see when we look into the eye of an elephant? Or, more to the point, what does the elephant see when it looks at us? Can the gaze of an elephant, like the gaze of Derrida's cat in *The Animal That Therefore I Am*, 'be, deep within her eyes, my primary mirror?'[27] This may be especially apt since elephants have joined humans as mammals that recognise themselves in mirrors.[28]

And what of the eyes of that poor beast, the dead elephant? What does that grandest of animals, that singular specimen, see through those dead eyes? Can those dead eyes be our mirrors? In passing, Derrida imagines an outrageous reversal of the gaze: 'One thinks of this elephenomenelephant that was no longer looking at them but could have seen them, with its own eyes seen the king see it in its own autopsy.'[29] What could this possibly mean – a dead elephant seeing the king looking, seeing the king usurping its grandeur through his autopsic gaze? What is the inversion of the gaze imagined by Derrida in this curious moment in *The Beast and the Sovereign*? We may get some clues from the 'The Force of Mourning', a eulogy for his friend and colleague Louis Marin, particularly from Derrida's analysis there of the 'inversion of the gaze' necessary for the 'failure' of mourning, which is to say, any mourning worthy of its name.[30] This operation of inversion would also be the excess or remainder of mourning beyond all autopsy, what absolute sovereignty cannot allow but is haunted by nonetheless.

Mourning escapes autopsy insofar as the revenant returns in its singularity, its irreplaceability, this impossible repetition of what cannot be repeated, this elephant, this very one, like Derrida's 'real little cat' who remains nameless in *The Animal That Therefore I Am* because to name is already to kill, to replace, to substitute. It is to substitute an eternal symbolic body for the mortal animal body, the body that is irreplaceable and therefore always also beyond the name, worthy of its name only insofar as it cannot be named. Its life and breath cannot be dissected. A 'failed' mourning would be an elephant mourning, perhaps even a fabled or impossible mourning, one that does not and cannot forget; one that never ends. As Derrida describes it, this 'failed' mourning is not the melancholia that Freud opposes to remembering or working through, melancholia as a form of repetition. For what is mourned, the singular living being now forever gone, cannot be repeated. Only an image can be reproduced. The singular being can only be reproduced through appropriations by the machines of nature (genetics) and culture (books or creations), yet these reproductions are incomplete traces of the deceased being. It is this revenant to which Derrida appeals, the other who resists assimilation or incorporation, not the ghost, the spectre or the phantom, those visible apparitions that appear to bring the dead back to life. But what remains invisible, secret, unavailable to autopsy is the life breath of that now-dead elephant. The revenant haunts us with what cannot be seen, the irreplaceability of this elephant, which returns to us even now in Derrida's counter-fable of the elephant and the king, but only as a trace.

'Successful' mourning, which is to say not mourning at all, is a type of autopsy insofar as it replays the absent other as so many memories, like pictures or movies shown on an interior screen. It subjects them to the light of memory as a series of images, sometimes literally photographs or videos, intended to conjure their visage, the face of the beloved. But, the revenant resists this autopsic model of mourning, of conjuring ghosts or apparitions, because it can only be felt and not seen – perhaps like the trunk of an elephant reaching for its dead friend or beloved. It cannot be projected on to the interior screen of my mind. Rather, it keeps its secrets and thereby takes me out of my mind, knocks me off my head, that capital representative of sovereignty and of philosophy.

Unlike the phantasm, spectre or ghost, Derrida argues that the revenant does not appear; it does not make itself visible and therefore capable of capture or mastery by our senses; it cannot be brought into the light or placed under the autopsic gaze. Rather, the revenant

> arises where there is no horizon [. . .] it allows itself to be dominated neither by a gaze, nor by a conscious perception in general, nor by a performative act of language [. . .] The 'revenant', however, comes and comes back (since singularity as such implies repetition) like the 'who' or 'what' of an event without a horizon. Like death itself.[31]

Derrida describes the inversion of the gaze through which his dead friend Louis Marin looks at him as the gaze of the revenant looking at him. The revenant looks at me and not I at him; he interpolates me; I do not assimilate, introject or incorporate him. Furthermore, the non-appearance of the revenant as event without horizon, as the secret that escapes autopsy, also shatters the interior space imagined to screen memories like so many picture shows of the mind. The inversion of the gaze that comes to us from the other is not a reciprocal looking. Neither is it the circulation of the gaze of the sovereign that moves from the dead elephant, to the king, to the witnesses, to the court historian, to the reading/listening public (or to Loisel, to Ellenberger, through Marin, to Derrida, to us, and so on). It is not the gaze that establishes sovereignty – the 'I can' – but precisely its inversion, what smashes the 'I can' and 'traumatises the interiority that it inhabits'.[32] Death describes the alterity of the other as infinitely out of our reach, just as much in death as it was in life. Life (and death) keeps its secrets from the prying eyes of autopsy. It remains uncanny even in the scene of autopsy, perhaps especially in the scene of the elephant autopsy with its grand beast and diminutive sovereign. It puts out the 'I' of the 'I can' and takes us out of our mind, particularly insofar as we imagine ourselves in possession of a mind's eye. The gaze of the revenant puts out the mind's eye. This is a counter-fable of an eye for an eye.

Reading the work of the late Marin, Derrida concludes,

> However narcissistic it may be, our subjective speculation can no longer seize and appropriate this gaze before which we appear at the moment when, bearing it in us, bearing it along with every movement of our bearing or comportment, we can get over our mourning *of him* only by getting over *our* mourning, by getting over, by ourselves, the mourning of ourselves, I mean the mourning of our autonomy, of everything that would make us the measure of ourselves.[33]

How do we bear it, the excess of this absence, a hole in the heart, the exorbitant gaze of the revenant that unsettles rather than recalls us to ourselves as sovereign agents?

Autopsy is just one way of avoiding the event of death, which is also to say the event of life, which is to say the event of mourning. The court scientists and the king look in vain at the remains of the grand beast without seeing the remainder always outside of their vision, the excess of life and death that resists their gaze and their sovereignty. They make a scene in order to cover up the fact that they cannot see what they are looking for, that the elephant refuses to reveal the secrets of his life, or more to the point, of life itself. The animal body refuses to yield all of its secrets to autopsy, whether that of the scientist as eyewitness or the philosopher gazing with his mind's eye. Even the elephant's dead blind eye sees more than they know, in Derrida's counter-fantasy of the gaze of the revenant.

Perhaps it is ironic that because elephants have very poor eyesight, they rely on touch, smell and hearing, the non-spectacular senses. These grandest of animals cannot see very well. Is, then, the gaze of the dead big elephant looking up at the living little king, witnessed to in Derrida's counter-fable, 'the gaze of a seer, a visionary or extra-lucid blind one' that Derrida invokes in *The Animal That Therefore I Am*; the gaze that shatters the hall of mirrors, the Cartesian theatre of theory and speculation, in which the *cogito* thinks it reflects only itself without any other, its own sovereignty, that clearest and most distinct of ideas, *cogito ergo sum*.[34] The *cogito*, another scopic machine of death, the mind's eye, focused on itself, making of itself a dead object, not unlike the elephant carcase exposed to the glaring lights of autopsy. An I for an eye. That is the calculated exchange in the economy of sovereignty, the eye of an elephant for the I of a king. But, not without remainder. Perhaps, then, the moral of Derrida's counter-fable of the grand beast and the diminutive sovereign, the big elephant and the little king, is that like an elephant, we mustn't forget the remains of that 'elephenomenelephant', the lost 'real' elephant as a revenant that haunts our fable of sovereignty, and our fable of elephant memory and of elephant mourning, even as we struggle to use one fable to take out the other.

Notes

1. Jacques Derrida, *The Beast and the Sovereign*, Vol. I, trans. Geoffrey Bennington (Chicago: University of Chicago Press, 2009), p. 282.
2. Derrida, *Beast*, I, p. 284
3. Jacques Derrida, *The Animal That Therefore I Am*, trans. David Wills (New York: Fordham University Press, 2008), p. 37.
4. Derrida, *Beast*, I, p. 273
5. Ibid., p. 296
6. See Jacques Derrida, 'Violence and Metaphysics', in *Writing and Difference*, trans. Alan Bass (Chicago: University of Chicago Press, 1980), pp. 84–92.
7. Derrida, *Beast*, I, p. 287.
8. Louis Marin, quoted in ibid., p. 294.
9. Ibid.
10. Derrida, *Animal*, pp. 3, 4, 33
11. Jacques Derrida, *Acts of Religion*, ed. Gil Anidjar (New York: Routledge, 2002), p. 86.
12. See Martin Heidegger, *Being and Time*, trans. John Macquarie and Edward Robinson (New York: Harper and Row, 1962), pp. 74, 208, 396.

13. Heidegger, *Being and Time*, pp. 138–44.
14. See Jacques Derrida, *La bête et le souverain* II (Paris: Galilée, 2010), p. 41.
15. Derrida, *La bête*, II, p. 41. 'An error by Joyce who thinks like everyone else that beasts do not die in the proper sense, do not wear mourning and do not bury.' See Jacques Derrida, *The Beast and the Sovereign*, Vol. II, trans. Geoffrey Bennington (Chicago: University of Chicago Press, 2011), p. 17.
16. Isabel G.A. Bradshaw, 'Not by Bread Alone: Symbolic Loss, Trauma, and Recovery in Elephant Communities', *Society and Animals*, 12.2, 2004, pp. 143–58. Bradshaw claims 'a zoo called a well-known, nonhuman animal communicator to consult with their elephants because of similar [aggressive, disruptive] irregular behavior. In conversation with the elephants, the consultant learned that a resident elephant who had died was removed before the remaining elephants could mourn the body of their dead companion of many years [. . .]. When the skull of the deceased was brought back to the elephant group, the elephants immediately gathered around and began a ritual of touch and caressing [. . .] Thereafter the elephants resumed "normal" behavior' (p. 149).
17. Bradshaw, 'Not by Bread', p. 147.
18. Charles Siebert, 'An Elephant Crack-Up?', *The New York Times Magazine*, 8 October 2006, www.nytimes.com/2006/10/08/magazine/08elephant.html (accessed 5 February 2013).
19. Daphne Sheldrick, 'Elephant Emotion' [1992], Sheldrick Wildlife Trust website, http://www.sheldrickwildlifetrust.org/html/elephant_emotion.html (accessed 5 February 2013).
20. See Marc Bekoff, 'Grief in Animals: It's Arrogant to Think We're the Only Animals who Mourn', *Psychology Today*, 29 October 2009, www.psychologytoday.com/blog/animal-emotions (accessed 5 February 2013); Bradshaw, 'Not by Bread'; G. A. Bradshaw and Allan Schore, 'How Elephants are Opening Doors: Developmental Neuroethology, Attachment and Social Context', *Ethology*, 113.5, 2007, pp. 426–36; Roger Highfield, 'Elephants Show Compassion in Face of Death', *The Telegraph*, 14 August 2006, http://www.telegraph.co.uk/news/1526287/Elephants-show-compassion-in-face-of-death.html (accessed 4 March 2013); Karen McComb, Cynthia Moss, Sarah M. Durant et al., 'Matriarchs as Repositories of Social Knowledge in African Elephants', *Science*, 292, 20 April 2001, pp. 491–4; Caitlin O'Connell-Rodwell, 'Ritualised Bonding in Male Elephants', *The New York Times*, 20 July 2011, http://scientistatwork.blogs.nytimes.com/2011/07/21/ritualized-bonding-in-male-elephants/ (accessed 4 March 2013).
21. Siebert, 'Elephant Crack-Up', p. 54
22. Gustave Loisel, *Histoire des menageries de l'antiquité à nos jours*, Vol. II (Paris: Octave Doin et Fils, Henri Laurens, 1912). According to Loisel, upon whose report Ellenberger and then Derrida rely, the elephant lying on the autopsy table reportedly was a trickster with a sense of humour that lived for three years at the Versailles menagerie until 'he' died in 1681; only at the autopsy did they discover that *he* was really a *she* elephant that apparently died of natural causes (or perhaps due to her captivity) (pp. 115–18).
23. Siebert, 'Elephant Crack-Up', p. 52.

24. For analysis of specific problems with wild elephants in Asia, see Heidi Riddle, 'Elephant Response Units (ERU)', *Gaja*, 26, 2007, pp. 47–53. Riddle explains that in parts of Asia, the Asian Elephant Specialist Group is using captive elephants to defuse tensions between humans and wild elephants (pp. 47–8). In China, the government is offering 'dinner halls' for wild elephants in the hope of luring them away from farms (p. 65).
25. Siebert, 'Elephant Crack-Up'.
26. See Charles Siebert, 'Orphans No More,' *National Geographic*, 220.3, September 2011, pp. 40–65; Bradshaw, 'Not by Bread'; Bradshaw and Schore, 'How Elephants are Opening Doors'; Siebert, 'Elephant Crack-Up'. Siebert reports that when young males do not have older role models and have been traumatised, they exhibit aggressive behaviour. But if older males are reintroduced into the herd, they stop their aberrant behavior ('Orphans No More', p. 55).
27. Derrida, *Animal*, p. 51.
28. Siebert, 'Orphans No More', p. 54.
29. Derrida, *Beast*, I, p. 282.
30. For an insightful analysis of this inversion of the gaze in mourning, see Kas Saghafi, *Apparitions – Of Derrida's Other* (New York: Fordham University Press, 2010).
31. Jacques Derrida, *For what tomorrow–: A Dialogue*, trans. Jeff Fort (Stanford: Stanford University Press, 2004), pp. 230–1, n. 34.
32. Jacques Derrida, *The Work of Mourning*, ed. Pascale-Anne Brault and Michael Naas (Chicago: University of Chicago Press, 2001), p. 160.
33. Derrida, *Mourning*, pp. 160–1
34. See Derrida, *Animal*, p. 4.

Chapter 7

Troubling Resemblances, Anthropological Machines and the Fear of Wild Animals: Following Derrida after Agamben

Stephen Morton

The animal names a conceptual problem for the Western philosophical tradition that cannot be grasped *as such*. From Aristotle and Descartes to Heidegger and Lacan, the animal is defined negatively in relation to the human: it denotes that which the human *is not*.[1] The statement often attributed to Aristotle that the human is *zōon logon ekhon* clearly exemplifies the way in which the animal defines the human through its exclusion from an anthropocentric Western philosophical tradition. In this sense, 'the animal' could be understood as the constitutive outside of 'the human'. Yet if 'the animal' is framed as a negative term, or a term without content, this does not mean that 'the non-human animal' has no being as such. On the contrary, the animal, or to be more precise the being of animals, marks a limit in human thinking: it is the otherness of animals and their mode of being in the world from which humans are excluded.[2]

It is this irresolvable problem or aporia in Western philosophy that Jacques Derrida sought to address in a lecture series he presented at a conference on 'The Autobiographical Animal' at Cerisy-la-Salle in 1997, published posthumously in 2008 as *The Animal That Therefore I Am*. As he puts it in a series of reflections on the significance of an exchange of gazes with his cat while he is naked in his domestic sphere: 'the gaze called "animal" offers to my sight the abyssal limit of the human: the inhuman or the ahuman, the end of man [. . .]'.[3] For Derrida, it is this 'abyssal limit' that is effaced in discussions of the animal from Aristotle and Descartes to Lacan and Heidegger. In his *Meditations*, for instance, Descartes refuses to address the difficult question of what a 'rational animal' is by excluding questions about the bodily life or animality of the human from his definition of the *cogito*. 'But what is a man? Shall I say a rational animal? No: for then I should have to inquire what an animal is, what rationality is, and in this way one question would lead me down the slope to other harder ones.'[4] By sidestepping the question, what is an animal, Descartes tries to efface the 'abyssal limit' between man and animal, and to present the human mind or *cogito* – the 'I am' – as a self-grounded concept. Yet, as Derrida goes on to explain, Descartes' formulation of the *cogito* is predicated on a complex metaphor, in which the excluded category of the animal/ body continues to mark, or in Derrida's words 'follow', the human mind.

More generally, Derrida has suggested that the use of the singular noun 'animal' as a master word for all non-human species in the Western philosophical tradition serves to highlight the sovereignty that humans claim over animals. The very word 'animal' is a 'name [humans] have given themselves the right and the authority to give to the living other'.[5] In saying this, Derrida not only draws attention to the way in which his earlier preoccupation with the logocentrism of Western philosophical economies of truth were also bound up with the anthropocentrism of Western philosophy; he also implies that the act of naming the animal is a particular kind of performative act that entails the performance of (human) sovereignty. The sovereign act of naming the animal that Derrida discusses in *The Animal That Therefore I Am* is developed further in his reading of Hobbes in *The Beast and the Sovereign*. Here, Derrida reflects on the way in which sovereignty in Hobbes 'presupposes the right of man over the beasts'.[6] Yet this sovereign claim of 'the human' over 'the animal' effaces the way in which the very name 'animal' eludes attempts to name or define it. In a similar way to Derrida's reflections on the sign in *Of Grammatology*, the animal could be understood as an 'ill-named thing [. . .] that escapes the instituting question of philosophy: what is. . .?'.[7] Derrida's reflections on the place of the animal in Martin Heidegger's thought shed significant light on the almost ungraspable distinction Heidegger draws between Being and beings, as we will see. But Derrida goes further than this. In the posthumously published seminars *The Beast and the Sovereign*, he suggests that the animal can be understood as a deconstructive figure – as a figure that raises questions about the anthropocentric foundations of the Western philosophical tradition and about the political sovereignty of humanity over the world. Indeed, Derrida's critical engagement with Giorgio Agamben in *The Beast and the Sovereign* can help to elucidate the singularity of the animal and its implications for political thought. Understood as a deconstructive figure, the animal not only troubles the Aristotelian distinction between *zōē* and *bios* that is so crucial to Agamben's writings on sovereignty, bare life and the anthropological machine, it also raises important questions about the place of the animal in the foundations and contours of political sovereignty. What, for example, can Derrida's thoughts on the beast and the sovereign tell us about the significance of the werewolf in Agamben's reflections on sovereignty? And how might Derrida's encounter with the animal interrupt the anthropological machine that Agamben associates with the Western philosophical tradition? For Derrida, 'the arbitrary suspension or rupture of right, runs the risk of making the sovereign look like the most brutal beast who respects nothing, scorns the law, immediately situates himself above the law, at a distance from the law'.[8] While the sovereign's 'mode of being-outside-the-law' may be quite different to that of a criminal or a beast, Derrida finds that the figures of sovereign, beast and criminal have a 'troubling resemblance'. Such a resemblance may seem to correspond with Agamben's suggestion that the figures of the sovereign and *homo sacer* are identical. Yet this would be to ignore the significance of Derrida's critique of Agamben's reading of the *zōē/bios* distinction. What is more, this 'troubling resemblance' has important implications for understanding the way in which colonial subjects have been framed as bestial figures in the classic texts of European philosophy and literature. As Gayatri Spivak has shown, the parallels Immanuel Kant draws between oxen and 'man-in-the-raw' in *The Critique of Judgement* bring the imperialist and anthropocentric determinants shaping Kant's reflections on the subject of moral and aesthetic judgement very clearly to the fore. In light of Spivak's marginal reference to the animal question, this essay considers how Derrida's readings of Agamben, Defoe and Heidegger in *The Beast and the Sovereign* can be seen to disclose the political implications of animals for understanding modern formations of sovereignty. By following Derrida's parenthetical reference to the fiction of J.M. Coetzee in *The Beast and the Sovereign*, the essay concludes by asking how Coetzee's literary representation of the animal and of violent forms of colonial sovereignty can shed light on Derrida's account of the sovereign violence that distinguishes between humans and animals.

Agamben and the empty space between 'the animal' and 'the human'

On a first reading, Derrida's critique of Agamben in *The Beast and the Sovereign* may appear to highlight the ways in which Agamben is complicit with the very anthropocentric discourse of sovereignty he seeks to criticise. For Derrida identifies specific traces of sovereignty in Agamben's own critical idiom, and his irrepressible tendency to assert that he was 'the first to say who *will have been* first'.[9] In Agamben's discussions of Hegel, Pindar, Löwith and Levinas, for example, Derrida notes how Agamben positions himself in the 'dubious' role of 'priest or master' who claims to be the first, and in so doing seems to forget Levinas's ethical injunction to respond to the other – an injunction that is exemplified in the polite phrase 'after you'.[10] Whereas Agamben wants to be the first, or the first to show that *x* will have been the first, Derrida suggests that it is both ethically and philosophically appropriate to follow, or to come after. In a coda to this session, Derrida proceeds to invoke a passage from the sixth book of Jean Jacques Rousseau's *Confessions* in which Rousseau offers an account of a visit to Moirans; during this visit, Rousseau met with a group of ladies who were part of a wedding procession, and adds that he felt obliged to dine with these ladies 'sous peine de passer pour un loup-garou' ['on pain of passing for a werewolf'].[11] Although Derrida does not expand on the significance of this example at this point, the implication of Rousseau's werewolf for Derrida's earlier reading of Agamben is clear: for if, as Derrida says, the 'law is always determined from the place of some wolf', the determination of the law is also troubled by figures that render unstable the secure distinction between 'the animal' and 'the human'.[12]

If this critical engagement with Agamben is postponed in the third session, it is pursued further in session twelve of *The Beast and the Sovereign*. Here, Derrida questions the rigorous distinction between *zōē* and *bios* that Agamben draws in *Homo Sacer* – a distinction that seems crucial to Agamben's formulation of 'bare life'. For Derrida, one of the problems with Agamben's formulation of bare life is that it seems to rest on an 'audacious' translation of Aristotle's concept of *zōē* as 'bare life' or 'life without qualities, without qualification, the pure and simple fact of living and of not being dead [. . .]'.[13] The problem with Agamben's translation for Derrida is that *zōē* 'designates a life that is qualified, and not "bare"'[14] As a consequence, Derrida claims that the 'subtle' distinction Agamben draws between the '"attribute of the living being"' and the '"specific difference that determines the genus *zōon*"' is 'untenable'.[15] The reason why this distinction is untenable, as Derrida proceeds to explain in a commentary on Heidegger, is that the originary sense of the word *logos* as force in Aristotle's definition of man as *zōon logon ekhon* has been forgotten in order to distinguish 'between an animal, a *zōon* supposed to be without reason, and a *zōon* supposed to be rational, the sovereign being posited as human'.[16] Derrida's use of the word 'untenable', from the French verb *tenir* or 'to hold', also recalls his critical discussion of the hand in the thought of Martin Heidegger: of what can and cannot be held in the hand, and what can be gestured to but not grasped. A detailed analysis of Derrida's thinking of the hand in Heidegger is beyond the scope of this essay, but suffice it to say that

Derrida's critique of Heidegger's hand takes issue with his sweeping assertion that 'the animal' can grasp, but it does not have a hand.[17] In Derrida's argument, Heidegger's claim is not only dogmatic because it 'presupposes an empiric or positive knowledge whose title, proofs, and signs are never shown [*montré*]'; it also 'takes no account of a certain "zoological knowledge" that accumulates, is differentiated, and becomes more refined concerning what is brought together under this so general and confused word animality'.[18] By using the word 'untenable' in his critique of Agamben's distinction between *zōē* and *bios*, then, Derrida implies that Agamben also fails to offer a sufficiently nuanced account of 'a certain "zoological knowledge"' in his formulation of biopolitics and sovereignty.[19] A further difficulty Derrida encounters in *Homo Sacer* concerns Agamben's claim that the introduction of bare life into the political order is the decisive event of political modernity, when bare or qualified life 'is as ancient as can be, immemorial and archaic'.[20] In Derrida's reading, Agamben's claims about the importance of bare life and biopolitics both for the age of political modernity *and* for the archaic foundations of the classical age point to the limitations of a conventional linear paradigm of history – a paradigm which, Derrida suggests, seems to residually inform Agamben's claims about the periodisation of bare life. If such a conventional, linear paradigm of history is synonymous with the history of sovereignty, Derrida attempts to interrogate the non-originary origin of that history by following the place of the animal in Western philosophy.

Derrida's criticisms of Agamben in *The Beast and the Sovereign* may strike readers as somewhat surprising when one considers that Agamben has broached similar questions about the distinction between 'the human' and 'the animal' in texts such as *Homo Sacer* (1995) and *The Open* (2002). In *Homo Sacer*, for example, Agamben invokes the figure of the werewolf to illustrate how the concept of the sovereign ban operates in defining the bandit or outlaw in Hobbes's state of nature:

> The life of the bandit, like that of the sacred man, is not a piece of animal nature without any relation to law and city. It is, rather, a threshold of indistinction and of passage between animal and man, *physis* and *nomos*, exclusion and inclusion: the life of the bandit is the life of *loup garou*, the werewolf, who is precisely *neither man nor beast*, and who dwells paradoxically within both while belonging to neither.[21]

In Agamben's account, the werewolf in Hobbes's state of nature inhabits a conceptually similar place to *homo sacer* in Roman law; for the werewolf designates 'a man who is transformed into a wolf and a wolf who is transformed into a man – in other words, a bandit, a *homo sacer*'.[22]

What the werewolf helps to clarify is the way in which the sovereign ban maintains a relation to that which has been abandoned: 'What has been banned is delivered over to its own separateness and, at the same time, consigned to the mercy of the one who abandons it – at once excluded and included, removed and at the same time captured.'[23] As in *The Beast and the Sovereign*, the werewolf serves to exemplify the non-relational relationship between the beast, the sovereign and the law.

It is in *The Open*, however, that Agamben appears to address the question of the animal in a sustained and explicit way. In common with Derrida, Agamben calls into question the tendency to posit a secure distinction between 'the human' and 'the animal' that is prevalent in Western philosophy. We have already seen, for example, how Descartes attempted to efface the 'abyssal limit' between man and animal, and to present the human mind or *cogito* – the 'I am' – as a self-grounded concept. It is significant too that Descartes frames the animality of the human – the living body – as a machine or automaton. In his *Treatise on Man and Passions*, Descartes described activities such as 'the digestion of food, the beating of the heart and arteries, the nourishment and growth of the limbs, respiration, waking and sleeping, the reception by the external sense organs of light, sounds, smells, tastes, heat, and other such qualities' as mechanistic behaviours that do not involve the human mind; in so doing, Descartes compared these human activities, which he designated as mechanistic, to animal behaviour.[24] It is comparisons such as these that have prompted Agamben to assert that 'Cartesian theory conceived of animals as if they were *automata mechanica*'.[25]

In Descartes' attempt to distinguish between the (animal) body and the (human) mind, one can also trace the operation of what Agamben has called the modern anthropological machine. In a discussion of the nineteenth-century German linguist Heymann Steinhal's effort to 'apply the methods of modern science to the study of Judaism', Agamben identifies how Steinhal attempted to distinguish between humans and animals by recourse to the category of language – the category that 'was presupposed as the identifying characteristic of the human'.[26] Steinhal 'tried to show how language could spring from the perceptual life of man and not from that of the animal'.[27] In so doing, he identified how the difference between a non-speaking animal and a speaking human is historically produced rather than 'already inherent in the psychophysical structure of man'.[28] Agamben names this historical process the 'anthropological machine':

> Insofar as the production of man through the opposition of man/animal, human/inhuman, is at stake here, the machine necessarily functions by means

of an exclusion (which is always already a capturing) and an inclusion (which is also always already an exclusion). Indeed, precisely because the human is already presupposed every time, the machine actually produces a kind of state of exception, a zone of indeterminacy in which the outside is nothing but the inclusion of an inside and the inside is in turn only the inclusion of an outside.[29]

In this extensive explanation, Agamben reveals how his engagement with the classical philosophical question of the relationship between man and animal is subordinate to his recurrent concern with the logic of inclusive exclusion that underpins modern forms of political sovereignty. Indeed, for Agamben the anthropological machine functions in a similar way to sovereignty: in the production of the opposition between man and animal, the human is 'presupposed every time', and it is this presupposition that produces 'a kind of state of exception' in which 'an already human being' is designated as 'not (yet) human' and is therefore excluded from itself. What is crucial for Agamben is not the animal *per se*, but the form of life that inhabits the caesura or empty space between the animal and the human: 'a life that is separated and excluded from itself – [. . .] a bare life'.[30]

Certainly, *The Open* develops some familiar themes in Agamben's thought. Specifically, Agamben's engagement with Martin Heidegger's reflections on the relationship between man and animal in his lecture series *The Fundamental Concepts of Metaphysics: World, Finitude, Solitude* exemplifies the way in which Heidegger's thought has informed Agamben's account of the state of exception. In *Homo Sacer*, Agamben clarifies how Heidegger's attempt to 'unconceal' the meaning of Being as the hidden foundation of Western metaphysics informs Agamben's own attempt to reveal 'bare life' as the hidden foundation of Western politics. In *The Open*, Agamben expands this concern with reference to the human/animal distinction. Towards the end of the chapter 'World and Earth', Agamben notes how 'the originary political conflict between unconcealedness and concealedness will be, at the same time and to the same degree, that between the humanity and animality of man'.[31] In Heidegger's thought, the distinction between the concealed and the unconcealed is crucial to the thought of *Dasein*; and one of the things that is concealed from 'humanity', Heidegger suggests, is its 'animality'. Agamben expands Heidegger's distinction between the unconcealed and the concealed by suggesting that 'Man suspends his animality and, in this way, opens a "free and empty zone" in which life is captured and a-ban-doned {*ab-bandonata*} in a zone of exception.'[32] In doing so, Agamben draws out (what he sees as) a biopolitical dimension in Heidegger's thought.

If, as Derrida has suggested, Agamben falls prey to an anthropocentrism in *Homo Sacer* which seeks to reinscribe a clear binary opposition between 'the human' sovereign and 'the animal', Agamben's reflections in *The Open* seem to be concerned with the ways in which certain forms of human life are relegated to the liminal category of bare life. As Kelly Oliver puts it,

> Agamben's own thinking does not so much open up the concept of animal or even open up man to the possibility of encountering animals as it attempts to save humanity from the anthropological machine that always produces the animal as the constitutive outside within the human itself.[33]

Yet the operation of the anthropological machine in Western thought also informs Derrida's own reflections on the animal question in Defoe and Heidegger in *The Beast and the Sovereign*, as we will see towards the end of this essay.

Reading *Robinson Crusoe* after Heidegger

Derrida's reading of a literary character in an eighteenth-century novel by an English writer, together with a published lecture series by a German philosopher of the twentieth century, may at first seem rather audacious in its apparent disregard for questions of historical and cultural context, as well as the disciplinary codes and conventions of literature and philosophy. Yet the grounds of comparison between Defoe's novel and Heidegger's lectures are hinted at in Derrida's comments on Heidegger's search for 'the true and proper path, the authentic *Weg* of philosophy itself'.[34] Robinson's circling of the island, and his encounter with a set of footprints in the sand (which he suggests later could be his own), prompt Derrida to reflect on the parallels between the direction or orientation of Heidegger's thought and Robinson's constant attempt to get his bearings on the island. What concerns Derrida specifically, he says, is 'the analogy between their respective ways of proceeding',[35] and this analogy provides a means of following the movements and orientation of thought in *The Fundamental Concepts of Metaphysics* and *Robinson Crusoe*. When Derrida renames Heidegger 'Robinson Heidegger', he is pointing to Heidegger's determination to stay on the correct philosophical path: to 'look metaphysics in the face without any detour'.[36] By following Crusoe after Heidegger, Derrida draws attention to the way in which Heidegger's attempt to follow the correct philosophical path is in a certain sense impossible. In trying to elaborate the proposition that the 'animal is poor in world', for example, Heidegger asserts that the 'proposition does not derive from zoology, but it cannot be elucidated independently of zoology either'.[37] Indeed, a proper philosophical understanding of Heidegger's proposition 'requires a specific orientation towards zoology and biology in general, and yet,' Heidegger insists, 'it is not through them that its truth can be determined'.[38] In a similar vein, Robinson Crusoe tries to stay on the right path in order to assert his sovereignty over the island, but sometimes finds himself thwarted in this endeavour, as the following extract suggests:

> I took another Way to come back than that I went, thinking I could easily keep all the Island so much in my View, that I could not miss finding my first Dwelling by viewing the Country; but I found my self mistaken; for being come about two or three Miles, I found my self descended into a very large Valley; but so surrounded with Hills and those Hills covered with Wood, that I could not see which was my Way by any Direction but that of the Sun, nor even then, unless I knew very well the Position of the Sun at that Time of the Day.[39]

Crusoe's disorientation on the island is further exemplified in his encounter with a set of footprints in the sand that could be his own. Crusoe's encounter with these footprints is not only a sign of his lack of geographical knowledge of the island, however. In Derrida's post-Heideggerian reading of Defoe's novel, Crusoe's terror of the footprints that he encounters on the island – a terror that is registered in his assertion that he 'stood like one Thunder-struck, or as if I had seen an apparition' – can be read as an expression of fear of his own death.[40] When Robinson takes flight to his makeshift 'Castle', he compares his emotional reaction to the footprints to that of a frightened animal: 'for never frighted Hare fled to cover, or Fox to Earth, with more Terror of Mind than I to this Retreat'.[41] The analogy Robinson draws between himself and animals does not end here. For, as Derrida suggests, Robinson's repeated reference to savages and cannibals is a displaced expression of 'the cruelty that Robinson seems to fear when he is afraid of dying a living death like a beast'.[42]

What Derrida implies here is that Robinson fears a death without the funeral rites that are deemed proper to 'the human'. In so doing, he also uses this moment in *Robinson Crusoe* to pose questions about Heidegger's understanding of the animal in *The Fundamental Concepts of Metaphysics*. If, as Heidegger claims, one of the things to distinguish 'the animal' and 'the human' is that 'the animal' cannot have access to death *as such*, Derrida raises questions about what the phrase 'as such' connotes, and suggests that Heidegger struggles to define what death as such actually means.[43] Through a close reading of Heidegger's lectures,

Derrida traces the use and significance of the German word *walten* – a verb that denotes force, but which Derrida glosses as 'the exercise of an archi-originary force, of a power, a violence, before any physical, psychic, theological, political determination [...]'.[44] *Walten*, in other words, is the groundless ground of sovereignty, and lacks determinate political and theological content.[45] As the thing that distinguishes beings from beings as such, *walten* 'is in a certain sense *nothing*'.[46] Yet it also has the power to produce difference:

> It is through this violence that breaks open ground or path, captures, tames that beings are discovered or revealed or unveiled, and appear as sea, as earth, as animal [...] The *als*, the *als-Struktur* that distinguishes man from the animal is thus indeed what the violence of *Walten* makes possible.[47]

Derrida's meticulous reading of Heidegger in *The Fundamental Concepts of Metaphysics* may appear to follow Heidegger's words to the letter. To take one instance, Derrida's suggestion that 'man' believes himself to exercise authority over a sovereign power or *walten* by which he himself is gripped and seized suggests that Derrida is also trying to follow the narrow philosophical path defined by Heidegger in order to disclose the quasi-transcendental operation of *walten*. And yet Derrida's engagement with Defoe's *Robinson Crusoe* also points towards different readings that stray from this path.

In a discussion of Rousseau's commentary on the Robinsonian ideal 'of an absolute identification of the sovereign and the people in a single person' in *The Social Contract*, Derrida describes this ideal as 'pre-political'.[48] This romanticised ideal of a solitary sovereignty is not entirely different from Heidegger's account of *walten* as a figure of sovereignty. For just as Defoe's utopian ideal of sovereignty is anterior to any determinate political content, so Heidegger's use of *walten* is 'stripped of all the anthropological, theological and political determinations of sovereignty'.[49] In this way, Derrida may appear to suggest that both Defoe and Heidegger understand sovereignty as the foundation of politics and history rather than having any determinate historical and political content as such. And yet the writing of Defoe and of Heidegger is irreducibly marked by its respective historical moments. As Derrida has indicated in a reading of Heidegger's rectoral address in *Of Spirit*, Heidegger's use of the word *geist* discloses the way in which the conceptual language of philosophy can become implicated in the right-wing politics of National Socialism.[50] Significantly, it is through an analysis of Heidegger's preoccupation with the difference between human and animal *Dasein* that Derrida broaches the concept of spirit. In a similar vein, Derrida's commentary on *Robinson Crusoe* in *The Beast and the Sovereign* makes clear how Defoe's novel is implicated in the British imperialist project: Derrida invokes James Joyce's observation that the novel prefigured 'an imperialist, colonialist sovereignty, the first herald of the British empire [. . .]'.[51] In this respect, Derrida's reading of Heidegger after Defoe could also be seen to disclose a trace of the political in Heidegger's thought, which Derrida started to follow in *Of Spirit*.

Subhuman animals and the violence of the anthropological machine

As Derrida suggests in his passing reference to Joyce's comment on *Robinson Crusoe*, the rhetoric of Western philosophy is profoundly marked by the geopolitical as well as the political context of its production. In *A Critique of Postcolonial Reason*, Gayatri Chakravorty Spivak has explored the correspondences between the rhetoric and concepts of Western philosophy and colonial representations of difference in detail. Commenting on Immanuel Kant's *Critique of Judgement*, Spivak has argued that 'philosophy has been and continues to be travestied in the service of the narrativization of history'.[52] In Spivak's reading, Kant's critical philosophy provides a rational justification for colonialism as a civilising mission. Such a reading is perhaps not surprising if one considers Kant's blatantly racist references to savages, negroes and Asians (to say nothing of his sexist remarks on gender, the sublime and the beautiful) in *Observations on the Feeling of the Beautiful and the Sublime* (1764–65).[53] It is perhaps for this reason that Spivak argues that the geopolitically divided subject of Kantian humanism is particularly exemplified in Kant's theory of the sublime. In 'On the Modality of a Judgement about the Sublime in Nature' (section 29 of the *Critique of Judgement*), Kant suggests that receptivity to ideas and moral feeling are available to all humanity; however, this claim is undermined by his subsequent assertion that: 'Without *development* of moral ideas, that which we, prepared by culture, call sublime presents itself to man in the raw [*dem rohen Menschen*] merely as terrible.'[54] Spivak picks up on the German adjective *roh* in Kant's original German text, noting that while it is normally translated as 'uneducated', this term in Kant's work refers specifically to 'the child and the poor'; the 'naturally uneducable' refers to women; and '*der rohen Menschen*, man in the raw' connotes 'the savage and the primitive'.[55] That the savage and the primitive experience the sublime 'merely as terrible' reveals how the category of human nature that produces the power of aesthetic judgement is not universal, but culturally specific to Europe. As Spivak puts it, 'It is not possible to *become* cultured in this culture, if you are *naturally* alien to it.'[56]

To further support her argument that Kant's critical philosophy provides a rational justification for colonialism, Spivak turns to the second half of the *Critique of Judgement*, 'The Critique of Teleological Judgement', in which Kant investigates 'the possibility of a purposiveness in nature and of an intelligent author of the world'.[57] In Kant's argument, the final purpose of nature or the existence of God cannot be known or cognised by the human subject *as such*; for the answers to these epistemological questions belong to the transcendent realm of what Kant called the supersensible. Some critics such as Douglas Burnham hold that 'judgment is forced to assume a supersensible realm underlying all purposive forms in nature, and all purposive activity in the subject'.[58] In Spivak's deconstructive reading of Kant, however, 'The Critique of Teleological Judgement' does not end with the assumption of a supersensible cause. Citing a passage from section 67 of the third *Critique*, Spivak intimates that Kant's quest for a purposiveness or final cause underlying nature is complicated by the example of the New Hollander (more commonly known as the Australian Aboriginal) and the man from Tierra del Fuego. Kant invokes these two figures to support his argument that the ultimate purpose or *telos* of nature is located outside the physical laws of nature. Kant recognises 'how cattle need grass, and how people need cattle as a means for their existence'.[59] Yet he adds the caveat that 'we cannot arrive at a categorical purpose in this way because we cannot see why people should have to exist (a question it might not be so easy to answer if we have in mind, say, the New Hollanders or the Fuegians)'.[60] Kant's parenthetical invocation of the New Hollander and the man from Tierra del Fuego may indeed support Spivak's observation that these figures are 'a *casual* object of thought' rather than a paradigmatic example in Kant's argument.[61] Indeed, these figures are invoked to support Kant's broader philosophical argument that it makes no sense to think of humans as a part of nature if we wish to account for the supersensible origin of nature. For Spivak, however, the relegation of the aboriginal to the category of the natural or the animal exemplifies what Kant means by man in the raw in his account of the sublime: 'We find here the axiomatics of imperialism as a natural argument to indicate the limits of the cognition of (cultural) man.'[62] In this respect, Kant's 'man in the raw' in the *Critique of Judgement* can be understood as an effect of an anthropological machine that differentiates between 'civilised' and 'natural' humans.

What Spivak has called her 'mistaken' reading of Kant may help to elucidate the political significance of Derrida's reading of Heidegger and Defoe.⁶³ Kant's theory of aesthetic judgement in the third *Critique* might appear to provide a set of axioms to justify the civilising mission of imperialism. However, this use of Kant is strictly speaking a travesty because it wrenches the terms of Kant's theory of aesthetic judgement out of its philosophical frame of reference. In a similar vein, by supplementing his reading of Heidegger with a discussion of Defoe's novel *Robinson Crusoe*, Derrida might be taken to imply that Heidegger's attempt to follow the correct philosophical path in his reflections on being and the experience of human and animal is predicated on the exclusion of non-philosophical questions related to history and politics. Rather than investigating that which is excluded from Heidegger's formulations, Derrida seems more concerned to elucidate the meaning of *walten* as the groundless ground of *Dasein* via a discussion of Robinson Crusoe's fictional sovereignty over his island. Indeed, it seems significant that Derrida's reading of *Robinson Crusoe* effectively overlooks the significance of Friday in Defoe's novel – even though Derrida explicitly acknowledges the colonial subtext of the novel, as we have already seen. Yet Derrida's parenthetical reference to the fiction of J.M. Coetzee also gestures towards a thinking of both the colonial and the anthropocentric aspects of the anthropological machine – even though this is a path that Derrida chooses not to follow. As he explains:

> ([. . .] Defoe's name is as though it meant enemy; and here I recommend that you read at least two or three magnificent novels by J.M. Coetzee, the great South African writer who wrote a novel called *Foe*, which presents itself as an oblique reading-rewriting of *Robinson Crusoe*, with embedded quotations, but also because Coetzee bears in his thought and his oeuvre the grave concern of the animal, I advise you to read also *The Lives of Animals* and *Disgrace*.)⁶⁴

By advising his audience to read Coetzee, Derrida announces that he does not plan to discuss Coetzee himself in the seminar; it is as if Coetzee's fiction is safely contained within the marginal space of a footnote. And yet by acknowledging the significance of Coetzee's fiction to his discussion of the human/animal dichotomy in Western philosophy and the colonial contexts of *Robinson Crusoe*, Derrida also encourages his audience/readers to follow this counterpath.

As a body of literary fiction and lectures concerned with the limits of (human) sovereignty, *Foe* (1986), *Disgrace* (1999) and *The Lives of Animals* (2002) might appear to depart from Derrida's philosophical readings of the beast and the sovereign in Heidegger and Defoe. Coetzee's *Foe* raises questions about Crusoe's sovereignty over the island by rewriting Crusoe's narrative from the point of view of Susan

Barton, a European female traveller in search of her daughter. In Coetzee's rewriting of Defoe's colonial classic, Friday is represented as a mute who has had his tongue removed. As a figure who has been deprived of the faculty of language, Friday's life narrative and consciousness is presented as unknowable, and yet it is the secret of how Friday's tongue was removed that impels the narrative. Barton asserts at one point that 'the unnatural years Friday had spent with Cruso had deadened his heart, making him cold, incurious, like an animal wrapt entirely in itself'.[65] By drawing this analogy, Barton implies that the experience of subjection to colonial sovereignty is not unlike the singularity of animal life. In *Disgrace*, the white, male South African protagonist, David Lurie, finds himself witnessing the euthanising of moribund dogs in a veterinary surgery after being dismissed from his job as a literature professor for sexually harassing one of his female students. Following the rape of his daughter, Lucy, at her home on a South African farm, and Lucy's decision to transfer ownership of the farm to Petrus, her former employee, Lurie compares the loss of white South African sovereignty over the land to being reduced to the condition of a dog:

> '[. . .] it is humiliating. But perhaps that is a good point to start from again. Perhaps that is what I must learn to accept. To start at ground level. With nothing. Not with nothing but. With nothing. No cards, no weapons, no property, no rights, no dignity.'
> 'Like a dog.'
> 'Yes, like a dog.'[66]

If Susan Barton's comparison of Friday's state of mind to that of an animal in *Foe* highlights his lack of agency and his subjection to the will of Mr Foe, David Lurie's comparison of his daughter's decision to relinquish the rights, property and power associated with white South African citizens during the apartheid era to the life of a dog clearly foregrounds the way in which the human/animal dichotomy has shaped narratives of European colonialism. In this respect, the animal can be read as a trope for the absence or loss of (human) sovereignty in *Foe* and *Disgrace*. In *The Lives of Animals*, by contrast, Coetzee broaches questions about the experience and consciousness of animals. In this lecture series, first delivered at Princeton University in 1997, Coetzee invents the fictional character of Elizabeth Costello, an eminent novelist who delivers a series of public talks on the animal at a college in the United States. In a controversial analogy, Costello repeatedly compares the human treatment of non-human animals to the Nazis' treatment of Jews in the Holocaust – a comparison that provokes an angry response from a poet called Abraham Stern, who accuses her of wilfully misunderstanding the 'nature of likenesses' and trading in cheap analogies.[67]

If both Defoe's *Robinson Crusoe* and Heidegger's *Fundamental Concepts* reproduce the operations of an anthropological machine that attempts to separate human and animal life, Coetzee's fiction provides a different frame of reference through which to address the political significance of Derrida's encounter with the animal in *The Beast and the Sovereign*. In a critique of the anthropocentrism of the analytic philosopher Thomas Nagel's attempt to comprehend the consciousness of a bat, Elizabeth Costello invokes an argument about the moral capacity of the sympathetic imagination:

> Sympathy has everything to do with the subject and little to do with the object, the 'another', as we see at once when we think of the object not as a bat ('Can I share the being of a bat?') but as another human being. There are people who have the capacity to imagine themselves as someone else, there are people who have no such capacity (when the lack is extreme, we call them psychopaths), and there are people who have the capacity but choose not to exercise it.[68]

Costello's appeal to a moral discourse of sympathy for the animal may seem to depart from the terms of Nagel's thought experiment, and it is this apparent disregard for the conventions of philosophical rigour that provokes the irritation of Costello's daughter-in-law, a trained analytic philosopher. To borrow a term from Spivak's reading of Kant, Costello's lecture on the lives of animals is a travesty. And yet Costello's attempt to feel sympathy for the non-human animal also helps to guide us along the Derridean counterpath I have been following in the reading of Heidegger and Defoe in *The Beast and the Sovereign*.

Against the powerful philosophical tradition that defines the difference between 'the human' and 'the animal' in terms of their power or ability to do something, Derrida invokes Jeremy Bentham's argument that 'the question is not, "can the animal do this or that, speak, reason, die, etc.?" but "can the animal suffer?"'.[69] In repeating Bentham's question, Derrida attempts to think the animal in non-anthropocentric terms – in terms that interrupt the operation of what Agamben has called the anthropological machine which underpins the Western philosophical tradition from Aristotle and to Heidegger. By posing a question about the suffering of animals, Derrida (following Bentham) is also posing a question about the ethical responsibility of humans to animals – a responsibility that is prefigured in his encounter with a cat in *The Animal That Therefore I Am*, but which is also developed in Derrida's elucidation of the category of *walten* in Heidegger. We have already seen how Heidegger used the term *walten* to denote the originary force or violence that differentiates between humans and animals. By suggesting that the difference between animals and humans is nothing but the arch-originary force or violence that differentiates between humans and animals, Derrida encourages readers to guard against such originary violence. In so doing, Derrida also questions the operations of an anthropological machine that defines certain humans as animals. And in this respect, Derrida may appear to be close to Agamben's position in *The Open*. Derrida's passing references to the Bush administration's foreign policy in Iraq and to Guantanamo Bay evoke a violent sovereign power that relegates certain forms of (human) life to the category of subhuman animals.[70] Yet to focus exclusively on Derrida's argument regarding the sovereign and the human who is relegated to the position of an animal would be to overlook the implications of Derrida's reflections on sovereignty and violence (*walten*) for certain non-human animals that are exposed to factory farming and other forms of industrial killing. We have already seen how Coetzee staged the violence of sovereign power for non-human animals through the controversial analogy that Elizabeth Costello draws between the Holocaust and the mass slaughter of animals. In a similar vein, Derrida has also compared the violent treatment of animals in factory farming and biomedical testing to 'the worst cases of genocide'.[71] In making this comparison, Derrida is not simply suggesting that the suffering of Jews in the Nazi death camps is equivalent to the suffering of animals in the factory farm; on the contrary, Derrida's point is that the violent logic of manufactured death that was first exemplified in the Nazi death camps has become normalised through practices such as the factory farming of animals. The identification of such a logic of industrialised death may not amount to an understanding of the suffering of non-human animals. But if this violent logic of industrialised death is situated in relation to Derrida's critique of the violence or *walten* that differentiates between humans and animals, it is possible to trace how the persistent undoing of the (human) subject in Derrida's reading of Defoe and Heidegger can mark the beginning of an ethical and therefore non-anthropocentric encounter with different forms of animal life.[72] It is this ethical and non-anthropocentric encounter with non-human animals that distinguishes Derrida's reflections on the animal question from those of Agamben. Whereas Agamben is concerned primarily with the way in which the animal sheds light on a form of (human) life that is excluded from the human community as its constitutive outside, Derrida is *also* concerned to question the anthropocentric foundations of violence that treat certain non-human animals as a form of superfluous life. As a posthumously published text,

Derrida's seminar notes in *The Beast and the Sovereign* may offer a somewhat fragmentary account of (human) sovereignty and the animal question. Yet, as this chapter has suggested, Derrida's critical reflections on the constitutive violence that differentiates between the human and the animal not only shed light on the non-anthropocentric dimension of his ethical thought; the persistent undoing of the (human) subject in Derrida's reflections on Heidegger and Agamben also offers a crucial contribution to understanding the necropolitical forms of sovereignty that continue to kill particular forms of animal life – whether human, subhuman or non-human.

Notes

1. Marie Louise Mallet, 'Introduction', in Jacques Derrida, *The Animal That Therefore I Am (More to Follow)*, trans. David Wills (New York: Fordham University Press, 2008), p. x.
2. For a further discussion of animal beings, see the essays collected in *parallax*, 12.1, 2006.
3. Derrida, *Animal*, p. 12.
4. René Descartes, *The Philosophical Writings of René Descartes*, trans. John Cottingham, Robert Stoothoff and Dugald Murdoc (Cambridge: Cambridge University Press, 1985), II, p. 17.
5. Derrida, *Animal*, p. 23
6. Jacques Derrida, *The Beast and the Sovereign*, Vol. I, trans. Geoffrey Bennington (Chicago: University of Chicago Press, 2009), p. 55.
7. Jacques Derrida, *Of Grammatology*, trans. Gayatri Chakravorty Spivak (Baltimore: Johns Hopkins University Press, 1976), p. 19.
8. Derrida, *Beast*, I, p. 39.
9. Ibid., p. 92.
10. Ibid., pp. 95–6
11. Jean Jacques Rousseau, *Oeuvres Complètes* (Paris: Gallimard, 1981), I, pp. 248–9.
12. Derrida, *Beast*, I, p. 196
13. Ibid., p. 326
14. Ibid., p. 327.
15. Ibid., p. 328.
16. Ibid., p. 339.
17. Jacques Derrida, 'Geschlecht II: Heidegger's Hand', trans. John P. Leavey, in *Deconstruction and Philosophy: The Texts of Jacques Derrida*, ed. John Sallis (Chicago: University of Chicago Press, 1987), pp. 161–96 (p. 173).
18. Ibid., p. 173.
19. Ibid.
20. Derrida, *Beast*, I, pp. 316–17
21. Giorgio Agamben, *Homo Sacer: Sovereign Power and Bare Life*, trans. Daniel Heller-Roazen (Stanford: Stanford University Press, 1995), p. 105.
22. Ibid., p. 106.
23. Ibid., p. 110.

24. René Descartes, *The Philosophical Writings of René Descartes*, trans. John Cottingham, Robert Stoothoff and Dugald Murdoc (Cambridge: Cambridge University Press, 1985), I, p. 108.
25. Giorgio Agamben, *The Open: Man and Animal*, trans. Kevin Atell (Stanford: Stanford University Press, 2004), p. 23.
26. Ibid., p. 34.
27. Ibid., p. 35
28. Ibid., p. 36.
29. Ibid., p. 37.
30. Ibid., p. 38.
31. Ibid., p. 73
32. Ibid., p. 79
33. Kelly Oliver, *Animal Lessons: How They Teach Us to Be Human* (New York: Columbia University Press, 2009), p. 230.
34. Jacques Derrida, *The Beast and the Sovereign*, Vol. II, trans. Geoffrey Bennington (Chicago: University of Chicago Press, 2011), p. 34.
35. Ibid., p. 35.
36. Ibid., p. 37
37. Martin Heidegger, *The Fundamental Concepts of Metaphysics: World, Finitude, Solitude*, trans. William McNeill and Nicholas Walker (Bloomington: Indiana University Press, 2001), p. 187.
38. Ibid., p. 187.
39. Daniel Defoe, *Robinson Crusoe* (New York: The Modern Library, 2001), p. 103.
40. Ibid., p. 142
41. Ibid.
42. Derrida, *Beast*, II, p. 145.
43. Ibid., pp. 122–3.
44. Ibid., p. 104.
45. Ibid., p. 278.
46. Ibid., p. 253.
47. Ibid., p. 288.
48. Ibid., pp. 23–4.
49. Ibid., pp. 278–9.
50. Jacques Derrida, *Of Spirit: Heidegger and the Question*, trans. Geoffrey Bennington and Rachel Bowlby (Chicago: University of Chicago Press, 1989).
51. Derrida, *Beast*, II, p. 16.
52. Gayatri Chakravorty Spivak, *A Critique of Postcolonial Reason: Towards a History of the Vanishing Present* (Cambridge, MA: Harvard University Press, 1999), p. 9.
53. Immanuel Kant, *Observations on the Feelings of the Beautiful and the Sublime and Other Writings*, ed. Patrick Frierson and Paul Guyer (Cambridge: Cambridge University Press, 2011).
54. Kant, cited in Spivak, *A Critique of Postcolonial Reason*, p. 13.
55. Ibid.
56. Ibid., p. 12.
57. Ibid., p. 20.

58. Douglas Burnham, *An Introduction to Kant's Critique of Judgement* (Edinburgh: Edinburgh University Press, 2000), p. 121.
59. Immanuel Kant, *Critique of Judgement*, trans. Werner S. Pluhar (Indianapolis: Hackett Publishing, 1987), p. 258.
60. Ibid., p. 258.
61. Spivak, *A Critique of Postcolonial Reason*, p. 26.
62. Ibid.
63. Ibid., p. 6.
64. Derrida, *Beast*, II, p. 46
65. J.M. Coetzee, *Foe* (London: Secker and Warburg, 1986), p. 70.
66. J.M. Coetzee, *Disgrace* (London: Harvill Secker, 1999), p. 205.
67. J.M. Coetzee, *The Lives of Animals* (Princeton: Princeton University Press, 2002), pp. 49–50.
68. Ibid., pp. 34–5.
69. Derrida, *Beast*, II, p. 245.
70. Ibid., pp. 260–1.
71. Derrida, *Animal*, p. 20.
72. See Ranjanna Khanna, 'Indignity', *positions: east asia cultures critique*, 16.1, Spring 2008, pp. 39–78.

Chapter 8

Derrida, Rousseau, Cixous and Tsvetaeva: Sexual Difference and the Love of the Wolf

Judith Still

As soon as you speak of loving there he is.
[...] In what way is the wolf lovable? It is not the wolf species that we love, it is not the wolf. It is *a* wolf, a particular wolf, a wolf-but, a surprise-wolf.

(Dès qu'on parle d'aimer il est là.
[...] Par où le loup est-il aimable? Ce n'est pas la race des loups que nous aimons, ce n'est pas le loup. Il s'agit d'*un* loup, un certain loup, un loup-mais, un loup-surprise.) (Hélène Cixous)[1]

The posthumous collection of Derrida's seminars, *The Beast and the Sovereign*, is principally concerned with the bestiary of political language, in which the wolf has a privileged place, usually outside the law and thus the *polis*, for example 'man' in the state of nature, a creature of appetites, free of social or political control, the outlaw.[2] However, the wolf shares this liminal position with the sovereign; the one who makes the law (or creates the social bond) is in some respects not included within it or subject to it: 'The law (*nomos*) is always determined from the place of some wolf. I shall call it *lyconomy*. No genelycology or anthropolycology without lyconomy.'[3] Derrida also repeatedly points his audience towards the private domain and to sexual difference including regular references to genre and gender (if only to draw our attention teasingly to la *bête et* le *souverain*), but this is much less developed in these seminars than the political aspect, even though there is always significant overlap between the two domains. He presents the figure of the sovereign as father, and vice versa, as *paterfamilias* or as *ipse* (self-same).[4] The wolf can be represented as all appetite, the one who is going to eat you up, and thus as the castrating father (according to Freud), but also the mother in the Wolf Man case history.[5] In this essay I shall expand on this question of lycological sexual difference, following the track of some of Derrida's intertexts from Plautus's *Asinaria* and Rousseau's *Confessions* to Hélène Cixous on Tsvetaeva and Pushkin in *L'Amour du loup*.

The first sentence or phrase of Derrida's seminar series on *The Beast and the Sovereign* is quite remarkable: '*La . . . le.*' This untranslatable couple of syllables, which might sound like a stutter, an inauspicious start, is initially translated into English as 'Feminine . . . masculine' with the French original in square brackets, which gets much closer to the connoted meaning than the sound or the literal meaning which might be rendered 'the . . . the'.[6] That rendition would lose not only the point but the subtle shift in the repeated sound – not a tuneful 'la . . . la' or a standard repeated definite article where the masculine prevails 'le . . . le', but 'la . . . le', so close and yet so different in this particular language – a point of terror for many Anglophone students of French, or even Anglophone teachers of French, the dreaded gender mistake.[7] English masks sexual difference at certain points where French reveals it (the sexed object), and vice versa (the sexed possessive, his or her); it also leans towards an objectification of the animal as 'it' where French can only ever render 'it' as 'il' or 'elle', making a distinction of gender and not a distinction between a person and a non-person. Derrida promises his audience, his pupils, echoing La Fontaine's deferral in 'The Wolf and the Lamb', that he will, soon ('tout à l'heure'), and, following the animal, stealthily as a wolf ('à pas de loup') show them the scene of sexual difference that his unconscious has detected in his choice of title for *La bête et le souverain*. Yet it could be argued that he does not (the uncanny *pas* of the wolf's step) quite make good his promise. For, while, unlike many commentators on sovereignty or indeed on animals or beasts, he does persistently allude to the question of sexual difference, he does not often bring it centre stage in this series of seminars, which enables many of his readers to pass it over entirely.[8] Yet even the wolf, especially the wolf, who is fascinating with respect to political writings throughout a long historical time span which draw on the wolf either as an image of man outside society (pre-social man, savages, outlaws) or as an image of the bloodthirsty tyrant, is gendered. Both the sovereign (as Derrida, following Benveniste, unpacks the word) and the outlaw are traditionally (hyper)-masculine even while either can deploy elements of femininity as part of the chain of significations they establish.[9]

Moreover the wolf figures in tales of relations between individuals, including relations between the sexes in which young girls may be warned that 'the worst wolves are hairy on the inside'.[10] Leaving aside the question of the she-wolf (*la louve*) for now, the fabulous he-wolf (*le loup*) frequently also allegorises hunting and predation in the private or personal sphere on which the *polis* is built, but which politics ambiguously overlooks. The 'insensibility' of the wolf – represented as silent, imperceptible and cruelly indifferent to the suffering of his prey – may be designed to terrify yet proves uncannily attractive in some legendary versions of the creature, in particular when he makes an exception for one particular lambkin.[11]

In this chapter, I ask what it is to love or be loved by a wolf (with Cixous), thereby also raising the question of the werewolf and other stories about men who are really wolves (with Marina Tsvetaeva).[12] Cixous's 'The Love of the Wolf' entwines itself with three texts by Tsvetaeva, two essays around her love for Pushkin ('My Pushkin' and 'Pushkin and Pugachev'), plus a long poem, *Le Gars*, based on a folk tale about a young girl, Maroussia, who falls in love with, and is loved by, a werewolf or vampire-like figure.[13] The way in which the lovely Maroussia shifts between vulnerable victim and ruthless match is both interesting and unsettling. Tsvetaeva's account of Pushkin and his hero, or anti-hero, Pugachev suggests furthermore that the potential for revolutionary political change may require love of the ferocious wolf.[14]

Like most animals having a significant role in the Western imaginary, the wolf has a certain conventional relationship to sexual difference as sexual opposition. This is largely the masculine wolf – a (sexual) predator devouring little lambs who need to be protected by 'shepherds' (who 'keep' them of course to eat them themselves in their own good time). The female wolf also crops up from time to time *either* as a good (foster) mother *or* occasionally as sexual predator. Figuring the wolf, for the twentieth-century women writers I am interested in, is a way of thinking through the relationship between women and the law (patriarchal law) as regards sexuality, appetite and language – and the role of fear in keeping distinctions, while laughter and desire may embrace what is feared. The problem for all the writers who struggle with this is how to engage with the seduction of the wolf without falling back into romance. But writing new, differently perverse romances at least responds to Cixous's injunction: 'Woman must write herself: must write about women and bring women to writing, from which they have been driven away as violently as from their bodies – for the same reasons, by the same law, with the same fatal goal.'[15]

A certain tradition: Plautus querying the domestic

Are women lambs or she-wolves who consume men? Are women treated as lambs, protected and controlled, in order to prevent them from turning into wolves? Thus sexuality would be policed, by terror, because it is feared, and fairy tales teach morals from an early age. Whichever came first, the wolf or the lamb, it is clear that women are mostly victims of male violence rather than the reverse. The Roman proverb 'man is a wolf to men' is often turned to mean that man is a wolf to women. In a novel about gang rape in Paris, *La Tournante*, Elisa Brune has 'the father's friend' say: 'We were taught that man is a wolf to men. It was to make us forget, I think, that first of all he is a wolf to women.'[16]

The phrase 'man is a wolf to men' is usually associated with Hobbes's political philosophy – which simply incorporates the subordination of women to their sovereign husbands, more or less analogically to the subjection of the people to the sovereign, of slaves to their masters, and animals to human beings. Hobbes, like others before him, has, however, simply borrowed this saying and turned it to his own ends – terrorising his reader with the thought of the violent chaos that would be the alternative to strong monarchs, husbands or masters. The earliest example that Derrida finds of this Roman commonplace is in *Asinaria*, a comedy 'of Asses' by Plautus, and Plautus is indeed often cited as the origin of the political-philosophical use of the phrase, although, in fact, in his play the phrase drifts from marketplace trickery into the domestic and the commoditisation of sex. Plautus was born in Sarsina, in the north of Umbria which was then a colony of Rome; he leared Latin and came to the capital at a young age.[17] He was then something of an outsider, a colonised subject, albeit in a cosmopolitan city famous for its origin with the adopted son of a wolf. In *Asinaria*, the stranger in the city is *said* to be the wolf – not actually a barbarian, not an absolute other, but your fellow human being who is unknown (for as long as he or she is unknown) to you and may try to cheat you in the market. However, in the *action* of the play it is not even a stranger, but your nearest and dearest who are most financially and sexually dangerous, and potentially violent. Mothers in particular are portrayed negatively as greedy, controlling women, but the men in question, husbands and sons, are also deceitful, lascivious and weak. There is a degree of bathos in this farce, relative to the Romans as noble wolves or even fierce and savage wolves on the battlefield, as Hobbes will show them – the battleground here is the *oikonomia* and a ludic power struggle between the sexes and the generations. Men are all cowardly creatures of appetite (wolves in that sense), and the home or the family is one of the hostile environments in which they prey on each other. The action moves between the home, the marketplace and the brothel – the brothel in a sense combining the other two.

The key sentence is placed in the mouth of a merchant (known only as *Mercator*): 'when one does not know him, man is not a man, but a wolf for man' (*lupus est homo homini, non homo, quom qualis sit non novit*, Act 2, scene 4, line 496).[18] Derrida points out that it is a scene of lending or giving credit, which is true in the sense of a merchant entrusting money to someone he does not know: 'me numquam hodie induces, ut tibi credam hoc argentum ignoto' (but notwithstanding, never will you induce me today to trust this money to you, a stranger).[19] We should note, however, that the merchant is not loaning money but simply making payment for some asses he has bought from Demaenetus, an old gentleman of Athens – he wants the latter to be present rather than simply handing over the cash to his steward who is a stranger to him. He is right not to trust the 'steward' since in fact it is Leonida, one of Demaenetus's slaves, who is masquerading as the steward. However, the presence of Demaenetus, treated by the merchant as a guarantee that all is well, in fact simply confirms the trick since Demaenetus wishes to get his hands on the money rather than let the steward hand it over to his wife who controls the purse strings – so he encourages and underwrites his slave's deception. The money is to go to his son to pay for a year's worth of favours from his beloved, Philaenium – who would give them to him for free but is forced into prostitution by her mother. Philaenium then treats the slaves Leonida and Libanus seductively in order to persuade them to give the money to her lover, and finally agrees to bestow her favours on Demaenetus for a night to show gratitude for the cash. I would point out that in the ancient Roman world brothels were called *lupanars*, literally dens of she-wolves. *Lupa* (she-wolf) was also a slang term for prostitute. In such ways men project predatory and voracious behaviour on to women who are visibly or audibly sexually active outside the marital law. Thus no one comes well out of the story – while the proverb specifies 'a stranger', most of Plautus's characters are above all 'wolves' to their spouses or children. We fear strangers but are most at risk from our nearest and dearest.

Enlightenment werewolves

In another, and very different, example of his series of cultural references, Derrida draws our attention to the fact that, at one point in his *Confessions*, Rousseau worries that he is becoming a werewolf because he reads so much. His confession that he was living as a *loup-garou* because of his passion for reading, is rendered living like 'an outlaw' in J.M. Cohen's English translation of the *Confessions*, outside society and thus outside the law as Derrida (delighted) indicates.[20] I would add that the *Petit Robert* dictionary quotes Rousseau to illustrate the old use of *loup-garou* (werewolf) to mean *sauvage, farouche, solitaire* (savage, wild, solitary). There is a link between the wolf (which is not companionably domesticated as the dog is) and solitude. Rousseau is writing about reading, but not speaking; the legendary werewolf, unlike a vampire, cannot talk when he is transformed – he is a lonely howling beast. Tsvetaeva will give the same wild and solitary character to Pushkin's Pugachev, as Cixous tells us: 'There remains the infinite solitude of the wolf, invisible and unrecognised except by himself' ('Il reste la solitude infinie du loup, non reconnu, invisible, sinon par lui-même').[21] On a visible level, throughout most of Pushkin's novel, *The Captain's Daughter*, Pugachev is surrounded by fellow rebels – his solitude is thus that which is as unrecognised as it is inevitable for the sovereign, outlaw, lover or wolf. While observers inform us that wolves are pack animals, and that any solitary wolf is usually a young male about to pair bond and then acquire a family which develops into a pack, it is often the exceptional lone wolf which captures the literary and mythic imagination.[22] Rousseau moves between private space (the choice to read voraciously) and political persecution as an example of lupine solitude. He tells his reader that he is perceived, and cruelly persecuted, as a wolf or lycanthrope, ferocious or mad, after the publication and condemnation of *Emile*.[23] Perhaps he can therefore empathise with the *sauvage* or the beast.[24]

Bestial cruelty and criminality, Derrida points out, is generally held to be the preserve of human rather than beast; he turns from Rousseau to Lacan, and the latter's classical assertion that what separates Man from the Beast is the Law.[25] Derrida tracks this human bestiality alongside human *bêtise* (stupidity) in Deleuze and Guattari, and alongside fraternity in Lacan:

> There remains the immense risk of what is still a fraternalism of the 'fellow'. This risk is double [...]: *on the one hand*, this fraternalism frees us from all ethical obligation, all duty not to be criminal and cruel, precisely, with respect to any living being that is not my fellow or is not recognised as my fellow, because it is other and other than man. In this logic, one is never cruel toward what is called an animal, or a nonhuman living creature. One is already exculpated of any crime towards any nonhuman living creature. And specifying, *on the other hand*, as Lacan does: 'It is a fellow that it [this cruelty] is targeting, even in a being of another species', does not change or fix anything. It is always my fellow that I am targeting in a being of another species. So the fact remains that I cannot be suspected of cruelty with respect to an animal that I cause to suffer the worse violence.[26]

Taking up Derrida's point about the alibi provided with respect to cruelty towards non-human living creatures (and thus lesser human beings too, in the end) by this 'uniquely human' quality of violence, I should note that Pushkin is well aware of the recorded atrocities committed by the historical figure Pugachev and his bands of Cossack and peasant fighters when he constructs his own Pugachev. Tsvetaeva comments on his ferocity, and the subsequent seductive appeal when Pushkin imagines his generosity to one young man, spared from the usual slaughter. Equally Tsvetaeva's lad ('le gars') will kill Maroussia's mother and brother to slake his appetite, and the girl is aware of the price to pay for their love. However, neither this bestiality nor their willingness to spare a beloved victim makes these figures peculiarly human or purely animal in Cixous's reading – rather it is the beast–human borderline which is made more complicated by her *rapprochements*.

The wolf is one of the most common creatures into which we imagine men metamorphosing in myths and legends. Ovid places Lycaon, transformed into a wolf by Jove, to whom he had offered a meal of human flesh, in the first book of *Metamorphoses*. We also have *Little Red Riding Hood* – the wolf masquerading as a grandmother – and our proverbs and fairy tales imagine the wolf as a master of disguise, even reinventing himself in sheep's clothing. The outlaw Pugachev is similarly elusive, sometimes taking on the role of a rightful sovereign Tsar Peter III. The Enlightenment *loup-garou* is both the real wolf that eats men *and* the man who turns into a wolf (thus opposites and similar), who is compelled to feast on human flesh, or imagines that that is the case.[27] The *Encyclopédie* article *loup-garou* is written by D.J., the chevalier de Jaucourt, an Enlightenment figure who writes against slavery and in sympathy with native American *sauvages*. He strongly rejects the idea of werewolves along with a poetic list of other fabulous and untranslatable monsters that used to haunt and terrorise the unenlightened:

> We should be eternally grateful to these enlightened centuries, even if the only blessings that they bestowed on us were to cure us of the existence of *werewolves*, spirits, lamias, monsters [*larves*], Liliths, shades [*lémures*], spectres, genies, demons, fairies, ghosts, imps, and other nocturnal phantoms so suited to troubling our souls, disturbing us, overwhelming us with fear and trembling.[28]

What is it we should really be afraid of? Other men? As Lacan interprets *homo homini lupus* in his *Ecrits*: 'cruelty implies humanity'.[29] In the *Encyclopédie* articles *lycanthrope* and *lycanthropie*, there is mention of the devil disguising men as wolves (not a real transformation), and then longer analysis of the sickness whereby men imagine they turn into wolves, and therefore adopt wolfish behaviour – and sometimes thereby convince others – as in the *Dictionnaire de l'Académie*.

The week before Derrida draws his seminar audience's attention to the passages in Rousseau's *Confessions* regarding the persecution (as if

Rousseau were a werewolf) following the condemnation of his *Emile*, he had highlighted a different passage in the *Confessions*.[30] In this case Rousseau was, as in the example of his appetite for reading, again in the private or domestic realm: he discusses his notorious shyness, particularly with respect to well-born or well-educated women, in relation to an episode in the late 1730s when he was about 25 years old. He tells his reader that he had to introduce himself to some brilliant ladies, who happened to be his travelling companions on the way to Montpellier, or he would have been taken for a *loup-garou* (translated into English as 'an absolute boor').[31] Here Derrida emphasises once again the relationship of the wolf to the law: Rousseau does not want to be unsociable and 'outside-the-law'.[32] I might note in addition the link, if only by negation, between the wolf and an erotic encounter – Rousseau begins by joining the ladies for meals, then gains some confidence in conversation, and finally begins an illicit amorous relationship with Madame de Larnage. His frankness about the fact that she is less beautiful as well as older than her newly wed friend may seem discourteous; however, Rousseau presents himself equally 'warts and all', and is clear about his strong emotional bond with this generous, sensitive and warm individual. What in Plautus could be cruelly comic is here translated into sensibility. Rousseau's youthful timidity is unexpectedly his greatest weapon in inspiring this more experienced woman to make the necessary advances while he, like a wild animal, is always about to make his escape from the snare. In Rousseau's famous discourse on inequality, he argues against Hobbes that wolves, and men in the state of nature, are fearful rather than aggressive. Like the young Rousseau in this episode in the *Confessions* they are always about to flee, rather than always about to pounce with slavering jaws. This is rather a different image of the wolf from the one Cixous and Tsvetaeva are celebrating, where the delicious thrill for the beloved/victim, like the child listening to a fairy tale, is supposed to be related to fear for their safety faced with a wolf rather than anxiety that the wolf will run away from them.

Rousseau's uncertainty about his position in legitimate society even leads him to disguise himself as a foreigner, an Englishman (Mr Dudding), in spite of the fact that he does not speak a word of English nor know anything about England, and thus he is uneasily at risk of being unmasked as an imposter.[33] His entrance into the field of romance means that he is no longer in danger of being labelled a *loup-garou*, and yet it is his very lone wolf or outlaw qualities that make him dangerously attractive to the woman who seems able to persuade him to make an exception for her. While she may not be quite a lamb, a woman's reputation is always vulnerable to a penetrating gaze such as that of the Marquis who accompanies the party. The period is one in which amorous liaisons of all kinds are common, yet social death is always a risk for women who transgress the law, as many fictional heroines discover. In fact the Marquis, whose merciless social wit would seem to make him a wolf to his fellow men, certainly in the shy and solitary Rousseau's eyes, is a sheep in wolf's clothing, who uses his sarcastic assaults on the young man's weaknesses as a suitor to disguise the fact that he has discovered their secret love affair.

Cixous, Tsvetaeva and Pushkin

While Rousseau's figural and real wolves in his *Discourse on Inequality*, and Rousseau himself as werewolf in his *Confessions*, are above all timid rather than aggressive and voracious, most modern rewritings of the figure of the wolf rejoice in the access it offers to exploring the pleasure and pain of eating and being eaten. The combination of wolf, carnivorous appetite and red-blooded sexual desire has more often been placed in the masculine – the wolfish sexual predator prowling for prey is typically represented as male, even in Plato with an older man pursuing a younger (the heteronormative being queered from the outset). Plato is the source for a rare staging in *The Beast and the Sovereign* of an erotic scene, a voracious *sexual* appetite. Socrates tells Phaedrus that the lover 'has an appetite and wants to feed upon you' then gives the verse 'as wolves love lambs so lovers love their loves'.[34] Derrida segues from one of his references to *Phaedrus* to a mention of Cixous's short essay 'The Love of the Wolf', which is cited as 'a text that ought to be quoted and studied *in extenso* for an infinite amount of time' – implying a hyperbolic appetite for analysis, although in fact Derrida devotes to it only one page out of the 460–odd pages of *The Beast and the Sovereign* before returning to La Fontaine.[35] Cixous's *Stigmata*, which includes 'Love of the Wolf', has a foreword by Derrida in the 2005 edition which speaks of the importance of drawing attention to stigmata, to the wound at the origin of writing, and affirms yet again his admiration for Cixous, both the person and the work: 'immense, powerful, so multiple but unique in this century'; today, in his eyes, 'the greatest writer in the French language'.[36] This book, he says, is 'a weave of poetic narratives, this unprecedented book overflows *our* language, the "French language", in every way while nonetheless cultivating and illustrating it in a rare and incomparably new fashion. A practically untranslatable fashion.'[37]

Derrida points out the wide range of intertexts in Cixous's piece (just as he himself has a range of interlocutors in *The Beast and the Sovereign*), and she does indeed make fleeting references to a variety of authors from Aeschylus to Kleist to show, for example, with a quotation from *Agammemnon*, how the adopted *sauvage* may start as a kitten but grow to be a lion. However, she herself sets it up more intimately in her 2003 version with her first words laid out like a dedication and enclosed in the arms of a parenthesis in French: '(*Ce texte qui suit les traces de Marina Tsvetaïeva est* un bon-d pour un loup secret.)'.[38] In the 1994 article, and thus in the English translation, the epigraph is simply '*This is a bo(u)nd for a wolf*', and only at the close of an added paragraph do we find: 'Following in Tsvetaeva's footsteps, this reading *is a bo(u)nd for a secret wolf*', reversing the use of italics.[39] In either case, the text is specifically following the tracks or traces of the Russian poet and playwright Tsvetaeva (1892–1941). I prefer animal tracks or non-specific traces to Cohen's choice of 'footsteps', which binds us to the human. It is also a *bon-d* for a secret wolf, which is a mysterious formulation; *un bon* is a good thing or man, or a bond or token, something which is good to be exchanged (appropriate for a work of language). The dash ties the good to a 'd' (Derrida's own initial) making it a *bond*, a leap or a bound, certainly appropriate for a wolf.

Cixous focuses largely on masculine predators in 'The Love of the Wolf': the wolf is 'le gars' (Tsvetaeva's 'lad'), Pugachev, Heathcliff or Othello. However, her 'analysis', perhaps better termed a poetic weave, as Derrida does, unsettles any comfortable reading of sexual difference as sexual opposition or heteronormativity:

> Tsvetaeva inscribes the genealogy of her own imaginary in a whole lineage of Pushkin's love mysteries. These always involve duels, dual relations that are so intense, so red-hot, so white-hot, that in the glare you forget even the dimension of sexual difference.[40]

> C'est dans toute une lignée de mystères amoureux de Pouchkine que Tsvetaïeva inscrit la généalogie de son propre imaginaire. Il s'agit toujours de duels, de relations duelles, si intenses, portées au rouge, au blanc, qu'on oublie même, dans l'éblouissement, la dimension de la différence sexuelle.[41]

For Cixous's Tsvetaeva, lambs can be boys (Grinev) as well as girls (Maroussia), and lambs can eat up wolves as well as be eaten by them. Duels here suggest lethal amorous couplings, but there is also a reference to history; Pushkin was killed in a duel with a French officer, d'Anthès. Tsvetaeva describes the impact on her of a painting that depicts this final duel (of many), which hangs in her mother's room in 'My Pushkin'.[42] In *The Captain's Daughter*, Pushkin depicts a duel between Grinev and

Shvabrin, who mocks Grinev's poetry and his love for Maria Ivanovna whom Shvabrin wants to seduce himself; and, in a figural sense, there are many more 'duels' in the texts.

In *The Beast and the Sovereign*, Derrida points to the undecidability between the subjective and the objective genitive in Cixous's paradoxically ambiguous title – the hovering between the love of the wolf for the lamb (whom he can eat up) and the lamb's love of the wolf (who loves the lamb). Unlike the version in *Stigmata*, I have chosen to retain the definite article in Cixous's title ('the' love of the wolf), in spite of the awkwardness in English, in order to keep the play between the two genitives. Sometimes English uses the present participle for this kind of ambiguity, 'loving Helen', but it does not work for a common noun such as wolf except in the plural (so we could have had 'loving wolves'), which would take away Cixous's amorous specificity (love of one particular wolf). These ambiguous genitives unsettle properties and the proper (of sexual difference) with their focus on the gift and love:

> What attaches the wolf to the lamb, she [Tsvetaeva] reckons, is the fact that he hasn't eaten him.[43] Painful mystery of the gift that returns through reflection: what the wolf loves in the lamb is his own goodness. It is thanks to the lamb that the wolf accedes to the plane of love – the love that gives itself without hope, without calculation, without response, *but* that nevertheless gives *itself*, seeing itself give itself.[44] The wolf given to a lamb of the Grinev type who doesn't even notice the enormity of the gift – that's really love.[45]

> Ce qui attache le loup à l'agneau, devine-t-elle, c'est qu'il ne l'a pas mangé. Mystère douloureux du don qui fait retour par réflexion: ce que le loup aime dans l'agneau, c'est sa propre bonté. C'est grâce à l'agneau que le loup atteint le plan de l'amour – celui qui se donne sans espoir, sans calcul, sans réponse, *mais*, quand même *se* donne, se voyant se donner. Le loup donné à un agneau genre Griniov qui ne remarque même pas l'énormité du don, ça c'est vraiment de l'amour.[46]

Derrida is particularly struck by the element of sacrifice in Cixous's account of the wolf's love for the lamb,[47] the Christ-like renunciation by the loving wolf:

> This wolf that sacrifices its very definition, its identity as a wolf, for the lamb, this wolf that doesn't eat the lamb, is it a wolf? Is it still a wolf? Isn't it a delupinised wolf, a non-wolf, an invalidated wolf? If it were a false wolf there'd be no interest. No, we've made no mistake, this wolf is a real wolf: right up to the last minute it might eat us, the axe doesn't falter, right up to the last minute.[48]

> Ce loup qui pour l'agneau sacrifie sa propre définition, son identité de loup, ce loup qui ne mange pas l'agneau, est-il un loup? Est-il encore un loup?

N'est-il pas un loup délupisé, un non-loup, un annulé? Si c'était un faux loup aucun intérêt. Non, ne nous trompons pas, ce loup est un vrai loup: jusqu'à la dernière seconde il pourrait nous manger, la hache siffle sans arrêt, jusqu'à la dernière seconde.[49]

The carnivore that ultimately sacrifices 'its' appetite may seem to draw Cixous closer to Renée Vivien's rewriting of the she-wolf in 'La Dame à la louve'. Yet there remain important differences. Derrida is struck by Cixous's play between force (kept as 'force' in Bennington's translation, which allows the necessary echo through the range of contexts, but which could sometimes be translated by 'power') and fear.

For Tsvetaeva the lupine relates to the blackness to which she is devoted in all its various forms. She remembers childhood walks, which ended at a famous statue of her beloved Pushkin:

> I loved the Pushkin Monument for its blackness – the reverse of the whiteness of our household gods.[50] Their eyes were totally white but the Pushkin Monument's were totally black, totally full. The Pushkin Monument was totally black, like a dog, still blacker than a dog because the very blackest of them always had something yellow above the eyes or something white under the neck. The Pushkin Monument was black like the piano. If they hadn't told me later that Pushkin was a Negro, I would have known, that Pushkin was a Negro.
> From the Pushkin Monument I also got my mad love for black people, carried through a whole lifetime.[51]

Tsvetaeva, writing in unhappy exile as a 'White' Russian, is pushing against the grain in her passion for blackness both symbolically and politically. Cixous notes that Tsvetaeva is transfixed by the 'blackness' of Pushkin (and Pugachev), which operates on a range of semantic levels, including ethical and political points, shades in a painting, the Black Sea or a reference to Othello's love for Desdemona. I could add the concrete detail that Pushkin's great-grandfather, Ibrahim Petrovich Hannibal (1696–1781), was Ethiopian, brought to Russia from Turkey in 1704 as a gift for the Tsar, who adopted him. Pushkin expresses pride in this remarkable African heritage and wrote an unfinished novel about his great-grandfather, whose early existence as a slave did not prevent him reaching the heights of military and diplomatic power.[52] This also fascinates Tsvetaeva who identifies strongly with anti-racist struggles,[53] although this particular political message is not explicit in the allusive and elusive Cixous text which operates more on the level of the poetic psyche.

Derrida has written extensively about fraternity, above all in *Politics of Friendship*. The social or political community of *semblables* excludes the animal and the woman – although women serve a purpose of mediating between men (perhaps preventing tedium) and enabling men to reproduce themselves; thus excluding women is an autoimmune reaction. In Tsvetaeva's *Le Gars* there is a section entitled 'Les Compères' which shows the voracity and violence of guests apparently come to celebrate the birth of Maroussia's son by the baron she has married in the absence of her beloved 'lad'. The lad warned her that she must spend five years without entertaining, but her weak husband has bowed to peer pressure and allowed his *semblables* to come into their home. They urge: 'Empty it and smash it up' ('Vidons-la, puis brisons-la') – 'la' (it) is of course a glass (*la coupe*), but the French gender system allows the ambiguity of imagining it is Maroussia who is to be emptied out and broken.[54] The *compères* are human wolves (*homo lupus homini*) with 'Brigands' teeth' – not the wolfish wolf who dazzles in the lad willing to sacrifice himself for his beloved. Theirs is the fraternity that Derrida finds in psychoanalytic accounts of the founding of society:

> When Lacan talks of this 'eternal fraternity', we must not hear in it merely the sort of edifying, irenic, pacifistic, and democratic praise which often denotes and connotes so many appeals to fraternity. [. . .] [Lacan] does not forget the murderous violence that will have presided over the establishment of the law, namely the murder of the father, thanks to which (thanks to the murder, thanks to the father, thanks to the murder of the father) the guilty and shameful sons come to contract, through a sort of at least tacit oath or sworn faith, the equality of the brothers. The trace of this founding criminality or this primitive crime, the memory of which is kept by the (animal) totem and the taboo – this murderous trace remains ineffaceable in any egalitarian, communitarian, and compassionate fraternity, in this primitive contract that makes of any compassionate community a *confraternity*.[55]

In other words this emphasis on the brother or the *semblable* neither addresses the question of the non-human nor the problem of 'all those who do not recognise their fellow in certain humans', the worst prejudices of race, class or sex (I would add), or even prejudice against one particular individual.[56] The baron's fellows can attack Maroussia and her child because she is a woman, and furthermore she is contaminated by her association with this being who is not a *semblable*: he is potentially the child of the vampire-werewolf. Likewise Rousseau is designated a (were)wolf before he is persecuted, and Vivien's lady can be left to die because of her she-wolf associate and association as well as her sex.

The appetites of the compeers are base ones:

'As long as into
My stomach goes
And flows out
Wine –
   who cares!'
('Pourvu qu'entre
Dans mon ventre
Et qu'en sorte
Vin –
   qu'importe !')⁵⁷

Finally they sum up with fraternity: 'Compères, fraternisons!', literally 'Compeers, let us fraternise' or 'Fellows, let us join in company'.⁵⁸

The dualism in Tsvetaeva, setting the poet against the world, which Cixous celebrates, could be argued to effect at least a partial and temporary displacement, perhaps like the sexual dualism in Vivien's fiction. It is not the kind of reversal that leaves hierarchies comfortably in place such as the Orwellian 'four legs good, two legs bad', because the poet dies – as the heroine so often dies whether in male- or female-authored fiction. In 'My Pushkin', for example, Tsvetaeva identifies lupine blackness (here, in Europe in 1937, given a racial materiality), death and poetry: 'The Russian poet – is a Negro, the poet – is a Negro and the poet – was struck down. / (Oh, God, how it all came together! What poet among those that were and those that are, *isn't* a Negro and what poet – hasn't been struck down and killed?)'.⁵⁹ The real social, economic and political forces which align with the cultural hegemony of *semblables* (and not only in a context when totalitarian regimes are particularly ascendant) make the gesture of reversal more resonant in its very impotence. Even Pugachev, whose Cossack peasant revolt is very successful for a time, seems doomed in hindsight to the failure which comes in due course. The marginality and vulnerability of the speaker is the context to, and pretext for, the text – suspending the efficacy of its judgement.

The outlaw, poet, rebel, wolf, lover stand outside, or on the margins of, society which holds together by fear as Hobbes shows us – we are made afraid to break the law, including the laws relating to gender ('*la ... le*').⁶⁰ Hobbes claims that outside society man is a wolf to men, but, even without tracking his source in Plautus, we could note with Rousseau that Hobbes shows that competitive social man is a wolf to men and women too – or instead. Yet the horror of the voracious wild is used to keep us within the law, and among those most like ourselves. Thus the romance of the lone wolf or the rogue individual, which remains a delight and a creative inspiration to the Cixousian or

Tsvetaevan reader, may yet help guard against the terror that lurks even in fraternal democracy.

Notes

1. 'L'Amour du loup' was originally published in a theatre review (*La Métaphore*) in 1994, then republished in a more concise form in Hélène Cixous, *L'Amour du loup et autres remords* (Paris: Galilée, 2003), pp. 17–40. 'Love of the Wolf', trans. Keith Cohen, in *Stigmata: Escaping Texts* (London and New York: Routledge, 1998), pp. 84–99 is a translation of the original expanded version. While I have consulted this translation, and reference it, I have preferred to retranslate the French myself – in some cases I indicate what might be at stake in the difficult translation decisions. Here 'Love of the Wolf', pp. 88–90; *L'Amour du loup*, pp. 24–5.
2. Jacques Derrida, *The Beast and the Sovereign*, Vol. I, trans. Geoffrey Bennington (Chicago: University of Chicago Press, 2009). *Séminaire La Bête et le souverain I (2001–2002)*, ed. Michel Lisse, Marie-Louise Mallet and Ginette Michaud (Paris: Galilée, 2008).
3. Derrida, *Beast*, I, p. 96.
4. Ibid., pp. 66–7.
5. 'Freud sees in the wolf, without hesitation, [...] a substitute for the castrating father, the more so in that the father often said in jest to the Wolf Man as a child, "I'm going to eat you." Later in the analysis, the mother becomes just as much a wolf, if not a she-wolf, as the father' (Derrida, *Beast*, I, p. 65).
6. Later '*La bête et le souverain. La ... le*' (e.g. pp. 97, 100) is rendered 'The [feminine] beast and the [masculine] sovereign. *La ... le*' (pp. 63, 65). There is no particularly elegant means in English of conveying what Derrida is doing.
7. See Nancy K. Miller, 'The French Mistake', in *Getting Personal: Feminist Occasions and Other Autobiographical Acts* (London: Routledge, 1991), pp. 48–55. His Majesty the ego, the internal external examiner checking for accuracy, upholds the law of gender and watches the Anglophone French academic, perhaps particularly women who hesitate sometimes to speak in public in any case, feeling that they are transgressing simply by opening their mouths, as Cixous relates in 'The Laugh of the Medusa', trans. Keith Cohen and Paula Cohen, in Elaine Marks and Isabelle de Courtivron, eds, *New French Feminisms* (Brighton: Harvester Press, 1985), pp. 245–64 (p. 251).
8. See Lynn Turner, 'When Species Kiss: Some Recent Correspondence between *animots*', *Humanimalia*, 2.1, 2010, pp. 60–85, and Kelly Oliver, *Animal Lessons: How They Teach Us to Be Human* (New York: Columbia University Press, 2009), for examples of reading Derrida on animal difference *and* sexual difference. Oliver makes some pertinent criticisms, saying 'philosophies of otherness from Freud through Kristeva repeat romantic gestures that exclude and abject animals [...] concepts of subjectivity, humanity, politics, and ethics continue to be defined by the double movement of assimilating and then disavowing the animal, animality, and

animals' (4); but it is not clear to me when Derrida would be guilty of falling into the traps that she elegantly outlines.
9. The absolute monarch, never mind the oriental despot who so often represents the European sovereign in the Enlightenment, is not a homogeneous or monolithic figure of virility – if we assume too much coherence in patriarchy we are likely to be over-optimistic about the power of gender-bending to subvert masculine authority.
10. Angela Carter, 'The Company of Wolves', in *The Bloody Chamber* (Harmondsworth: Penguin, 1988 [1979]), pp. 110–18 (p. 117).
11. Derrida, *Beast*, I, p. 6.
12. Chapter 3 of my forthcoming book *Derrida and Other Animals: The Boundaries of the Human* (Edinburgh University Press) analyses women's writing from early in the twentieth century, as well as contemporary feminist writing, raising the question of the wolf–woman conjuncture from a gynocentric perspective, and/or by complicating sexual difference along with other differences. The main examples, apart from Cixous and Tsvetaeva, are Renée Vivien, Angela Carter and Carol Ann Duffy. In terms of biography as well as writing these writers are interesting for their oppositional sexuality, and their complicated relationship to maternity and to appetite. For Vivien, see my 'Renée Vivien's "La Dame à la louve" and the Freedom to Choose', in Margaret Atack, Diana Holmes, Diana Knight and Judith Still, eds, *Women, Genre and Circumstance: Essays in Memory of Elizabeth Fallaize* (Oxford: Legenda, 2012), pp. 96–108.
13. *Le Gars* (Paris: Des Femmes, 1992, preface by Efim Etkind). After reading *The Vampire* by A.N. Afanasyev in his collection of popular tales, Tsvetaeva wrote a long Russian poem in 1922 on this theme; it took three months, then a further eight months to transpose it into a French poem – which is this book. While a vampire traditionally sucks blood, the 'gars' devours his prey like a wolf. 'My Pushkin' and 'Pushkin and Pugachev' are both translated in J. Marin King, ed. and trans., *Marina Tsvetaeva, A Captive Spirit: Selected Prose* (London: Virago, 1983), pp. 319–62, 372–403.
14. Pushkin's desire for revolt, for rebellion against Tsar Nicholas, thrusts him towards the lupine outlaw Pugachev whose 'mighty spell' he falls under; in the character of Grinev he will forgive Pugachev any atrocity, argues Tsvetaeva. See 'Pushkin and Pugachev', pp. 384–5. I leave aside the complex question of the relation between Tsvetaeva and the Russian revolution.
15. Cixous, 'The Laugh of the Medusa', p. 245.
16. Elisa Brune, *La Tournante* (Paris: Editions Ramsay, 2001), p. 135, my translation. Thanks to Dylan Sebastian Evans for drawing this text to my attention.
17. Derrida, *Beast*, I, p. 61.
18. Titus Maccius Plautus, *Amphytryo, Asinaria, Aulularia, Bacchides, Captivi*, trans. Paul Nixon (Cambridge, MA, and London: Harvard University Press and Heinemann, 1916). There is an issue of 'who' or 'what' in translation; it seems obvious to translate the phrase as 'when one does not know him, man is not a man, but a wolf for man' – but Derrida points out that it is grammatically possible to say 'wolf [the wolf] is a man for man, which is

not a man, when one does not know him'. Is the wolf 'who' or 'what'? (*Beast*, I, pp. 61–2).
19. Derrida, *Beast*, I, p. 61.
20. Ibid., p. 64. Jean-Jacques Rousseau, *The Confessions*, trans. J.M. Cohen (Harmondsworth: Penguin, 1953), p. 47.
21. Cixous, 'Love of the Wolf', p. 98; *L'Amour du loup*, p. 39.
22. See Garry Marvin, *Wolf* (London: Reaktion Books, 2012), pp. 19–24. Gilles Deleuze and Félix Guattari do focus on the pack or band rather than the lone wolf or werewolf, but do not follow natural history in seeing this as an extended family – they prefer to imagine the pack growing by infection: 'Propagation by epidemic, by contagion, has nothing to do with filiation by heredity, even if the two themes intermingle and require each other' ('1730 – Becoming-Intense, Becoming-Animal, Becoming-Imperceptible...', in *A Thousand Plateaus*, trans. Brian Massumi [Minneapolis: University of Minnesota Press, 1987], p. 241).
23. Jean-Jacques Rousseau, *Confessions*, in *Oeuvres complètes*, ed. Bernard Gagnebin and Marcel Raymond, 5 vols (Paris: Gallimard, 1959–95), I, p. 591.
24. Derrida, *Beast*, I, pp. 100–1.
25. Ibid., pp. 102–34.
26. Ibid., pp. 107–8.
27. See 'Lycanthropy', in *Dictionnaire de l'Académie* (1762) to which Derrida refers (*Beast*, I, p. 100).
28. *Encyclopédie, ou Dictionnaire raisonné des sciences, des arts et des métiers, par une société de gens de lettres*, ed. Denis Diderot and Jean D'Alembert, 35 vols (Paris and Neufchâtel: Briasson, 1751–80), my translation. 'Lamies' are fabulous monsters who were reputed to devour children; 'larves' and lémures' are spirits of the dead who pursue the living. See Marina Warner, *No Go the Bogeyman: Scaring, Lulling and Making Mock* (New York: Farrar, Straus and Giroux, 1998), for an account of various bogeymen and their female equivalents such as Lamia (pp. 28, 82).
29. Jacques Lacan, *Ecrits: The First Complete Edition in English*, trans. Bruce Fink (New York: Norton, 2002), p. 120. Quoted in Derrida, *Beast*, I, p. 97.
30. Rousseau, *Oeuvres complètes*, I, pp. 248–9.
31. Rousseau, *Confessions*, p. 236.
32. Derrida, *Beast*, I, p. 96. He does not refer back to *Of Grammatology*, but we might be irresistibly reminded of his writing on Rousseau and the supplement, including the particular solitary supplement of masturbation. See *Of Grammatology*, trans. Gayatri Chakravorty Spivak (Baltimore: Johns Hopkins University Press, 1974).
33. See Geoffrey Bennington, *Dudding: Des Noms de Rousseau* (Paris: Galilée, 1991).
34. Plato, *Phaedrus*, in *The Dialogues of Plato*, trans. Benjamin Jowett (London: Sphere, 1970), II, p. 257.
35. Derrida, *Beast*, I, p. 210.
36. Jacques Derrida, 'Foreword', trans. Eric Prenowitz, in Hélène Cixous, *Stigmata* (London and New York: Routledge, 2005), p. ix.
37. Ibid.
38. Cixous, *L'Amour du loup*, p. 17.

39. Cixous, 'Love of the Wolf', p. 84.
40. Ibid., p. 91.
41. *L'Amour du loup*, p. 27.
42. Tsvetaeva, 'My Pushkin', pp. 319–20.
43. Cohen's translation uses 'it hasn't eaten it' for 'il ne l'a pas mangé' – where the wolf has not eaten the lamb. This allows the ambiguity that the lamb might be female (Maroussia) or male (Grinev) – the lack of a final 'e' on 'mangé' means that the lamb is not simply feminine (the word is masculine). I have settled for the masculine *person* as Grinev is the dominant example in the paragraph. To refer to these figures of animals with the neuter 'it' is a decision that the animal is not a person, which is a decision that the French does not have to make.
44. It is a complex decision how to translate Cixous's reflexives: 'se donne' translated on each occasion by Cohen as 'gives of itself'.
45. Cixous, 'Love of the Wolf', p. 98.
46. Cixous, *L'Amour du loup*, p. 39.
47. Derrida, *Beast*, I, p. 210.
48. Cixous, 'Love of the Wolf', pp. 93–4.
49. Cixous, *L'Amour du loup*, p. 32.
50. The translator, Marin King, suggests that this may refer to a bust of Zeus in her father's study.
51. Tsvetaeva, 'My Pushkin', p. 324.
52. *The Blackamoor of Peter the Great* (1827–28); see *The Collected Stories*, trans. P. Debreczeny (London: Everyman, 1999), pp. 3–40.
53. See Tsvetaeva, 'My Pushkin', pp. 324–6.
54. Tsvetaeva, *Le Gars*, p. 94.
55. Derrida, *Beast*, I, p. 107.
56. Ibid., p. 108.
57. Tsvetaeva, *Le Gars*, pp. 94–5.
58. Ibid., p. 95
59. Tsvetaeva, 'My Pushkin', p. 320.
60. Derrida, *Beast*, I, pp. 39–43.

Chapter 9

Deconstructing Sexual Difference: A Myopic Reading of Hélène Cixous's Mole

Marta Segarra

The mole occupies quite a prominent position among 'animals in deconstruction'. Although its presence is not as important as that of the cat, the silkworm or its former kin in the now abandoned order *Insectivora*, the hedgehog, the mole's polyvalent role (which has unstaged those of other animals) has been pointed out by Nicholas Royle in his inspiring essay entitled 'Mole'.[1] Moles emerge on the surface of texts by Freud, Kafka, Jacques Derrida and Hélène Cixous, authors whom we may consider as belonging to the so-called 'demenagerie' of deconstruction.[2] Royle's 'Mole' begins with a quotation from Derrida citing Freud's expression 'with a mole-like progression', and recalls *Hamlet* and two of Kafka's short stories which feature a mole, 'The Burrow' and 'The Village Schoolmaster', also known as 'The Giant Mole'.[3] This essay takes all these moles into consideration, including Royle's, and adds to this labour a new sow – which also may be a boar – the Mole (*La taupe*), a character in Hélène Cixous's *The Blindfolded Fiancée or Amelait*. This play was written in 2004 but was staged for the first time in 2011, and has never been published in French.[4] Cixous is familiar with Kafka's, Freud's and Derrida's oeuvre, and her own mole is heir to those created by these fellow writers, as well as to that of Shakespeare in *Hamlet*. In fact, Cixous's text could be considered a playful rewriting of *Hamlet*'s story: Amelait, its leading role, directly refers to Amleth, the legendary hero of the *Historiae Danicae* by Saxo Grammaticus, compiled at the end of the twelfth century – which is known as the oldest ancestor of Shakespeare's *Hamlet* – as well as being a version of this name when pronounced in French. Amelait is, moreover, a signifier prone to puns such as *âme-lait* (or milky soul, as Judith G. Miller translates it), *âme-laid* (ugly soul), or 'a melee'.[5] The first and the third of these possibilities, among others, concern sexual difference; my own analysis of Cixous's mole will focus on this issue, which, as it will be argued, is inherent in the figure of the mole as such.

If we first examine the word 'mole' (although the text is written in French, Cixous is certainly well aware of the multiple contents of the English 'mole'), it is notable that its primary meanings work in two different, even opposite senses: 'mole', as a spot on the skin, concerns the surface of the body; it is also related to the interior or the subterranean of the body ('an abnormal mass in the uterus, especially when containing fetal tissues', *Merriam-Webster*) as well as the interior of the earth (since animal moles live and work underground). As Royle notes, each of the appearances of a mole in *Hamlet* follows one of these two senses, even though they take a figurative scope. In the first occurrence, when Hamlet says, referring to the Danish people, 'That for some vicious mole of nature in them' (I.iv.24), 'mole' alludes to a fault or a defect in Danish character and customs. In the second, the hero says to the Spectre 'Well said, old mole', adding 'Canst work i'th'earth so fast? / A worthy pioneer!' (I.v.170–1), apparently alluding to the courage of his father. However, these two seemingly divergent directions, which correspond to different etymological Proto-Indo-European roots, rejoin in several aspects. First, 'mole' as a spot on the skin derives from the same Greek root as 'miasma', something coming from the exterior that pollutes the body's interior; the first *Hamlet*'s mole could also evoke a hidden or interior default of Danish 'soul'. It can also be added – although Cixous may not have been aware of this – that the Spanish equivalent of 'mole', as a spot, is *lunar*, which obviously derives from *luna* (moon). Here we come again to the sense of 'mole' as something monstrous (as in 'mooncalf', also evoked by Royle), related to eccentricity ('lunatic') and madness (Amelait as well as Hamlet are, or feign to be, mad). In French, this signifier is also related to vision – which is a key issue for the mole, as we shall see – as Cixous herself develops in one of her most recent books, *Le Voyage de la racine alechinsky*: 'Glasses [*lunettes*, literally 'small moons'] have an incalculable influence. A bit of moon and of its follies always mingles in the look of the person who resorts to the power of this supplement.'[6] To finish our wandering in this perhaps diverting tunnel, with a shortcut that sends us back to the beginning, I will briefly note that a variant of the Spanish *lunar*, when referring to round spots or dots on tissue, is *topo* – the Spanish term for 'mole' as an animal.

Topo sends us also back to the French *taupe*, since both come from the same Latin word, *talpa*. *Talpa* is a masculine noun, as is the Spanish *topo* or the Catalan *talp*, but has undergone a feminisation in French, 'under the influence of feminine nouns in -a' (such as 'Derrida', we might playfully add), according to the *Dictionnaire historique de la langue française*.[7] *Taupe*, as a transgender word, fits well with the transsexual or intersexual nature of the mole: in many mole species, the females have 'masculinised genitals', that is 'gonads with testicular and ovary tissue instead of normal ovaries'.[8] Moreover, this particular feature – which makes of the mole such a Cixousian animal as the *méduse* or jellyfish, which is often hermaphrodite – has been related, by scientists, to the 'extra thumb' also characteristic of the mole, that is to say, to touch.[9] The best-known feature of moles is indeed their poor eyesight (in French, *myope comme une taupe* is the equivalent of the English expression 'blind as a bat'), a handicap compensated by an excellent sense of smell and touch. Physically, these senses are represented through the nearly invisible eyes of the mole (some people even believe that it has no eyes nor ears, which are often completely covered by its fur) and its extremely big paws in relation to the size of its body and hindlimbs. Finally, and very relevant to both Cixous's and Shakespeare's plays, the mole is also associated with excessive female sexuality, since the French *taupe* also means 'prostitute' or 'slut', as does the English 'mole' through its near homophone 'moll'.

This labour – the collective term for moles – in all its variants can be found in *The Blindfolded Fiancée*. First of all, as is stated in the 'Prologue', the play can be summarised through these questions: 'Who is the cause where is the cause / Is it inside is it outside? / Are we inside are we outside?'[10] Cixous's text problematises the distinction between interior and exterior, on a narrative/fictional level: Shakespeare (as the 'author' of the story) and his team are characters in the play, but also in it are other writers who record the events or decide their course, such as Amelait himself or his friend Horatio. In Miller's words, this feature shows 'the difficulty of peeling away all the layers of fiction'[11] in the story. In a funny *mise en abyme*, since *The Blindfolded Fiancée* can be considered a variation on Shakespeare's tragedy, Amelait reproaches his mother for never having read *Hamlet*.[12] However, Cixous's play contains so many *mises en abyme* that we cannot call it simply 'a play within a play'. All of them have a dazzling effect on the spectators/readers, who finally cannot tell who is outside or inside the story, or on which side they are themselves. On the other hand, readers who are familiar with Cixous's oeuvre soon notice that *The Blindfolded Fiancée* is closely related to a narrative 'fiction' that she published in 2002, *Manhattan*.[13] Many of its characters reappear in Cixous's play: the naive 'fiancée' who is tricked by a mad – or at least pretending to be – lover, her German and realistic mother, the enthralling Letter – personified in the play – and even, as it will be shown later, the mole – appearing as a squirrel in Central Park in *Manhattan*.

All these cross-references (as usual in Cixous, there are also hints to the *Odyssey*, the Bible, *Ulysses*, *The Divine Comedy*, to name only a few), which are sometimes literal echoes of sentences picked from a vast conscious and unconscious literary memory, radically debase the distinction between the 'real' and the 'fictional' or 'literary' spheres, and may be identified as what Nicholas Royle calls 'dramaturgic telepathy'. Dramaturgic telepathy consists of 'a sort of telepathic repetition of utterance', 'transposing or translating otherwise the boundaries and marks of classification supposedly separating one character from another, one scene from another'.[14] In a 'mole-like progression', dramaturgic telepathy burrows crossing tunnels which follow a 'logic indissociable from the mole' in Royle's words.[15] He relates this logic to the figure of the spectre as developed by Jacques Derrida, which deconstructs 'the sharp distinction between the real and the unreal, the actual and the inactual, the living and the non-living, being and non-being ("to be or not to be", in the conventional reading)',[16] thus bringing us back to *Hamlet*.

The Blindfolded Fiancée emphasises, in many ways, the ambiguous nature of the spectre (already present in *Hamlet* as Royle observes), such as pointing out that Amelait's father was already a 'revenant' when he was still alive, as he himself claims.[17] Also remarkable is the unnumbered scene 'The Pictures', where the Spectre[18] is displaced, in Amelait's mind, by a more spectral figure of the father than himself: his pictures. The Spectre fails to get Amelait's attention, in spite of the Mole's help, because his son is completely absorbed in looking at the pictures of himself. Much has been written about the relationship between photography and death, and Cixous herself tackles this issue in relation to her mother's snapshots, in *Si près*.[19] What is most striking in the play are the mirror effects multiplying the reflections, oppositions, passages, creating a really intricate maze, similar to the one Kafka portrayed in 'The Burrow'. Like Kafka's, Cixous's poetic imagination burrows a *real* tunnel, called the *puits de néance*, a powerful signifier which may be translated as 'well of nothingness', although *néance* is a neologism in French, from *néant* (nothingness) and the suffix *-ance*, which conveys a sense of duration and incompleteness, of which Cixous is fond.

The last two scenes of *The Blindfolded Fiancée* take place in this subterranean labyrinth, where Amelait finds the spectre of his father and, though he succeeds in ridding himself of its burden, he finds his own death there. The hero's trip to this ominous place is likened to a descent into Hell, or a fall into the father's tomb, as Amelait's mother has predicted: 'By many errors and much goodwill, he [the father] wants to pull you underground.'[20] However, the undermining of the opposition between interior and exterior earlier commented upon opens into a similar complication of the pair life/death. To begin with, this underground maze can be identified with 'the kingdom of moles', which is in turn assimilated to death by the French phrase *aller visiter le royaume des taupes* ('to visit the kingdom of moles'), meaning to die. The Mole is thus the king – or the queen – of this realm, and as such she will be the only survivor, and even have a long life, according to the last sentence of the play. (This can also be considered a proof of the centrality of the mole in *The Blindfolded Fiancée*, which is, by the way, inhabited by many other animals.) The mole, like the spectre, thus destroys the barrier between living and non-living. In Cixous's oeuvre, this transgressive being is also embodied by another animal, the squirrel, which plays the lead in a 'primal scene' often depicted or alluded to throughout her work. *The Blindfolded Fiancée*, as well as *Manhattan*, for instance, describe this uncanny *Urszene*: a squirrel seems to be half-buried in the ground, since its head and trunk are under the soil, whereas its completely still bottom and tail are visible for the observer, who believes that the animal in this strange position is dead.[21] But in a flash, the squirrel takes its body out of the ground and 'resuscitates'. The same scene, following Cixous's interpretation, is depicted by Goya in his *Half-buried Dog*, one of her favourite paintings, in which a dog seems to be in the process of sinking into the sand, or otherwise rising from it. These two immensely powerful images represent the continuity between life and death, and also the impossible distinction between past, present and future: Goya captures this dog in 'the minute where time overturns. And hup! The future enters', in Cixous's words.[22] Moreover, the squirrel, the dog and the mole embody two seemingly contradictory meanings: the weight – which can be sometimes considered a burden by the person carrying it – of memories of the beloved dead (who are always 'improperly buried',[23] according to the writer), as well as the capacity of literature and art to revive these beloved beings, saved thus from oblivion – which might then be judged as the only actual death.

A mole with similar features can be found in Kafka's diary. Some weeks before he wrote his unfinished short story 'The Village Schoolmaster' or 'The Giant Mole', the author reported in his diary the story of a premonitory mole: his brother-in-law realised that a mole was digging a tunnel under his feet, in a trench (the entry is dated November 1914), and took this as a sign warning him to escape. The soldier who replaced him was killed by a bullet.[24] In this story, thus, the mole appears as the kingdom of the dead's queen, or at least as a spectral messenger of death, who, instead of her usual delivery, brings life to Kafka's brother-in-law.

The figure of the spectre, as already mentioned, also represents this ambiguity between death and life. According to Jacques Derrida, the spectre, unlike the 'spirit', is 'neither soul nor body, and both one and the other',[25] and has 'the tangible intangibility of a proper body without flesh, but still a body of some*one* as some*one other*'.²⁶ In relation to the reading of *The Blindfolded Fiancée* offered here, Derrida's sentence is rich in pertinent suggestions about the senses of vision and touch. We shall return to them later, but first, it is important to notice that what is also at stake in this statement is the relationship between the subject and the other. In Cixous's text, this binary pair is also problematised, through the figures of the spectre and the mole. Amelait's tragedy lies in the impossibility of re-enacting his father's figure by emulating him, equalling or even surpassing his supposed qualities as a man and as a king and warrior. The son complains that he cannot live his life because of this haunting paternal figure who forces him to take revenge for his supposed murder. But we may also understand that Amelait re-enacts his father's selfish behaviour in his love relationship with Reguine. This identification between old Amelait and his son is especially striking at moments, such as in the scene 'The Pictures', when the Spectre addresses Amelait in a symmetrical way, since they share the same name: 'Can you hear me, Amelait, it's me, Amelait, who calls you'; or in the last scene, the confrontation between the Spectre and the hero, when the former asks his son: 'I ask you Amelait forget yourself and remember me [*oublie toi et souviens moi*]'.²⁷

However, another character, the Mole, intervenes in what otherwise might be considered a relationship between Amelait and his double – although it is impossible to discern who is the 'original' and who is the 'alter ego' or the double of the former, since the chronological distinction, as we have seen, between past, present and future is also altered. The Mole, who appears at the beginning as Amelait's pet, always carried in a cage, soon manifests a more complex meaning and personality, if this word can be used. In the Prologue, and although Amelait forcefully states that he hates to leave her behind, he walks out of the scene without her. In Prologue 2, the Mole vanishes, taken away by the Spectre. She reappears in scene vi, where she begins to signal every appearance of the Spectre, and also to speak, at first by repeating only the last words uttered by Amelait. The Mole seems thus to be a sort of extension of the Spectre, as well as of Amelait, or perhaps a bridge between their two spheres, the world of the living and the realm of the dead, as Kafka's mole in the trench. But, like Echo the nymph, the Mole's apparently simple repetitions of Amelait's words convey other meanings. First of all, she seems to be 'a pet compass, pointing always to the truth', as Lynn Turner says of Anna Freud's dog.²⁸ However, in light of Turner's subtle analysis, here the role of Cixous's mole is a more ambivalent one. At the end of scene vi, the Mole completes the Spectre's last sentence, inaudible to Amelait – as well as to the audience – and when Amelait doubts its accuracy, she retorts: 'If I'm lying, finish the sentence yourself.'[29] In this and other cases, we wonder who is the master and who is the 'subject' in this relationship; the audience may likewise question, at the end of the play, who haunts whom in the pair formed by old and young Amelait.

In a similar way, the Mole can be considered a double of the Spectre, since she tries to call Amelait's attention whenever the Spectre appears, as well as being a double of Amelait himself in his tense relationship with his mother: the servants who take care of the Mole in the Prologue assume that she is nourished with milk, a fact that correlates with Amelait as 'milky-soul', but also with his mother, who, according to her son, has always lacked 'the milk of maternal tenderness'.[30] For his part, Shakespeare, himself a character in the play, seems to see in the Mole an incarnation of Amelait's life, precisely when he says: 'Has he forgotten the mole? Trying so hard to forget his mother, / He would end up forgetting to live';[31] later in the play, we find an echo of this premonition when the mother tells Amelait: 'One day you will kill yourself in your mole.'[32]

Nevertheless, all the characters of the play may be identified with the Mole; in Prologue 2, Shakespeare exclaims: 'In the heart of every character / A mole in a cage / A cage in a badly-lit room', an idea repeated by Amelait as he addresses the Mole before dying: 'You have always been in the cage that was my heart.'[33] If we follow this path, the conclusion that in fact Amelait does not really die at the end of the play is plausible, since Horatio succeeds in saving the Mole from Laerte's hate, and the animal goes to live with Reguine. Amelait's last words are addressed to the Mole: 'If you could spend some time in Reguine's room, I would be very grateful . . . I am sure that she will adore you', and he shows her how to return Reguine's kisses.[34]

This funny but somewhat troubling scene shows the sexual implications of the mole, too. The Mole in *The Blindfolded Fiancée* may thus be seen as an image of Amelait's sex, of his 'real and metaphorical penis' in Cixous's words, speaking of Jacques Derrida's *Circumfession*. It is worth quoting in full this passage from 'Tales of Sexual Difference':

> [Derrida] is one of the rare 'men', or perhaps the only one, to risk his active body in the text. A body movement on the order of circling around inscribes and is inscribed in *Circumfession*. You yourself [she addresses Derrida] circle around this real and metaphorical penis, this blinded, wounded, healed, resuscitated, etc., penis, you circle around this sex . . .[35]

The circling movement described here as a characterisation of Derrida's writing and thinking may be assimilated to a 'mole-like progression' in a burrow similar to Kafka's, where the main room would be that of the mole itself. In this passage, Cixous seems at first to oppose 'exterior' male sex to an 'interior' female one, when she asks: 'What would "a woman" do where for you there is penis?', answering: 'If I work with body and text, I work (from) the interior. But "my sex" is this interior earth we listen to. If there is an organ, it is the imagined, felt organ that serves as a sex: *the heart*.' However, the writer soon dismantles this opposition between (male/masculine) exterior and (female/feminine) interior when she concludes: 'the heart is the most mysterious pleasure organ, the sublime sex common to the two "sexes"'.[36]

The mole certainly has a phallic shape, with its eyeless and earless rounded head, and it is this sense that Amelait's mole seems to follow in several scenes. Gerutha finds it a disgusting beast, complains about its smell,[37] refuses to acknowledge its identity as a mole, calling it sometimes a 'rat', and other times a 'ferret' or a 'polecat', and tries to convince Amelait to get rid of his animal companion. Amelait himself seems to have ambivalent feelings towards the Mole, since he often leaves her behind in spite of his declared affection for her; in scene ii, too, infuriated by his mother, he looks for a rat to kill, instead of attacking his mother. Finally, the above-mentioned *Urszene* with the squirrel can also have a sexual meaning: when the squirrel 'resurrects', Amelait encourages Reguine to caress it, but makes her touch his own hand instead.[38]

This gesture sends us back to Kafka, who, in an unpublished letter to Milena, implicitly identifies his own hand with a mole he has captured; the mole, when he lets it go, instantly vanishes into the ground ('as it dove into the water', he writes). He adds: 'I will never dare reach out my hand to you, young lady, my dirty, trembling, clawed, hesitant, nervous, moist hand.'[39] This mole/male, 'deaf, blind sex', in Gerutha's words referring to old Amelait, can also embody, however, Reguine's or Gerutha's sex.[40] For we must not forget that the Mole is mainly female: its subterranean, nocturnal nature refers to this 'interior earth' that Cixous relates to woman's sex in 'Tales of Sexual Difference'. What can make it repugnant is that, coming from the interior, it appears at the exterior, following the principle of abjection: substances hidden in the interior of the body such as milk, blood, sweat or sperm (all of which explicitly or implicitly appear in Cixous's play) become abject when they emerge outside. Similarly, all beings that inhabit the margins, that do not fit in any category, are considered abject. Daniel Mesguich, in his staging of *The Blindfolded Fiancée*, smartly supports this idea, invoking popular culture by presenting the Spectre as a vampire and the Mole as a manga-fashion humanimal creature. Both of these characters are abject, in the sense that they are 'in-between', between death and life, between species.

As for the Mole, not only is it assimilated to many other animals, as we have seen, such as the squirrel, the rat, the ferret, and the worm, but it constantly changes sex and species: 'Depending on the hour and the mood, it's a boy or a girl mole, or a cat, a mouse, a woman, a best friend, a cherished sister,' according to Amelait, who concludes: 'my heart is tender and divided'.[41] (This conclusive sentence also reminds us of the equivalence between the mole and the heart mentioned earlier.) The permanent shifting of species and categories, which evokes a 'philosophy of indecidability'[42] in Cixous's words, referring simultaneously to Derrida's silkworm and to Alechinsky's root, makes of the mole the very image of sexual difference, as defined by Cixous. In addition, this quotation from *The Blindfolded Fiancée* resonates with the following, from 'Tales of Sexual Difference', which alludes to the multiplicity of beings one can find in what appears to be a single individual:

> But I know from experience [. . .] that very often a 'woman' is not a woman nor a 'man' a man, that very often a 'woman', a 'man' is an ensemble of x elements. I know a woman who is at second glance an ensemble of five little boys and one little girl. As for the following glances . . .[43]

These 'networks of identifications always trembling and always exchanged between men and women and . . .'[44] can be seen as liberating, but also menacing, as Laerte seems to think when he states 'Here we have the time when men change species / We become wolves, sexes, saints.'[45] These three avatars relate to love in the Cixousian universe: her text 'Love of the Wolf' takes up the fable of the wolf who loves the lamb so much that it devours it, in order to weave an extremely rich and subtle discourse on love as fear/desire of devouring, and fusion with the other.[46] Thus, the relationship between Amelait and Reguine can be assimilated to that of the wolf and the lamb, with no certainty about who is one or the other. If Amelait seems to be the one who rules, who decides, who manipulates the frail, victimised young woman, Reguine is the one who survives at the end and who keeps the Mole. Moreover, Amelait complains that she wants him 'purified, cleaned of my dead and my ghosts [. . .] wiped, bleached, diminished from my rotten half'.[47] Reguine does not love Amelait as such, but rather an image of him. This selective love is represented by the missing tooth she wants him to replace; in a similar fashion, Amelait loves an idealised image of his father that he himself has constructed. Both are, in fact, blind to the beloved person's actual presence; in the other's place, they love a reflection or a ghost.

The theme of blindness is very relevant in the play, as it is in Cixous's – and Derrida's – world. In *The Blindfolded Fiancée*, all the characters are actually blindfolded, in relation to others and also to themselves. In the unnumbered scene, which is all about seeing, as its title ('The Pictures') reflects, Gerutha says to Amelait: 'Your father was a blind man who didn't see that he didn't see.' But this blindness is constitutive of human beings, we cannot escape it; as Hélène Cixous formulates, '*wisdom*' only 'begins with knowing that we cannot stop ourselves, being blind, from believing we are what we are while knowing that we know nothing of what we are, which Shakespeare had already told us'.[48]

Blindness is embodied by the mole, who apparently lacks eyes, or else is considered the epitome of shortsightedness, as in *myope comme une taupe*. But if the mole also incarnates sexual difference, as posited here, we must conclude that sexual difference is not associated with vision but more likely touch, a sense that is also represented by the mole through its big paws. However, we must not jump to the conclusion that touch would simply replace vision; in any case, it would be a special kind of touch, between a 'don't-touch' and an 'almost-touching' (which constitutes a definition of 'real love').[49] In fact, concludes Cixous, '*tact itself*' is '*a phantom touching*',[50] a phrase which sends us back to the 'tangible intangibility' of the spectre as defined by Derrida.[51]

The Blindfolded Fiancée's mole, in this way, would incarnate sexual difference inasmuch as she represents the passage, through the paths and tunnels that she burrows which connect (in non-linear, intricate, multiple ways) the identifications that constitute the ensemble we call 'me' and 'you', 'the other', bearing in mind that there is no binary opposition between 'me' and 'the other', nor between man and woman. Sexual difference (or 'D. S.' as Hélène Cixous calls it in French, making a pun that has been widely commented upon)[52] can thus be identified with 'movement itself, reflection, the reflexive *Se*'.[53] *Se* is a 'personal pronoun used in particular with reflexive verbs', as the translator of this text, Eric Prenowitz, clarifies in a note, giving, not coincidentally, the example of '*se toucher* = to touch oneself/one another'.

If sexual difference is 'ungraspable' and can never be fixed nor 'photographed',[54] we may think that it does not (any more) exist despite exterior appearances, as if molehills only bore witness to an empty and useless burrow. On the contrary, Hélène Cixous ascribes this untraceability to the high speed of the passages, shifts and metamorphoses that constitute us. She thinks, notwithstanding, that sexual difference leaves traces in 'texts': 'That is where "D. S." leaves traces that last long enough for us to have the time to note them, time we do not have in the quick of reality.'[55] For his part, Derrida puts forward the following 'hypotheses', which complement one another. The first is 'every fabulous narrative recounts, stages, teaches sexual difference or offers it for interpretation'.[56] Since the *The Blindfolded Fiancée* can be certainly read as a fable, both in the sense of 'a legendary story of supernatural happenings', as well as in the sense of 'a narration intended to enforce a useful truth; *especially*: one in which animals speak and act like human beings' (*Merriam–Webster*), this hypothesis would support our own assumption that the mole embodies sexual difference. Derrida's second hypothesis concerning the traceability of sexual difference states 'as soon as there is sexual difference, there are words or rather traces to be read'.[57] This formulation can be understood literally, bringing it closer to Cixous's statement about texts being the only place where sexual difference is traceable, or it can be read in a more figurative way. In this second case, these 'words' or 'traces' would be inscribed on the body, as Cixous also suggests in 'Tales of Sexual Difference', for instance when she talks about the membrane taken away by circumcision as 'a sort of immense manuscript'.[58]

This link between writing and the body implies that the mole, in addition to embodying sexual difference, may also stand for writing itself – as in the case of the C.J. Cherryh novel analysed by Lynn Turner. This link is endorsed by the fact that writing (a term which also includes painting and other forms of art) comes, furthermore, from an 'original wound' on the artist's body-soul,[59] a wound that writing holds open, while taking care of it. This seemingly contradictory gesture is described by Cixous through the formulation *entretien de la blessure*: the lips of the wound must remain open in order to be able to *speak*,[60] but also as a sign that we are a 'little bit opened' by and to the other.[61] It is also in this sense that we can understand Cixous's statement that we are all 'a little bit signed'.[62] This wound is located in the very depths of the artist's heart, in the secret inner self, but we can read its traces on the exterior, inscribed on the 'skin', as does Kafka's invented machine in his short story 'In the Penal Colony'.[63]

These traces or *letters* – both in the sense of units of the alphabet that form words, as well as messages from a correspondence – are thus identified with the subject or the 'being', since *lettre* (letter), and *l'être* (the being) are homophonous in French, an ambiguity with which Cixous plays in several of her texts.[64] Judith G. Miller posits that *The Blindfolded Fiancée* is 'focused on "to write and to be" (*lettre et l'être*) rather than on "to be or not to be" (*être ou ne pas être*)',[65] but perhaps Amelait's dilemma is rather 'to write or not to write', or else, as expressed in the play: 'So, this is the question: To say everything or not to say everything?'[66] This sentence is uttered by the Letter addressed from Amelait to Reguine, which is personified as a *real* character in the play, in order to stress its autonomy (it never arrives where it is expected), its effect of *destinerrance*, as theorised by Derrida.⁶⁷ In Daniel Mesguich's staging, the actress playing this character was wrapped in the letter's pages, as if they were layers of her skin rather than clothes, and peeled them off one after the other in order to read each of them. Meanwhile, under the Letter's influence, Reguine feels that she is travelling through a 'tunnel' or a 'gut';⁶⁸ this last word reinforces the impression that the Letter is a being, and more precisely an animal being. Reguine's mother, trying to thwart its power, uncannily repeats (as she was not there when Reguine spoke these words): 'It's not a letter, it's a tunnel', and evokes the animals it contains, calling it also a 'zoo'.⁶⁹ Writing is, once again, associated with animals, and, at the same time, with an animal's burrow, through the image of the tunnel and the gut – the original French word, *boyau*, meaning also 'narrower gallery connecting two main galleries in a mine'.⁷⁰

That image leads us back to the mole as the incarnation of writing, an activity in turn associated with the Mole's passages between death and life. According to Amelait's mother, a writer is always 'talking to revenants',⁷¹ and we may add that the language he or she uses is itself a revenant: Amelait says only once that the Mole's name is Chana.⁷² Readers may wonder what this name evokes for Cixous; though she might not have been aware of this at the time of writing the play, Chana is the name of a 'revenant language', a language spoken by an aboriginal nation of Argentina which had been considered extinguished since the beginning of the nineteenth century, but arose from assumed death a few years ago. In 2005 a 71-year-old man, called 'the one who keeps memory' in Chana, revealed that his family had kept this language alive for more than 200 years without telling anyone, due to fear of contempt or even racist aggression, until he finally decided to unearth this treasure in order to preserve it.⁷³

Writing would, then, keep secret and reveal, or bury and unearth at the same time, precious nourishment for the soul-body, as the mole does with worms and small animals stored alive in the galleries of its burrow. In this sense, Derrida quotes in 'Ants' a text from Cixous's *Jours de l'an* which says 'I write underground, like an animal, burrowing in the silence of my chest . . .'.⁷⁴ That implies, too, how the writer or the artist works in the dark, like the mole, steering by ear and touch, not by sight in these subterranean passages of the burrow-text⁷⁵ – or, as Cixous says, referring to Derrida, advancing 'as an Indian walks, with a wild step, [. . .] an animal step'.⁷⁶ If there is sight, in any case, it would be an inner or in-sight, and never a *prévision* ('pre-vision', which means 'foresight' in French): Cixous claims that 'true artists' can be distinguished by the 'specks of impurity' or the 'blind spots' – the *moles*, thus – which subsist in their works, proving, therefore, that they do not foresee what they effectively do.[77] This special type of vision is close to touch, or at least to the 'phantom touching' or the 'almost-touching' that has been commented upon here, which Cixous links to myopia.[78] On the other hand, this writer's tread, or 'mole-like progression', has been linked to *écriture féminine* or to what would be a 'feminine' way of approaching things and beings. In fact, we do not need the adjective in order to establish that, again as the ambiguously sexed mole, the 'poet' – man or woman – escapes 'phallocratic destiny' by 'see[ing] through the opacity'.[79]

To conclude our own mole-like wanderings into Cixous's burrow, we might instead take the viewpoint of readers and argue for an analogous progression when reading. This would lead us to plead for a *myopic reading*, not shortsighted in the usual sense of a reader who cannot see the forest for the trees, stubbornly focusing on small and maybe meaningless details, but a reading which advances by ear, by touch, without foreseeing its path or looking at maps but rather losing itself in the text's tunnels, experiencing 'how someone who almost cannot see, "sees"'.[80]

Notes

1. Nicholas Royle, 'Mole', in *The Uncanny* (Manchester: Manchester University Press, 2003), pp. 241–55, reprinted in the present volume. This essay was first published in French, translated by Ian Maclachlan and Michael Syrotinski, in Marie-Louise Mallet, ed., *L'Animal autobiographique. Autour de Jacques Derrida* (Paris: Galilée, 1999), pp. 547–62.
2. See Anne Emmanuelle Berger and Marta Segarra, eds, *Demenageries. Thinking (of) Animals after Derrida* (New York and Amsterdam: Rodopi, 2011).
3. Franz Kafka, *The Complete Short Stories* (London: Vintage, 1992), pp. 325–59, 168–82.
4. Judith G. Miller translated two scenes of *La Fiancée aux yeux bandées ou Amelait* and included them in the section called 'The Theater of Hélène Cixous. Remembering, Refashionings and Revenants', in Marta Segarra, ed., *The Portable Cixous* (New York: Columbia University Press, 2010), pp. 215–77.
5. Judith G. Miller suggests these translations of 'Amelait' ('Theater of Hélène Cixous', p. 221).
6. Hélène Cixous, *Le Voyage de la racine alechinsky* (Paris: Galilée, 2012), p. 39.
7. Alain Rey, ed, *Le Robert. Dictionnaire historique de la langue française* (Paris: Dictionnaires Le Robert, 1998), III, p. 3768.
8. See Christian Mitgutsch, Michael K. Richardson, Rafael Jiménez et al., 'Circumventing the Polydactyly "Constraint": The Mole's "Thumb"', *Biology Letters*, 8.1, 2012, pp. 74–7, http://rsbl.royalsocietypublishing.org/

content/8/1/74.full.pdf+html?sid=ffde55af-9990-47df-baa3-0cf306d2f48e (accessed 5 February 2013).
9. Ibid.
10. Pages will be indicated only when they correspond to Judith G. Miller's already mentioned partial translation. Otherwise the translation is mine and the only reference given will be that of the scene.
11. Miller, 'Theater of Hélène Cixous', p. 222.
12. Cixous, *La Fiancée aux yeux bandés*, sc. ii.
13. Translated by Beverley Bie Brahic as *Manhattan. Letters from Prehistory* (New York: Fordham University Press, 2007).
14. Royle, 'Mole', pp. 249–50.
15. Ibid., p. 250.
16. Jacques Derrida, *Spectres of Marx: The State of the Debt, the Work of Mourning, and the New International*, trans. Peggy Kamuf (New York: Routledge, 1994), p. 11.
17. Cixous, *La Fiancée aux yeux bandés*, sc. xvi–xvii.
18. I use 'Spectre' with a capital *s* only when referring to the character – the same for the M/mole.
19. Originally published in 2007 (Paris: Galilée) and translated by Peggy Kamuf as *So Close* (Cambridge: Polity Press, 2009). In relation to photography, see Elissa Marder, 'Photolectures', in Bruno Clément and Marta Segarra, eds, *Rêver croire penser: autour d'Hélène Cixous* (Paris: Campagne Première, 2010), pp. 190–9.
20. Cixous, *La Fiancée aux yeux bandés*, sc. 'The Pictures'.
21. Ibid., sc. iii.
22. Cixous, *Le Voyage*, p. 76.
23. Cixous, *Manhattan*, p. 14.
24. See Claude David, 'Notes et variantes', in Franz Kafka, *Œuvres complètes* (Paris: NRF, 'Bibliothèque de la Pléiade', 1980), II, p. 975.
25. Derrida, *Spectres of Marx*, p. 6.
26. Ibid., p. 7.
27. Cixous, *La Fiancée aux yeux bandés*, sc. xvi–xvii.
28. Lynn Turner, 'Animal Transference: A "Mole-like Progression" in C.J. Cherryh', *Mosaic*, 44.3, 2010, p. 166.
29. Miller, trans., 'Theater of Hélène Cixous', p. 277.
30. Cixous, *La Fiancée aux yeux bandés*, sc. ii.
31. Ibid.
32. Ibid., sc. 'The Pictures'.
33. Ibid., sc. xvi–xvii.
34. Ibid.
35. Originally published as 'Contes de la différence sexuelle', in Mara Negrón, ed., *Lectures de la différence sexuelle* (Paris: Des Femmes-Antoinette Fouque, 1994), pp. 31–68. A fragment of this text, translated by Eric Prenowitz, was included in Segarra, ed., *The Portable Cixous*, pp. 48–60. I am grateful to Eric for having granted me access to the full version of this translation, still unpublished in its entirety. I quote from his translation and give the page references of the French original edition, here p. 51.
36. Ibid.
37. Cixous, *La Fiancée aux yeux bandés*, sc. vi.

38. Ibid., sc. iii.
39. David, 'Notes et variantes', p. 975.
40. Cixous, *La Fiancée aux yeux bandés*, sc. 'The Pictures'.
41. Miller, trans., 'Theater of Hélène Cixous', p. 274.
42. Cixous, *Le Voyage*, p. 19.
43. Cixous, 'Contes de la différence sexuelle', p. 57.
44. Ibid., p. 37.
45. Cixous, *La Fiancée aux yeux bandés*, sc. iii.
46. First published in the journal *Métaphore*, 2, 1994, pp. 13–37. Republished in Cixous's book *L'Amour du loup et autres remords* (Paris: Galilée, 2003), the text was translated as 'Love of the Wolf' by Keith Cohen, in *Stigmata. Escaping Texts* (New York: Routledge, 1998), pp. 84–99. This text is commented upon by Derrida in his seminar *The Beast and the Sovereign*, Vol. I, trans. Geoffrey Bennington (Chicago: University of Chicago Press, 2009).
47. Cixous, *La Fiancée aux yeux bandés*, sc. xiv.
48. Cixous, 'Contes de la différence sexuelle', p. 58.
49. Cixous, 'Love of the Wolf', p. 95.
50. Ibid.
51. Derrida, *Spectres of Marx*, p. 7.
52. 'D. S.' in French is homophonous to *déesse* ('goddess').
53. Cixous, 'Contes de la différence sexuelle', p. 56.
54. Ibid., p. 35.
55. Ibid., p. 58.
56. Jacques Derrida, 'Ants', trans. Eric Prenowitz, *The Oxford Literary Review*, 24, 2002, p. 19. The original edition of this text, entitled 'Fourmis', was published in the same collection as 'Contes de la différence sexuelle' by Cixous, as a response to it (in Mara Negrón, ed., *Lectures de la différence sexuelle* [Paris: Des Femmes, 1994], pp. 69–102).
57. Derrida, 'Ants', pp. 20–1.
58. Cixous, 'Contes de la différence sexuelle', p. 39.
59. Cixous, *Le Voyage*, p. 71.
60. *Entretien de la blessure. Sur Jean Genet* is the title of one of Cixous's most recent essays (Paris: Galilée, 2011).
61. Cixous, 'Contes de la différence sexuelle', p. 40.
62. Ibid.
63. Kafka, *The Complete Short Stories*, pp. 140–67.
64. Such as 'Letter-beings and Time' ('Les lettres et le temps'), a lecture given by Hélène Cixous at the University at Albany-SUNY in 2007, translated by Peggy Kamuf and included in Segarra, ed., *The Portable Cixous*, pp. 85–95.
65. Miller, 'Theater of Hélène Cixous', p. 221.
66. Cixous, *La Fiancée aux yeux bandés*, sc. v.
67. Jacques Derrida, *The Post Card. From Socrates to Freud and Beyond*, trans. Alan Bass (Chicago: University of Chicago Press, 1987).
68. Cixous, *La Fiancée aux yeux bandés*, sc. v.
69. Ibid.
70. According to the *Trésor de la Langue Française informatisé* http://atilf.atilf.fr (accessed 5 February 2013).
71. Cixous, *La Fiancée aux yeux bandés*, sc. vi.
72. Ibid.

73. Verónica Toller, 'Blas el chaná, tató olle nden', *El Día de Gualeguaychu*, 26 May 2007, http://www.eldiadegualeguaychu.com.ar/guardin-de-las-historias-y-costumbres-de-su-raza/ (accessed 5 February 2013).
74. Derrida, 'Ants', p. 37.
75. Nicholas Royle, commenting upon Kafka's 'The Burrow', states 'It is the condition of having a burrow, of being in the burrow that is the text'; 'Mole', p. 251.
76. Cixous, 'Contes de la différence sexuelle', p. 36.
77. Cixous, *Le Voyage*, p. 47.
78. Especially in 'Savoir', a text published together with Derrida's 'A Silkworm of One's Own', in Hélène Cixous and Jacques Derrida, *Veils*, trans. Geoffrey Bennington (Stanford: Stanford University Press, 2001), pp. 1–16.
79. Cixous, 'Contes de la différence sexuelle', p. 55.
80. Cixous, *Le Voyage*, p. 40.

Chapter 10

Your Worm

Peggy Kamuf

> Poor worm, thou art infected!
> (Shakespeare, *The Tempest*, III.i.2)

Verso

Worm. A simple word, a humble word, common as dirt. It is such a lowdown, ordinary thing that one might well ask what it is doing here. Was it invited to take part or did it just turn up? Perhaps it wormed its way in, as one says of those who insinuate themselves, for example, into another's confidence or home. Worms are sinuous, hence the insinuation. One has to admit, however, that for such a simple word, 'worm' displays an interesting complexity, flexibility, suppleness, or sinuousity. For, demonstrably, it is not only a noun and the name of something dirt-common; it can also bend itself into many shapes of verbs, active and passive, transitive and intransitive, in a manner that, while perhaps not unique in the language, shows a great virtuosity.

Maybe I am trying to worm out of the question that was just put: How did it get here, this worm, this word, part noun, part verb, or perhaps even the one always insinuated in the other?

≈

(Drop through the dictionary's wormhole and you'll find that 'worm out of', meaning 'to evade or escape in indirect or subtle fashion; wriggle', is but one of several insinuatingly similar constructions with the worm verb; both Webster's and the *OED* list at least four others, which all have the form of 'to worm X out of Y', where X and Y are interchangeably persons and things: thus one may worm a person out of his money or worm money out of a person; one may worm secrets out of someone, but also worm someone out of her position. The space of worm-action is thus configured as strangely reversible, without certain distinction of inside from outside. You will also note the verb's predilection for certain prepositions or adverbs: commonly these are in, into, out, out of, through, but also up, down, about, along and combinations thereof, as in James Cooper's *Last of the Mohicans*: 'I little like that smoke which you may see worming up along the rock above the canoe.')[1]

≈

But enough worming about. I come back to the question: what is worm doing here, appearing so abruptly, without introduction, thus so impolitely? To begin as I did by pronouncing merely the word 'worm' sounds not at all nice. Actually, it's not the sound that could make one squirm; phonically, 'worm' emits a soothing, almost mantric resonance as it hums across the tongue and warms the lips. But isolated, without any context, it might very well be an epithet, a curse, unless it is an apostrophe, an address – if one may permit oneself to address a worm or even to invoke it as a proper name, Worm. Or else, since the noun is so thoroughly wormed through with the verb – and vice versa ('and vice versa' says already something wormlike) – it could as well be a strange imperative, a command, or even some kind of prayer or supplication. To be sure, no dictionary is going to sanction all these possibilities, but by definition, so to speak, inventive language has never waited upon dictionary definition, on the contrary. To paraphrase Jacques Derrida's great text on invention and its im-possibility, 'Psyche: Invention of the Other', the question is: What, then, am I going to be able to invent *with* – *about, through, up, along* – this 'worm' that has positioned itself, so unexpectedly, in my path?[2]

≈

(I must open right away another parenthesis in order to recount how I had got no further than this with my worm, that is, with 'Your Worm', when an message from my friend Nicholas Royle reminded me of the beginning of another text by Derrida, 'Telepathy', which alludes apparently to a dream that the signatory has already recounted to his unnamed addressee. Here is how the text opens, in Royle's translation:

> So, what do you want me to say, I had a premonition of something nasty in it, like a word, or a worm, a piece of worm that would be a piece of word, and that would be seeking to reconstitute itself by slithering, something tainted that poisons life. And suddenly, precisely there, only there, I started to lose my hair, no, to lose some hair that was not necessarily mine, perhaps yours. I was trying to keep it by making knots that, one after the other, came undone

only to re-form themselves further on. I felt, from a distance and confusedly, that I was searching for a word, perhaps a proper name [. . .] Rather it was the term that was searching for me, it had the initiative, according to me, and was doing its best to collect itself by every means [. . .][3]

This worm-word dream now seems to me the most overdetermined place on the programme, on to which I have stumbled in my sleep, as it were, while I thought I was heading somewhere else, as I'll explain as soon as I worm my way out of this parenthesis.)

≈

So I was saying something about the path on which the worm-word showed up, if not for the first time, then with a kind of importunity that I could not get around. I came upon it in a passage of Hélène Cixous's formidably inventive text *Insister à Jacques Derrida*, which I undertook to translate some years ago.[4] Of all the bombs in this writing set to go off as soon as a translator treads on them, there was one that worried me even and perhaps especially in my sleep. This particular explosion took the form of the anagram, ananym or palindrome of *rêve* inverted into *ver*. The reversal is invoked explicitly only once but it is early on, virtually at the same moment the text turns to face, so to speak, the subject of dreams.

> Le Rêve . . . Ce personnage, cet autre texte. Ce Visiteur . . . Gros de secrets, infiniment désirable, ver à transformation. Ver renversant.[5]

> Le Rêve . . . This character, this other text. This Visitor . . . Bursting with secrets, infinitely desirable, a transformation worm [*ver*]. Amazing reversible *ver*.[6]

Of course, *ver* is not simply the noun whose sense is more or less translatable as worm. It is also the syllable *ver-* in, for example, *renverser*, reverse, version, *vers*, verse or line of verse, the preposition *vers* (towards), all of which are traceable to the Latin *versus, versum*, turn. In the preceding chapter of this book, Cixous had mined these and many other *ver-* words – for example conversation, verso – keeping in view as she did so the text by Derrida that would come to be titled 'Un Ver à soie' and that Geoffrey Bennington translated as 'A Silkworm of One's Own'.[7] So there is your *ur*-worm, if you will, but for Derrida as well in 'Un Ver à soie' the *ver*-syllable ricochets throughout the language, turning up not only in the reversible turns of *versus*-words, but also landing on *vérité*, verdict and, improbably, on the rare word *veraison*, which derives neither from *versus* nor *vermis* – the latter being the common root of your English and your French worms – nor yet from *veritatem, verus*, but from still another homonym in French here, *vert*, the name of the colour green.⁸ Add to this wriggling mass the very element of the verbal, verb, verbalisation, then let the unpredictable German prefix *ver-* overwrite and disseminate endlessly all these lines of strict Latin descent (for example, *Vermögen*), and you have opened a fine can of word-worms. (I am going to set it aside for the time being, but it will be squirming around in the background.)

What worried me and wormed its way into my sleep was the passage into English of the dream's reversibility in the figure of the Worm. I confess that I desired to find and to reproduce in English the extreme economy of the palindromic anagram, *Rêve* ⟵⟶ *Ver*, a mad desire since its impossibility defined very precisely the line of irreducible language difference on which translation, if ever there is any, must take place. At the same time, however, a vaguely sensed contrary motion pulled in the direction not of economy but of proliferation, a space of proliferating reversibilities, not in the contained space of some container – a can, whether opened or closed – but as the medium of difference, the space of differencing and differentiation. Dream space, in other words, where the worm turns.

≈

Proverbs: 'Tread on a worm and it will turn'; 'Even a worm will turn.' In *Henry VI, Part III* (II.ii.19), Clifford puts it thus: 'The smallest worm will turn, being trodden on.' What is proverbial in these sayings is the connection between worm and turn, which is not just an assonance but also perhaps a lost, buried pun on the *ver-* of *versus, vertere*, to turn, and the *ver-* of *vermis*, worm, probably from an Indo-European root, *kverm*, to creep, slither, crawl. In any case, in the proverbs the turn figures the reversibility of values and positions: high/low, proud/meek, master/slave, oppressor/victim, mighty/weak and so forth. It is not just that, through a reversal of the hierarchy, the lowly, trodden-upon worm can turn into the opposite and the oppressor, but also that worm situates the medium of this overturning, the space of its action and passion.

Worm would thus be at once one of the terms in a reversible opposition, and, as the always opened possibility of reversibi*li*ty, it is unopposable, beyond, before or outside opposition. When Hamlet says, for example, 'your worm is your only emperor for diet' (IV.iii.28), it is particularly the insistence on the uniqueness, the only-ness, and not just the the exalted title of emperor, that situates your worm beyond the reversible oppositions in which it can also both eat and be eaten, like any other king or beggar:

> *King Claudius*: Now, Hamlet, where's Polonius?
> *Hamlet*: At supper.
> *King Claudius*: At supper! where?
> *Hamlet*: Not where he eats, but where he is eaten: a certain convocation of politic worms are e'en at him. Your worm is your only emperor for diet: we fat all creatures else to fat us, and we fat ourselves for maggots: your fat king and your lean beggar is but variable service, two dishes, but to one table: that's the end.
> *King Claudius*: Alas, alas!
> *Hamlet*: A man may fish with the worm that hath eat of a king, and eat of the fish that hath fed of that worm.
> *King Claudius*: What dost thou mean by this?
> *Hamlet*: Nothing but to show you how a king may go a progress through the guts of a beggar. (IV.iii.17–31)

≈

(Here another parenthesis, wormhole, or mole tunnel. The king's 'progress through the guts of a beggar' is just one of the echoes one may hear with 'Mole', a chapter in Royle's *The Uncanny*. 'Mole' begins by opening a first parenthesis and will progress by enclosing each of its paragraphs in enlarged brackets. I cite the first lines of the first parenthesis or tunnel:

> ('after a mole-like progression': how am I [N.W.O.R.] going to read this, eat or keep it, keep it by eating it? I have gathered the words together, like so many worms, I've bitten their heads, to immobilise them if only for a while, and I have placed them here, in my first tunnel. I'm worn out. The question of delay, detour, digression, deferred action, marked here in the first place by the lunar crescents of a tunnel '( )', known in English as parentheses, brackets or, perhaps most crepuscular, lunulae. Worms of words, squirming in the dark, and me worn to shreds . . .)[9]

The speaker identified by Royle's initials, capitalised and in square brackets [N.W.O.R.], says that he has bitten the heads of words 'like so many worms'. With that simile, an assimilation appears to initiate a transformation of the speaker into a word-worm consuming creature, but likewise, similarly, one who is consumed by words, taken over, taken in by them, ingested and spat out in shreds. For besides the repetition of words that are like worms and 'worms of words', in these few lines the narrating I twice says that he is 'worn': 'worn out' and 'worn to shreds'. It is as if N.W.O.R. is the one who has been bitten in the head, in the initial initial of his name, turned on his head, NWOR now reading 'worn' and undergoing thereby a de-capitalisation, if not a total removal then at least an immobilising displacement of the head that precipitates the proper name's fall into a used-up language where one size is worn by all: anonymity, the loss of name, the passion of wearing and wearing out, of headless words that can be kept still 'only for a while' before they take over once more the initiative, heedlessly, headlessly, shredding as they go, mole-like, worm-like, gnawing their way through the pillars supporting the capital initials of identity.

One last word before closing down this tunnel: that word is 'your', as in '*your* worm is *your* only emperor for diet.')

≈

For imagine that W.S. had written instead, 'the worm is the only emperor for diet.' A good line, but not nearly so good, not nearly so funny – comical and strange – as 'your worm', 'your only'. Who is the you of this 'your'? No one in particular, of course, and therefore anyone who hears the address of the second person. Its use is allied to what is called the *ethical dative*, which the OED illustrates with further citations from Shakespeare, and once again from *Hamlet*, the graveyard scene (V.i.169), where the first clown says: 'Your water is a sore Decayer of your whoreson dead body.' And a few lines earlier in the same scene, the same clown answers Hamlet's question about 'how long a man will lie i' the earth ere he rot', saying:

> I' faith, if he be not rotten before he die – as we have many pocky corses now-a-days, that will scarce hold the laying in – he will last you some eight year or nine year: a tanner will last you nine year. (V.i.159–63)

This 'you' is used, says the OED, with 'no definite meaning, as indirect object', which identifies it as the ethical dative. One may well ask why Shakespeare's play clusters these uses in a graveyard or in Hamlet's jokes in such bad taste about the dead Polonius.

≈

Palindromic reversibility of dreaming, or rather of *rêver*, *rever-*, five-letter palindrome turning round the pivot of the maternal name, Éve, Eve: on that pivot everything turns in the texts of Cixous. From waking to sleeping and back again, from writing to dreaming and back again, from eve/Éve to *rêve* and back again, and again, everything turns as if on the point of a 'v', *la vie des lettres, une vie en lettres*, that is, life, *la vie*, in literature. I cite this time another text of Cixous's, 'Letter-Beings and Time':

> E, V, E In the beginning as in the end, without end without beginning, Eve the name of the initial final rebeginning
> Eve palindrome...[10]

Éve, the pivotal eve, allows all the reversals and re-reversals or *rêver*sals to cross over and back, over and back, for her name also assigns her the duty of the watch, the evening watch, as well as of the wake-up call. The pivot of the palindrome keeps watch over the reversibilities from the centre point of the *veille*, which draws out the sound of the French letter 'v', pronounced 'vay'. Éve *veille*, she keeps watch, but also she awakens, *éveille*, not herself, for she is always awake on watch, but the other dreamer who has gone into the deep abyss from which there might be no return, no waking were it not for the *éveil* that is is called up and called to:

> H dreams. *H rêve*.
> It occurs to me that if as H I undertake every night the journey to the side of death or the other life, journey destined to risk many deaths, if I dare what I do not dare, if I desire what I fear it is because, in the end, Eve is there, she keeps watch in the end. At the end of the end. I emerge slimy snotty and dead from an abyss. Perhaps I died definitively this time. The between two times. I hoist myself into the deshiscence of time. Myself mouth agape into the cleft between two years. Mouth empty. Thought does Eve still keep watch? Telephone call. Wager. I am hiatus. Hiata. Not even: hiata. H. Mute H. Telephone rings. Rings. In the end, Eve, who holds the beginning, answers 'Good day!' Therefore I am. Words come to my lips. De-hisce my tongue.[11]

But there is another crossing that the principle of the palindromic Eve or of the 'v'/*vie* cannot assure, no matter how watchful. When it comes to the idioms that make up the writer-dreamer's life in letters, it is necessary to remain on one side or the other of a divide, which is therefore finally a more impermeable frontier than that between life and death, waking and dreaming, this world and the other world. Translation it is called, the carrying over from here to there, shore to shore as over a bridge, but even though the traffic there may flow both ways, the translating bridge cannot effect its transfers through palindromic reversal. Rather, from one shore to the other, the crossover is not built on the struts of reversible words. What there is, however, is desire, and once again dream, the dream of 'being understood in more than one language'.

> It is very hard for me to write this letter because it dreams of being understood in more than one language, it wants that to be, it must be it cannot be, it is condemned in advance to remain caught in the golden snares of French, that is its lot, its kingdom its fate, in the magic forests of French. If it exits them so as to heave itself dripping and laughing onto the shore/the bank of (the English language) the English/the American that it never stops thinking about, it loses the song the speech of its initial language.[12]

Hear how the writing of the letter must plunge into the river of the idiom, its own and only idiom, for that is its lot, its fate, its share. It is 'caught in the golden snares of' its French idiom, that is, in its 'rets dorés'. These three rhyming syllables are eligible to undergo a reversing rearrangement, which they do before the sentence concludes when *rets dorés* is echoed, quasi-palindromically, in *forêts*, forests. But the dreamed-of crossing over to an English or American shore must be given up or else 'lose the song the speech of its initial language'.

And yet the evocation of the river, with its golden snares, and the forest, with its magic charms, also calls up another medium between languages, that of a common store of mythological figures, which are at once figures of speech and narrative figures. The desire to cross prompts a plunge into this shared memory story of names and the text calls out suddenly 'Ondine, do you remember?' Ondine, the common proper name of a water nymph, like all nymphs was/is immortal. Was immortal, because she traded immortality for the love of a mortal, and yet she also is immortal, for Ondine lives on as name for an impossible crossing to the other shore. It so happens that Ondine is also a *veilleuse*, one who keeps watch over sleep, not, however, as its protector but rather as its curse. To the mortal husband who had sworn that his every waking breath would be his pledge of love and faithfulness to her, Ondine recalls the pledge upon discovering his infidelity: 'You swore faithfulness to me with every waking breath, and I accepted your oath. So be it. As long as you are awake, you shall have your breath, but should you ever fall asleep, then that breath will be taken from you and you will die!' 'Upon surrendering herself to translation, upon being translated', as Cixous might have said in translation, Ondine becomes the enforcer of the difference between the shores, between waking and sleeping, life and death, but also and above all, first of all, the one's idiom and the other's.

≈

'V' locates the palindromic pivot at work and in play in Cixous's dream-life-in-letters, and it is untranslatable, necessarily. Instead, v, *vie*, *v*, *veille*, the letters, the sounds echo according to a principle of homonymy, between speakers and idioms, like the call and response of Narcissus and Echo, or their echoes in Zohra and Hélène.[13] An echo is a kind of repetition, a doubling that does not merely repeat the same because it also responds. Like Echo, translation doubles in order to respond. The palindromic 'v' at the center of Eve and of *rêver*, the condition of reversibility, has its double and its echo in English as *double v*, that is, as double u, and its initialling letter 'w', which, however it is pronounced or named, is in French already the mark of a certain foreignness, non-Frenchness. So while *vers* are the very substance of the poetic in French, the translation into *worms* has already taken us to the other shore. To *Hamlet*'s shore, to be sure, and beyond it, to the wide lands full of worms under Shakespeare's earthy language. But worms have fed many other poetic and dream idioms in English or American. By way of homage to the might of Cixous's *rêver*sible v/*vie* in letters and so as to respond otherwise to its expressed desire to reach the other shore of translation, I offer a very brief excursion in the company of two other English-language poets who found words for worms.

≈

Following Hamlet's use of an ethical dative, 'your worm', we ended up in conversation with the gravedigger. The association seems quite natural, if not indeed the way of all flesh. Although the underground of the dead, the graveyard and the tomb are perhaps the most frequent sites of Emily Dickinson's lyrics, it is above ground that these poems most often locate worms. And here, under the sun, the common topos of the triumphant worm or what Edgar Allan Poe called the conqueror worm, in a poem by that title, is almost entirely absent. Rather than feeders and still less 'your only emperor for diet', Dickinson's worms are primarily food and fed upon; the poet repeatedly offers them up to her beloved birds, as in this evocation of a woodpecker:

> His bill an auger is,
> His head, a cap and frill.
> He laboreth at every tree, –
> A worm his utmost goal.[14]

Or again, in this well-known opening stanza:

> A bird came down the walk:
> He did not know I saw;
> He bit an angle-worm in halves
> And ate the fellow, raw.[15]

In another poem, however, this same scene of bird-eats-worm induces a reversal and thus opens up the ethical angle:

> Our little Kinsmen – after Rain
> In plenty may be seen,
> A Pink and Pulpy multitude
> The tepid Ground upon.
>
> A needless life, it seemed to me
> Until a little Bird

> As to a Hospitality
> Advanced and breakfasted.
>
> As I of He, so God of Me
> I pondered, may have judged,
> And left the little Angle Worm
> With Modesties enlarged.[16]

The last lines reverse a judgement of value made most explicit in the previous stanza: 'A needless life, it seemed to me.' The revision of this judgement is reflected in the substitution of 'the little Angle Worm', capital A, capital W, for what had at first been refused a name, mocked and dismissed with the wonderfully funny line, 'A Pink and Pulpy multitude.' 'As I of He, so God of Me / I pondered, may have judged.' Through a speculative analogy, whose transcendent or quasi-transcendent medium is God or the name of God, Worm and I, He and me reverse positions, thereby enlarging the scope of ethical pondering to encompass life in one of its apparently lowest, smallest, humblest forms. But this enlargement occurs precisely at the pivoting point of reversal. It is thus no less or undecidably a becoming or a making-smaller. 'And left the little Angle Worm / With Modesties enlarged.' The grammar of these final two lines allows the same phrase, 'With modesties enlarged', to be read in the exactly opposed senses of increased and decreased modesty, thus enlargement and diminution, the one, I, with my modesties enlarged, i.e., more modest, the other, He, with his modesties enlarged, i.e., less modest. Through an enlargement that is also and at once, undecidably, a shrinkage, a scaling up that at the same time scales down, this 'little' poem (and the qualifier 'little' is repeated in each stanza) touches on the measureless border of measured, oppositional space, beyond which your Worm turns to meet your God in the medium of *différance*.

If we looked at another Dickinson lyric that begins 'In Winter in my Room / I came upon a Worm – / Pink, lank, and warm –' and that recounts the sudden transformation of the Worm into a mottled snake 'ringed with power' and having the power of speech, we would hear unmistakable echoes of Milton's serpent in his insinuating conversation with Eve.[17] In Dickinson's version, however, the startled woman is alerted to danger, shrinks and then flees before 'Propitiation's claw': 'I shrank – "How fair you are!" / Propitiation's claw – / "Afraid," he hissed / "Of me?" / "No cordiality"'.[18] The last of the poem's thirty-nine lines states, in the flattest manner possible, 'This was a dream', whereupon the poem seems to denounce itself as having merely mimicked the power to welcome the language and reversible logic of dreams. Indeed, if we follow Cixous when she identifies the Dream as 'This character, this other text. This Visitor [...] Bursting with secrets, infinitely desirable, a transformation worm', then 'In Winter in my Room', which refuses to welcome the Visitor ('as he was a worm / And worms presume / Not quite with him at home –'), would be something like an anti-dream-poem, that is, a stage on which to flee the reversibility of the transformation worm-verse that has sneaked into our sleeping lady's chamber.

≈

'In Winter in my Room' (w/r/m/r/m) replays Milton's tragedy as comedy, the Fall of Eve as prelude to the dream in which the latter-day heroine recognises and flees the counterfeit voice of Evil: 'O Eve, in evil hour thou didst give eare / To that false Worm, of whomsoever taught / To counterfet Mans voice' (*Paradise Lost*, VIII, 1067–9). In the space of Milton's Christian epic, when the worm turns it is towards its false nature, a counterfeit elevation, an undeservedly enlarged modesty, for it pulls itself erect up off the ground on which it is meant to crawl in perpetual humility. Earlier in Milton's poem, however, it is not the worm's evil falsity but its – or rather their – perpetuity that is evoked. 'Th' undying Worm' is the phrase Milton puts in the mouth of the Son of God in Book VI when the latter pledges that he will 'drive down' Satan's rebellion: 'and shall soon, / Armd with thy might, rid heav'n of these rebell'd, / To this prepar'd ill Mansion driven down / To chains of Darkness, and th' undying Worm, / That from thy just obedience could revolt' (VI, 737–40). The phrase 'undying Worm' is at least a double quotation, a quotation within a quotation. Because it is spoken by the Son, it recalls perhaps first of all the verses in the Gospel of Mark where Jesus is quoted admonishing his disciples to pluck out an eye or cut off a hand if it offends thee or be prepared otherwise to 'go into hell, into the fire that never shall be quenched: / Where their worm dieth not, and the fire is not quenched' (Mark 9:43–4). These words are repeated verbatim three times in the space of six verses and each time there appears to be an anacoluthon in the switch from second-person address to the third person of 'their worm'.

> 43: And if thy hand offend thee, cut it off: it is better for thee to enter into life maimed, than having two hands to go into hell, into the fire that never shall be quenched:
> 44: Where their worm dieth not, and the fire is not quenched.
> 45: And if thy foot offend thee, cut it off: it is better for thee to enter halt into life, than having two feet to be cast into hell, into the fire that never shall be quenched:
> 46: Where their worm dieth not, and the fire is not quenched.

47: And if thine eye offend thee, pluck it out: it is better for thee to enter into the kingdom of God with one eye, than having two eyes to be cast into hell fire:
48: Where their worm dieth not, and the fire is not quenched.

What I just called an anacoluthon, 'their worm' where one would expect 'your worm', is in fact the signal of the quotation. The repeated line cites the final verse of the last chapter of Isaiah. The angry God's last words call up a terrible sight as a perpetual warning for 'all flesh' to obey his commandments or else suffer the fate of those who, like Milton's Satan and the rebel angels, defied his supremacy:

> And it shall come to pass, that from one new moon to another, and from one sabbath to another, shall all flesh come to worship before Me, saith HaShem. And they shall go forth, and look upon the carcasses of the men that have rebelled against Me; for their worm shall not die, neither shall their fire be quenched; and they shall be an abhorring unto all flesh. (Isa. 66:23–4)

Both Isaiah and Mark, say the commentators, are alluding to Gehenna, which is derived from the Hebrew name for the valley or ravine of Hinnom, a place near Jerusalem once famed for Moloch worship and human sacrifice, especially of children by fire, before it became the local garbage dump where the corpses of criminals refused burial as well as animals and other refuse were burned. Just as these refuse fires never went out, so too were the maggots constantly renewed.

≈

'That's the end,' as Hamlet says. And as such it would be irreversible, if indeed it is an end and not something else as well or instead, for example, a beginning or a re-beginning.

> E, V, E In the beginning as in the end, without end without beginning, Eve the name of the initial final rebeginning
> Eve palindrome ...

≈

Imagine now that, having been led into the very depths of hell by your worm or their worm, we could emerge on the other side and begin to read again, for example in the oeuvre of Cixous, according solely to the pivotal letter *v*, and first of all its insistence as vibrating initial: *voir, voiles, voyage, visage, vol, voler, volcan, venir, veine*, so many v's, *vies, veilles*.[19] Would we then be reaching for some truth, some *vérité* of an experience of life-in-letters that Cixous signs and bids us to countersign at the point of reversibility of your *ver*, your *worm* or in whatever language that gives one, that gives *you* to receive thought *ethically*? That is, always in view of response to another, not me, another me, before me and also beyond me?[20] Is the *ver renversant* a species of this truth, of this verity, and not just a species, but *the truth, la vérité*?

In the remarkable and riveting conversation in letters between Cixous and Frédéric-Yves Jeannet published under the title *Rencontre terrestre,* Jeannet at one point retrieves a sentence from Cixous's 1991 text *L'Ange au secret* and sends it back to the author for her response. The sentence reads 'Mon projet était de dire la vérité', 'My project was to tell the truth.' In her reply, sent from Arcachon in August 2002, listen and you can hear the insistence of the pivoting *v, vie, envie, veille* driving, dividing and watching over the desire for 'what is called *vérité*'.

> First a commentary on 'my project was to tell the truth.' There, right away, me, the subject, divides. There is someone in me who *wants* [*veut*] to tell the truth, desires, wishes [*a envie*], aspires, but *in* this same someone watches [*veille*] someone who has no illusion concerning the vanity of this desire, and who knows that Truth [*Vérité*] is the pretty name of illusion, which does not prevent desiring what is called *vérité*.[21]

Recto

Let's turn back to 'A Silkworm of One's Own' so as to read differently this turn of the ethical dative: your worm. Derrida's text begins turning a worm this way and that with its title, *Un ver à soie,* four words that combine to invoke at least four different things or worms: (1) a member of a species of worm that produces silk, silkworm in English; (2) by means of the homophone *soi*, which is a third-person objective pronoun, a worm of one's own, an appropriated worm, belonging to some self, some *soi*, for example, a breeder of silkworms; (3) the same construction, *à soi*, also says the worm is its own worm, a worm itself as a self: it is a life form, which is to say the possibility of relating to itself and of auto-affection: 'The living [*vivant*] is the possibility of auto-affection, of time and delay: what, in self-affection, will have been able to touch itself'; (4) thus, the title names *a* worm, indefinite but singular, just one worm, each time.[22] It is each time *un vivant*, a living being, its *own* auto-affection of life, its own appropriation of life.

The title, then, disseminates across this text at least four figures or ideas of worms. Your dative worm, however, does not seem to appear there yet. But the construction *à soi* is or *recalls* a dative, that is, a movement of giving X to Y, although this movement gets taken over by the appropriating sense of *soi*, self, oneself. In Derrida's text, however, the dative sense of *à soi* is uncovered in a most palpable form, that of the prayer shawl or tallith that Derrida touches and talks to every day. He calls it 'mon tallith à moi', 'my own tallith' but which will have been given to me, to him, by an ancestor on Yahweh's order: 'It will be *your* fringe, and when you see it, you will remember all Yahweh's commandments, you will carry them out.'[23] As Derrida remarks, the signal of appropriation – *your* fringe, 'my own tallith', '*my* shawl' – comes undone from the moment the order is given and received to wear it. 'One says "*my* shawl" only by obeying Yahweh's order.'[24] My shawl is not mine because the other has commanded 'it is yours', 'this is your shawl'.

Or, if I may translate: this is your worm. *Un ver à soie* authorises such a translation, I believe. Indeed one could say it performs it in the course of the fabrication of itself as work. It is *like* the fabrication or operation of a silkworm, *un ver à soie*, which is described so vividly in the work's last pages or secretions. These extraordinary paragraphs, printed in italics, deserve to be read as one of Derrida's greatest *poèmes en prose*. One might even propose to title it 'Sériciculture', a rare word that is used three times in the poem and each time in a different sense. If we follow its displacement, we can see that the word itself is doing some work; indeed, perhaps it is working to divest itself of its own name.

In its last pages, the text switches into italics so as to recount 'a true childhood memory' that invaded the writer as he began to drift into sleep after reading Cixous's 'Savoir'. As a true memory of childhood, it is what he calls 'l'envers d'un rêve', the underside of a dream. Like Cixous's 'Le Rêve . . . Ver renversant', this phrase turns on the pivoting syllable *ver-*, which has so far taken the text through the vocabulary of *verdict* and *vérité* with its *voile*. Other than in its title, however, the main text up to this point has more or less omitted using or mentioning the word *ver*, worm.[25] One exception occurs in the following passage, which first introduces the term sericulture or *sériciculture*:

> – Truth, if we need it and if you still care, still seems to wait. In sericulture before the verdict, another figure . . .
> – Sericulture, you mean the culture of silk?
> – Patience, yes, the culture of the silkworm, and the quite incomparable patience it demands from a *magnanier*, the sericultivator.[26]

Already here, before the term is taken up again in the italicised poem at the end, the sense of this rather rare word, sericulture, is made to float among three or four ideas: (1) the culture or growing of silk; (2) the culture of the silkworm, with its already double genitive, objective and subjective; and (3) the patient culture or cultivation demanded from the silkgrower.

These senses and still others are going to be deployed again in the italicised poem, starting from the first occurrence just after Derrida begins to recount his true childhood memory of cultivating silkworms. Right away this memory is interrupted to report on the word 'sericulture': '*I now discover that that's called sericulture (from Seres, the Seres, it appears, a people of Eastern India with whom there was a silk trade).*'[27] The name is thus a kind of antonomasia, the metonymised proper name of a people, a human name. Sericulture designates, in other words, something proper to man. And yet, when the word is repeated on the next page, the poem has displaced this proper sense of what is proper to man: '*Sericulture was not man's thing, not a thing belonging to the man raising his silkworms. It was the culture of the silkworm* qua *silkworm.*'[28] This shift towards the subjective genitive, towards the worm's own production of a work outside itself and yet from which it cannot be separated, occurs by means of what Derrida calls, very cautiously, his appropriation of the worm's invisible, secret 'operation'.

> *I would observe the invisible progress of the weaving, a little as though I were about to stumble on the secret of a marvel, the secret of this secret over there, at the infinite distance of the animal, of this little innocent member, so foreign yet so close in its incalculable distance. I cannot say that I appropriated the operation, nor will I say anything other or the contrary. What I appropriated for myself without turning it back on myself, what I appropriated for myself over there, afar off, was the operation, the operation through which the worm itself secreted its secretion ... Sericulture was not man's thing, not the thing belonging to the man raising his silkworms. It was the culture of the silkworm* qua *silkworm.*[29]

The operation of the other animal, its self-production as silk, remains afar off, over there, at 'the infinite distance of the animal', at the 'incalculable distance' of the secret of its secretion. Thus Derrida must signal the problem with saying he appropriated it. 'I cannot say that I appropriated the operation, nor will I say anything other or the contrary.' This appropriation did not abolish the distance and the absolute secret of the other animal's operation. It was rather a *figure* of that operation which I appropriated 'without turning it back on myself', that is, without undoing the turn of the trope, or, if you will, the turn of the worm. Recall that when Derrida first uses the term sericulture in 'A Silkworm', he calls it a figure: 'In sericulture before the verdict, another figure ...' Sericulture figures, then, 'the culture of the silkworm *qua* silkworm', a self-production of self that the text calls 'a becoming-silk of silk', where the homophony of *soie/soi* authorises hearing also a becoming-self of self.

We can thus see how the displacement of this figure of sericulture – not proper to man but the silkworm's own – takes place, strangely enough, through the operation of appropriating the other's operation! I say we can see it, but everything about the one and the other operation, the one's and the other's, is invisible. Invisibility is the limiting condition of this appropriating figuration, its possibility in its impossibility.

> *I would observe the progress of the weaving, of course, but basically without seeing anything. Like the movement of this production, like this becoming-silk of a silk I would never have believed natural, as this extraordinary process remained basically invisible, I was above all struck by the impossible embodied in these little creatures in their shoebox.*[30]

A no less invisible process let us watch as weaving progresses on the page, made up of the silky strands of the poem's sentences. This progression also layers different times of narrating and narrated, building up a thickness of reference and self-enveloping quotation. There is likewise a shift from first to third-person narration. These layers are remarked in a passage that builds to '*all the crawling bits of words with* ver', close to the close of the text. In the same passage, one finds a certain 'novel of sericulture', which is the last occurrence of the name:

> *This philosophy of nature was for him, for the child I was but that I remain still, naiveté itself, doubtless, but also the time of infinite apprenticeship, the culture of the ready-made* [la confection], *made* [confectionnée] *according to fiction, the autobiography of the lure,* Dichtung und Wahrheit, *a novel of education, a novel of sericulture that he was beginning to write with a view to addressing it to himself, to stand up in it himself in a Sabbath of colors and words: the word* mûrier *was never far from ripening and dying* [mûrir ... mourir] *in him, the green* [le vert] *of the mulberry whose green color he warded off* [conjurait] *like everyone in the family, a whole history and war of religions, he cultivated it like a language, a phoneme, a word, a verb* ...[31]

There follow, in parentheses, lines and lines of words with *ver-*, which he began to cultivate as a boy keeping worms [*vers*] alive with green [*verts*] mulberry leaves, even as he began to write 'a novel of sericulture' in which to '*stand himself up in a Sabbath of colors and words*':

> (*green* [vert] *itself, and greenery* [verdure], *and going green* [verdir], *and worm* [ver] *and verse* [vers] *and glass* [verre] *and rod* [verge] *and truth* [vérité], *veracious or veridical* [vérace ou véridique], *perverse and virtue* [pervers et vertu], *all the crawling bits of words with* ver- *in even greater number, that he will celebrate later and recalls here, one more time, without veil and without shame.*[32]

This swirl of worm-words is suspended in a complex temporal frame, which is at once prospective and retrospective: there is the perspective of looking ahead like the apprentice he was then, learning the craft or trade of sericulture, but as seen by one who looks back at the other looking ahead. This is the perfect set-up for irony, and notes of it are indeed sounded here (*'naiveté itself'*, *'culture of the ready-made'*, *'autobiography of the lure'*, *'novel of sericulture'*). But these notes end up being absorbed by the poem's affirmation *'without veil and without shame'* of the work that has cultivated in so many senses so many *vers*.

The repetitions of 'sericulture' across the poem are doing some work, I suggested. The displacement of the word's sense does not just undo the antonomasia that put the name of man to the worm's own operation. It aligns sericulture with the possibility of the purest poetry:

> *Sericulture [...] was the culture of the silkworm* qua *silkworm. Secretion of what was neither a veil, nor a web (nothing to do with the spider), nor a sheet nor a tent, nor a white scarf, this little silent finite life was doing nothing other, over there, so close, right next to me but at an infinite distance, nothing other than this: preparing itself to hide itself, liking to hide itself, with a view to coming out and losing itself, spitting out the very thing the body took possession of again to inhabit it, wrapping itself in white night. With a view to returning to itself, to have for oneself what one is, to have oneself* [s'avoir] *and to be oneself* [s'être] *while ripening but dying thus at birth, fainting to the bottom of oneself, which comes down to burying oneself gloriously in the shadow at the bottom of the other: 'Aschenglorie ... grub ich mich in dich und in dich.'*[33]

The lines spin themselves out like an enshrouding tallith or cocoon. That is their sero- or seripoetic operation.[34] And it buries itself in you and in you, for it is your worm.

Notes

1. James Fenimore Cooper, *The Last of the Mohicans* [1826] (New York: Barnes and Noble, 2003), p. 216.
2. Jacques Derrida, 'Psyche: Invention of the Other', trans. Catherine Porter, in *Psyche: Inventions of the Other*, ed. Peggy Kamuf and Elizabeth Rottenberg, I (Stanford: Stanford University Press, 2007), pp. 1–47.
3. Jacques Derrida, 'Telepathy', trans. Nicholas Royle, in Kamuf and Rottenberg, eds, *Psyche*, I, p. 226.
4. Hélène Cixous, *Insister of Jacques Derrida*, trans. Peggy Kamuf (Edinburgh: Edinburgh University Press, 2007).
5. Hélène Cixous, *Insister à Jacques Derrida* (Paris: Galilée, 2006), p. 86.
6. Cixous, *Insister of Jacques Derrida*, p. 128.
7. Jacques Derrida, 'A Silkworm of One's Own', in Hélène Cixous and

Jacques Derrida, *Veils*, trans. Geoffrey Bennington (Stanford: Stanford University Press, 2001), pp. 17–92.
8. But also, as Claudia Simma notes, *ver* is the Spanish and Portuguese verb meaning 'to see'. See her fine essay 'Ver(s): Toward a Spirituality of One's Own', in *Demenageries: Thinking (of) Animals after Derrida*, ed. Anne Emmanuelle Berger and Marta Segarra (Amsterdam and New York: Rodopi, 2011), p. 90.
9. Nicholas Royle, 'Mole', in *The Uncanny* (Manchester: Manchester University Press, 2003), p. 241 (reprinted in this volume).
10. Unpublished translation of 'Les Lettres et le temps', which is also unpublished in French. A fragment of the translation by Peggy Kamuf, 'Letter-Beings and Time', is included in *The Portable Cixous*, ed. Marta Segarra (New York: Columbia University Press, 2010), pp. 85–95.
11. Ibid.
12. Ibid.
13. See Hélène Cixous, *Si près* (Paris: Galilée, 2007), and 'Letter-Beings and Time'.
14. *The Poems of Emily Dickinson*, ed. Thomas H. Johnson (Cambridge, MA: The Belknap Press of Harvard University Press, 1979), Poem 1034.
15. Ibid., Poem 328.
16. Ibid., Poem 885.
17. Ibid., Poem 1670.
18. Ibid.
19. In 'Silkworm', Derrida wonders about all 'the words in V that sometimes return, from beginning to end of [Cixous's] *Savoir*'. He lists 110 such words and then asks: 'But what is she fabricating in this fabric? What is she fabricating with these V's? Imagine someone wanting to translate them, translate their warp and their woof! Good luck and courage to this new royal weaver! For translation always fails when it gives up giving itself over to a certain alliance of lips and meaning, of palate and truth, of tongue to what it *does*, the unique poem' (p. 101, n. 2).
20. The ethical dative is commonly described as signalling the interest of the thing said for someone or other. It thus implies a response, an address, a giving-to-someone, who may be the speaker himself or herself: 'Cry me a river' employs a first-person ethical dative.
21. Hélène Cixous and Frédéric-Yves Jeannet, *Rencontre terrestre* (Paris: Galilée, 2005).
22. Derrida, 'Silkworm', p. 66.
23. Num. 15.39, qtd. in 'Silkworm', p. 43.
24. Ibid., p. 44
25. Curiously, in the inventory of v-words in *Savoir* (cf. n. 8), Derrida remarks the absence of *voile* in the feminine – that is 'sail', rather than 'veil' – but not of *ver*, worm.
26. Derrida, 'Silkworm', p. 31
27. Ibid., pp. 82, 87–8, italics original.
28. Ibid., pp. 83, 89, italics original.
29. Ibid., p. 89, italics original.
30. Ibid., p. 88, italics original.
31. Ibid., italics original.

32. Ibid., pp. 90–1, italics original.
33. Ibid., pp. 89–90, italics original.
34. As in 'sero te amavi', the epigraph from Augustine's *Confessions* that Derrida sets as the first word of his text after its title. But also *sero-* as in serology, the study of blood serum, the practice of diagnosing disease based on antibodies in the blood that signal the presence of a virus, that is, of 'a little perverse and pernicious worm, neither living nor dead, which carries delayed death in its self-multiplication' ('Silkworm', p. 91).

Chapter 11

Mole

Nicholas Royle

He will return, that is certain: do not ask him what he is looking for down there, he will tell you himself of his own accord, this seeming Trophonius and subterranean, as soon as he has 'become a man' again. Being silent is something one completely unlearns if, like him, one has been for so long a solitary mole. (Friedrich Nietzsche)[1]

'Kafkaesque' has taken on an uncanny meaning for many among us; perhaps it has become a universal term for what Freud called 'the uncanny', something at once absolutely familiar to us yet also estranged from us. (Harold Bloom)[2]

Then all the stories would have to be told differently, the future would be incalculable, the historical forces would, will, change hands, bodies; another thinking as yet not thinkable will transform the functioning of all society. Well, we are living through this very period when the conceptual foundation of a millennial culture is in process of being undermined by millions of a species of mole as yet not recognised. (Hélène Cixous)[3]

('after a mole-like progression': how am I [N.W.O.R.] going to read this, eat or keep it, keep it by eating it?[4] I have gathered the words together, like so many worms, I've bitten their heads, to immobilise them if only for a while, and I have placed them here, in my first tunnel. I'm worn out. The question of delay, detour, digression, deferred action, marked here in the first place by the lunar crescents of a tunnel '( )', known in English as parentheses, brackets or, perhaps most crepuscular, lunulae.[5] Worms of words squirming in the dark, and me worn to shreds. 'After a mole-like progression [*après un cheminement de taupe*]': this is a quotation from Derrida's 'Freud and the Scene of Writing'. It comes in the course of his meditation on pathbreaking, in particular regarding Freud's supposition of the logic of the memory-trace (*Erinnerungsspur*) as not yet 'conscious memory' and a notion of the '*itinerant* work of the trace, producing rather than following its route, the trace which traces, the trace which breaks open its own path'.⁶ He goes on: 'The metaphor of pathbreaking, so frequently used in Freud's descriptions, is always in communication with the theme of the *supplementary delay* and with the reconstitution of meaning through deferral, after a mole-like progression, after the subterranean toil of an impression. This impression has left behind a laborious trace which has never been *perceived*, whose meaning has never been lived in the present, i.e. has never been lived consciously.'⁷ The mole might appear to be a promising figure for the trace. The mole, then, as the impossible figure, figure of the trace in Derrida's impression of the Freudian impression, the mole as the ghost of archive fever. Why a mole? What is the pertinence or impertinence of a mole here? As I said, I'm worn out, I'm going to sleep for a little now . . .)

(What do animals dream of? We all know what Freud says about that – 'I do not know what animals dream of', he says in *The Interpretation of Dreams*, with that apparent naivety that is so lovable and yet in this case perhaps also so problematic. 'I do not know what animals dream of', he says. 'But a proverb, to which my attention was drawn by one of my students, does claim to know. "What", asks the proverb, "do geese dream of?" And it replies: "Of maize." The whole theory that dreams are wish-fulfilments is contained in these two phrases.'⁸ Then there are two footnotes (one added in 1911, the other in 1914) in which Freud remarks: 'A Hungarian proverb quoted by Ferenczi [1910] goes further and declares that "pigs dream of acorns and geese dream of maize." . . . A Jewish proverb runs: "What do hens dream of? – Of millet".'⁹ Doesn't the whole of *The Interpretation of Dreams* tremble here, in this question of animals' dreams, in this edgy configuration of ignorance ('I do not know what animals dream of') and desire (Freud's theory, 'the whole theory that dreams are wish-fulfilments')? Is Freud not an animal? And if geese and pigs and hens dream and in their dreams confirm the Freudian hypothesis, what or who is the subject of the wish: can there be wish, a desire for wish-fulfilment without an 'I'? I'm tunnelling, I'm dreaming of worms, I'm dreaming of a completely new tunnel . . . ( )

('Those, and I am one of them, who find even a small ordinary-sized mole disgusting, would probably have died of disgust if they had seen the giant mole that a few years back was observed in the neighbourhood of one of our villages, which achieved a certain transitory celebrity on account of the incident.' Thus opens what is usually referred to in English as 'The Village Schoolmaster' but also known by the title 'The Giant Mole' (1914–15), a text described by its English-language translator, Edwin Muir, as being among Kafka's most 'gravely incomplete'.¹⁰

The gravely incomplete: such, perhaps, would be the condition of a discourse on the mole. 'The Giant Mole' is less about the creature evoked in its title than about the mad agonistics of writing about it: the narrator and the village schoolmaster both write pamphlets concerned to prove 'the existence of the mole', and despite the narrator's avowed desire to support the schoolmaster they fall into a dispute that is apparently interminable.[11] The mole, it seems, exists only in the writings of this strange discoupled couple; and the pamphlets they write are themselves examples of the text in which they appear: the mole is textual, a writing-mole. And it is always already in retreat, burrowing away in a curious sort of textual-cum-'bestial oblivion': the most one hears or sees of it is in that opening sentence I quoted a moment ago.)

(In *The Natural History of Moles* (1990), Martyn L. Gorman and R. David Stone write: 'Once a suitable volume of soil has been accumulated the mole turns within the tight confines of the tunnel, either sideways or by somersaulting, and begins to push it back down the tunnel away from the working face. To do so, it places one of its forepaws diagonally to the body, rather like the offset blade of a bulldozer [elsewhere the authors talk of the Old World moles whose forelimbs "have evolved into powerful digging tools and are turned permanently outwards from the body, like a pair of oars protruding from a rowing boat": no time to engage here with the whiffs of anthropocentrism coming downstream from *The Wind in the Willows*, with the prosthetico-catechresis whereby one's limb would be a supplementary tool or machine, or more broadly with the supposition, implicit here as well as elsewhere in Gorman's and Stone's book, that "metaphor . . . is what is proper to man"][12] and with two or three powerful thrusts of the body it moves the soil along the tunnel. It then changes over forepaws and continues its Herculean task until it reaches a *previously dug side tunnel* leading to the surface [I underscore the narratological *Nachträglichkeit* here: the necessary but out-of-place irruption of the reference to the "previously dug side tunnel"]. The soil is pushed up this sloping lateral shaft and out onto the surface to form a molehill. The mole then returns to the tunnel face and continues to dig . . . The result of all this unseen labour is a line of molehills marking the route of the subterranean passage.'[13] After a mole-like progression, after the subterranean toil of an impression: this, for Derrida, is Freud's greatest discovery. As he says in 'Freud and the Scene of Writing': 'The irreducibility of the "effect of deferral" – such, no doubt, is Freud's discovery.'[14] And in *Archive Fever,* in the context of an account of 'deferred obedience' which does not fail to make reference to Shakespeare's *Hamlet* (a reference to which I will try to somersault or come back in a moment or three), Derrida writes: 'the logic of the after-the-fact (*Nachträglichkeit*)' is 'at the heart of psychoanalysis', above all because it 'disrupt[s], disturb[s], entangle[s] forever the reassuring distinction between ... the past and the future, that is to say, between the three actual presents, which would be the past present, the present present, and the future present'.[15] 'After a mole-like progression, after the subterranean toil of an impression': is this to be read from the point of view of being above ground or chthonically, from the point of view of man (say) or from the point of view of the mole? This very question is disturbed, embroiled, undermined by the law of supplementary delay. Each 'after' is 'at the same time', but one 'after' can never not be after the other ... No autobiography without a name or mole. The me is in the mole, the mole in me. '250 million years ago ... dinosaurs were not totally alone ... for scampering about in the leaf litter, amongst their great feet, were small furry animals whose descendants would, in the fullness of time, inherit the earth.'[16] I quote Gorman and Stone, *The Natural History of Moles*: what could 'fullness of time' mean, after a mole-like progression? And what of inheriting, without theology? Yes, the 'mole' in 'me', in what is called 'my' language, 'my' lifedeath caught up in 'mole'-effects. Which will entail, among other things, the task of reading 'mole', of thinking 'mole' as the secret that Derrida calls 'the functional possibility of homonymy',[17] of finding myself inscribed in the 'mole', not only as the so-called name of an animal, but also as identifying mark or stain, a fault or blemish, as foreign body or enemy within, and even as monstrosity (the 'mole' as 'false conception', a usage dating back to 1611, according to the *OED*, and synonymous with 'mooncalf').[18])

(Derrida's 'Freud and the Scene of Writing' is concerned with thinking otherwise what he calls 'Hallucination as speech and hallucination as writing':[19] Latin, *hallucinari*, to wander in the mind. It is a matter of what would be (in Derrida's words) 'before the distinction between man and animal, and even before the distinction between the living and the nonliving'.[20] A few of the many piquant formulations from the concluding paragraphs of his wanderings: 'We must be several in order to write, and even to "perceive"'; 'The *sociality* of writing as *drama* requires an entirely different discipline'; 'we must think of this scene [of writing] in other terms than those of individual or collective psychology, or even of anthropology'.[21] The scene or stage of the world would be that of 'the trace that is not yet language or speech or writing or sign or even something "proper to mankind"'.[22] Stop privileging a certain model of writing: that's what one's nose tells one, and Derrida is always led by the nose, close to or under the ground, on the scent of the trace.[23] 'There is no society without writing (without genealogical mark, accounting, archivalization), not even any so-called animal society without territorial mark. To be convinced of this, one need merely give up privileging a certain model of writing.'[24])

(*On* or, better perhaps, *under* the stage: a question of the chthonic. What truth can I make of *Hamlet* in relation to the autobiographical animal? In *Spectres of Marx* Derrida does not, apparently, devote much attention to the figure of the mole in Shakespeare's play.[25] He seems to recognise the terrible, earthy darkness identifiable with this figure; but his only reference is in the form of a peculiar ellipsis, a contorted paralipsis, an admission of the apparent need to leave the mole out of account. He situates it in passing as something not even calling to be singled out for being passed over in silence. The allusion to the mole is subsumed or encrypted, as it were, within an observation about that 'fretful porpentine' (I.v.20) to which the Ghost of Hamlet's father refers.[26] Derrida writes: 'Every *revenant* seems to come from and return to *the earth*, to come from it as from a buried clandestinity (humus and mold, tomb and subterranean prison), to return to it as to the lowest, toward the humble, humid, humiliated. We must pass by here, we too, we must pass over in silence, as low as possible to the earth, the return of an animal: not the figure of the old mole ("Well said, old Mole"), nor of a certain hedgehog, but more precisely of a "fretfull Porpentine" that the spirit of the Father is then getting ready to conjure away by removing an "eternal blazon" from "ears of flesh and blood".'[27] I would like to propose that this is what could be called a taupological ellipsis (for the suggestion of the word 'taupology' I am indebted to Ian Maclachlan who, with Michael Syrotinski, will have mined in advance everything I am saying here, if anything is being said: to them I would like, finally, humbly to dedicate this text – but where and in what language?). This ellipsis seems to me to be in communication with another, more general 'gap' in *Spectres of Marx*, namely the 'massively unavoidable' question of animals. I am thinking here of a singular tunnel that opens up immediately following Derrida's remark that 'no degree of progress allows one to ignore that never before, in absolute figures, have so many men, women, and children been subjugated, starved, or exterminated on the earth'.[28] In lunulae he adds: (And provisionally, but with regret, we must leave aside here the nevertheless indissociable question of what is becoming of so-called "animal" life, the life and existence of "animals" in this history. This question has always been a serious one, but it will become massively unavoidable).[29] What is the time of the 'massively unavoidable'? Has it come? Derrida defers, he leaves aside the question of the animal and animals, even while acknowledging that it is 'indissociable' from everything he is saying. The massively unavoidable question is a ghost that haunts *Spectres of Marx*. I want to explore it by way of a smaller-scale question: what happens to the mole in *Spectres of Marx* and how does it relate to the more broadly political 'vision' of this book? The autobiographical here has to do with feeling: one's feeling (as Derrida puts it) 'projects itself necessarily into the scene I am interpreting . . . it is never possible to avoid this precipitation, since everyone reads, acts, writes with *his or her* ghosts, even when one goes after the ghosts of the other'.[30] 'Mole' appears twice in Shakespeare's play. On the first occasion, in Act I scene iv, Hamlet is with others on the watch, in a state of anticipation regarding the possibility of seeing his father's Ghost, and he is criticising the Danish propensity for drunkenness: 'So, oft it chances in particular men / That for some vicious mole of nature in them, / As in their birth, wherein they are not guilty / (Since nature cannot choose his origin), / By their o'ergrowth of some complexion, / . . . / . . . /Shall in the general censure take corruption / From that particular fault' (I.iv.23–36). 'Mole' here is taken to mean 'fault', 'defect', 'stain' or 'blemish'. It's there at the origin: a mole in one's birth. The second occasion, shortly after this, is when the Ghost has come and gone, but announces chthonically, from *'under the stage'* (I.v.157), 'Swear by his sword', and Hamlet exclaims: 'Well said, old mole. Canst work i' th' earth so fast? / A worthy pioneer!' (I.v.169–71). Already, then, the 'mole' is internally divided, divided on its 'first' appearance. As M.M. Mahood suggested in 1957, in her discussion of the 'vicious mole of nature': 'Since the *mole* as a burrowing animal is in Shakespeare's mind before this episode of the play ends ('Well sayd olde Mole'), it is perhaps not too far-fetched to indicate, in the word's use here, a nuance of "something that undermines from within" as well as the obvious meaning of a surface blemish.'[31] The second 'mole' comes before the first. The mole begins by coming back. 'Mole' is moled, mined from within: it mines the 'mine', even before Hamlet's characterisation of the mole as 'worthy pioneer' or 'miner', and before his later agonistic assertion of the 'I' against Rosencrantz and Guildenstern ('But I will delve one yard below their mines / And blow them at the moon', III.iv.210–11). It ghosts the Ghost's words when describing the effects of the poison as it 'courses through / The natural gates and alleys of the body' (I.v.66–7). 'So did it mine', the Ghost says, 'And a most instant tetter bark'd about, / Most lazar-like, with vile and loathsome crust / All my smooth body' (I.v.70–3). There's a mole in me and mine. When Hamlet says 'Well said, old mole', the ghost becomes a mole but this mole is already spectralised. The out-of-joint tonality of this moment in the play, the irruption of what J. Dover Wilson called 'Hamlet's levity with his father's spirit',[32] constitutes what I would like to call, after Derrida or after Joyce, a peephole or portal. In *Spectres of*

Marx Derrida speaks of Hamlet's expression 'The time is out of joint' as opening 'one of those breaches, often they are poetic and thinking peepholes [*meurtrières*], through which Shakespeare will have kept watch over the English language'.³³ This figure of the peephole bears an uncanny resemblance to that of the portal of which Stephen speaks in Joyce's *Ulysses*: 'A man of genius makes no mistakes. His errors are volitional and are the portals of discovery.'³⁴ This, it may be remembered, is the same passage in which Joyce recalls the apocryphal story (published in Nicholas Rowe's Preface of 1709) that Shakespeare himself played the mole ('Shakespeare who has studied *Hamlet* all the years of his life which were not vanity in order to play the part of the spectre'; and in which Joyce works with the molecular particles of 'mole' in 'molecules': 'Wait. Five months. Molecules all change. I am other I now …')³⁵ Portal: the opening of a tunnel. An air hole or breach. The word 'portal' comes in, or out of, *Hamlet*. As the Ghost disappears for apparently the last time, disappears as if forever, Hamlet exclaims to his mother: 'Why, look you there, look how it steals away. / My father, in his habit as he liv'd! / Look where he goes even now out at the portal' (III.iv. 136–8). Even now: does this ghost-mole go out or go in? The mole is at the portal. The chiasmus of ghost becoming mole and mole becoming ghost is suspended here.)

(Derrida speaks, in *Spectres of Marx* and elsewhere, of the 'visor effect'. He defines this in terms of the formulation that 'we do not see who looks at us' and asserts that 'it will be presupposed by everything we advance on the subject of the spectre in general, in Marx and elsewhere'.³⁶ In 'The Time Is Out of Joint', the visor is integral to what Derrida offers, in passing, as a definition of deconstruction: 'Deconstruction is just visiting – and from the visitation one passes quickly to the visor, to the visor and haunting effect in *Hamlet* – return to Hamlet's father.'³⁷ In *Archive Fever* the visor effect is attached to Derrida's definition of the archive: the archive, he says, 'is spectral *a priori*: neither present nor absent "in the flesh", neither visible nor invisible, a trace always referring to another whose eyes can never be met, no more than those of Hamlet's father, thanks to the possibility of a visor.'³⁸ And in the context of his account of deferred action, and more specifically deferred obedience in Freud and Yerushalmi, he observes: 'The phantom thus makes the law – even, and more than ever, when one contests him. Like the father of Hamlet behind his visor, and by virtue of a *visor effect*, the spectre sees without being seen.'³⁹ All of this is slightly curious. If I contest a certain aspect of what Derrida is saying here I will of course be testifying to its truth. The word 'visor' does not occur in *Hamlet* and the suggestion of Hamlet's father concealing himself 'behind his visor' would appear to be a misreading.⁴⁰ As is evident from the following exchange between Hamlet and Horatio: *Ham*. Then saw you not his face? / *Hor*. O yes, my lord, he wore his beaver up. / *Ham*. What look'd he, frowningly? / *Hor*. A countenance more in sorrow than in anger. / *Ham*. Pale, or red? / *Hor*. Nay, very pale. / *Ham*. And fix'd his eyes upon you? / *Hor*. Most constantly. (I.ii.228–34) Of course Derrida knows all this: he refers to this passage in *Spectres of Marx* in order to push through his point, which has to do with the *possibility* of the visor (or beaver): 'Even when it is raised, *in fact*, its possibility continues to signify that someone, beneath the armour, can safely see without being seen or without being identified.'⁴¹ Derrida toils at the visor-effect, as if preferring not to countenance this 'countenance more in sorrow than in anger'. Why does he put so much emphasis on something that runs counter to the words that actually appear in Shakespeare's text? Is it possible (such would be the feeling I have, and one of the possibilities I am interested in excavating here) that his concern with the visor-effect is traced, spectralised, 'supervised' by a certain mole? Isn't that above all what the figure of the mole evokes, at least in the West, namely an uncanniness around the question of seeing, an uncertainty about whether the mole sees or not, or, if it sees, how it does? Might this in turn throw another light or another sense on the logic according to which Hamlet addresses the figure with the visor-effect as a mole? Shakespeare will present the mole as blind, for instance in *The Tempest*, when that other mole, the 'moon-calf' (II.ii.107) Caliban warns Stephano and Trinculo of their proximity to the mole called Prospero: 'Pray you, tread softly, that the blind mole may not / Hear a foot fall: we are now near his cell' (IV.i.194). But the mole has eyes, it is just that they are largely hidden in fur. As Sir Thomas Browne remarked, in his *Pseudodoxia Epidemica*: 'that [moles] have eyes in their head is manifest unto any, that wants them not in his own.'⁴² I can feel it now, it's the visor-effect.)

(When Hamlet says 'Well said, old mole' he refers to the Ghost's saying 'Swear by his sword' (I.v.169), in other words to the only statement that the Ghost ever makes that is explicitly addressed to someone other than Hamlet: such is the significance of the word 'his'. The Ghost's repeated imperative 'Swear' (I.v.157, 163, 189) is not marked in this way. What is going on in this performative *en abyme*, this speaking well of speaking well of speech addressed to the other, the speech of a mole, at once interrupting and supplementing the performative?⁴³ There is perhaps another haunting of the mole, by the mole, in *Spectres of Marx*, I mean in the speech or writing of another spokesperson for the mole, that is to say Marx himself. Marx's trope erupts in the 'Eighteenth

Brumaire' when he is describing the experience of being, as he sees it, in the middle or rather the purgatory or limbo of revolution: 'But the revolution is thoroughgoing. It is still journeying through purgatory. It does its work methodically. By 2 December 1851, it had completed one half of the preparatory work; it is now completing the other half . . . And when it has done this second half of its preliminary work, Europe will leap from its seat and exultantly exclaim: Well grubbed, old mole! (*Brav gewühlt, alter Maulwurk!*)'[44] 'Old mole' here, as Bataille suggested, appears to be 'Marx's resounding expression for the complete satisfaction of the revolutionary outburst of the masses' and can be understood 'in relation to the notion of the geological uprising as expressed in the *Communist Manifesto*'.[45] Marx's exclamatory trope consists partly in the shift from saying to digging, searching, finding food ('grubbing'), and partly in the theriomorphic figuration of the completion of the revolution. In its programming of the future, catapulting the future into the past tense, and in its crucial elision of the notion of speech act, injunction and promise ('well said'), Marx's text perhaps speaks out against what has been called the opening of the future itself, that messianic that comes from 'the being-promise of a promise' and that Derrida so patiently explores in *Spectres of Marx*.[46] The mole, if there is one, comes from the future. I want to feel my way into a 'return of the animal' in *Spectres of Marx*, a return that would not, however, like Marx's rhetoric, involve a metaphorical appropriation and effective objectification of the animal (mole as figure of the people or of the revolution) but would attempt to articulate slightly differently the taupological ellipsis in Derrida's book, concerning the 'massively unavoidable question' of the animal and animals. This ellipsis takes the form of a tunnel: it is placed in parentheses. The context of this seems to me significant. In a tunnel Derrida expresses his regret for not speaking of the animal, and this tunnel immediately precedes that moment in the text when he offers the most explicit 'working definition' of the New International: the New International, he says, 'is a link of affinity, suffering, and hope, a still discreet, almost secret link, as it was around 1848, but more and more visible, we have more than one sign of it. It is an untimely link, without status, without title, and without name, barely public even if it is not clandestine, without contract, "out of joint", without coordination, without party, without country, without national community (International before, across, and beyond any national determination), without citizenship, without common belonging to a class'.[47] The New International, I would like to suggest, is not separable from the question of 'so-called "animal life"'. If there is a New International, it is not human, or at least not confined to the human.)

(Hamlet's praise for the Ghost's speech ('Well said, old mole') is, before anything else, a bearing witness to the thought that a mole can speak. The seeming madness of this testimony can be linked up with something else that is marked in the 'mole' and in the 'well said'. I have tried elsewhere to burrow away a little at what I call dramaturgic or theatrical telepathy, that is to say 'the provocative oddity, encountered elsewhere in Shakespeare's plays, of a sort of telepathic repetition of utterance, apparent displays of telepathy or thought-transmission which no amount of textual scholarship or editorial argumentation will efface'.[48] It breaks out all over the place in *Hamlet* and it is perhaps inseparable from the figure of the mole. At stake here would be the possibility of another way of thinking 'the *sociality* of writing as *drama*'. The phrase 'Well said', for example, is itself a sort of ghost, or mole, that comes back. It is put into the mouth of Polonius, in a quite different context, but just thirty-four lines after Hamlet uses it: '"You shall do marvellous wisely, good Reynaldo, / Before you visit him [i.e. Laertes], to make inquire / Of his behaviour." Reynaldo: "My lord, I did intend it." Polonius: "Marry, well said, very well said"' (II.i.3–6). Dramaturgic telepathy would entail transposing or translating otherwise the boundaries and marks of classification supposedly separating one character from another, one scene from another. It would mean trying to think differently what is happening when, for instance, Hamlet's 'private' vow to 'speak daggers to [his mother], but use none' (III.ii.387) is picked up in the closet scene in his mother's exclamation, 'O speak to me no more. / These words like daggers enter in my ears' (III.iv.94–5); or when, in the same scene, the Queen notes Hamlet's 'bedded hair, like life in excrements, / Start up and stand an end' (III.iv.121–2) and thus eerily 'repeats' the Ghost's earlier evocation of Hamlet's 'each particular hair to stand an end / Like quills upon the fretful porpentine' (I.v.19–20); or when the Queen's dismissal of Hamlet's experience of the Ghost ('This is the very coinage of your brain', III.iv.139) refers back to Hamlet's numismatic phrase, to his verbal coinage at the moment the Ghost first cries under the stage: 'Ah ha, boy, say'st thou so? Art thou there, truepenny?' (I.v.158). To elaborate the notion of dramaturgic or theatrical telepathy in greater detail lies beyond the scope of the present text. I would say only this for now: rather than frame *Hamlet* according to the conventional boundaries of characterology, scenes and acts, and imagery (above all 'animal imagery'), wouldn't the logic of dramaturgic telepathy be a spectral logic, a logic indissociable from the mole? Wouldn't dramaturgic telepathy lead into a thought of spectral speech or writing within which the mole as much as the human 'speaks', that is, into a thinking of the trace impossibly figured in the mole, into a thinking of the secret as that which is 'no more in speech than foreign to speech'?⁴⁹ Nothing happens in *Hamlet* without a prior and radical putting into question of the opposition of the human and the animal, the living and the non-living, a questioning that begins with the (im)possible identification of a ghost ('Who's there?') and the ghostly negation of a mouse ('Have you had quiet guard?' 'Not a mouse stirring', I.i.10–11). I cannot get further into that labyrinth today. I'll stay here, in the outer labyrinth.)

(After a mole-like progression, after the subterranean toil of an impression, in the winter of 1923, who or what is the 'I' in the very great late text, also regarded as incomplete, 'The Burrow'? Everything is in this Kafka text, in the portal of its title and of its first sentence: 'I have completed the construction of my burrow and it seems to be successful.'⁵⁰ In the almost completely incredible, completely seductive voice of a burrowing animal (one whose mole-like characteristics lead me to want to call Kafka's story exemplary of a certain *animology*), in a trembling appearance of completion and of success that by the very terms of the description ('it seems') can be neither complete nor successful, the 'I' tells a fable about the anthropomorphism that permits this fabulous case of a speaking animal. It is an 'I' that reflects on itself and on the performativity of its speech, and that elaborates a deconstructive, animological discourse. 'Here is my main entrance, I said in those days, ironically addressing my invisible enemies and seeing them as already caught and stifled in the outer labyrinth': this 'I' knows that it is doing things with words, ironically, and that those it is addressing are not only invisible but already dead.⁵¹ And it proceeds to unfold a tale which suggests that, within the anthropomorphic projection, to speak or write as an anonymous, singular, autobiographical animal is to encounter the fabulous origins of the 'I' in a doubling or division. Such is the bizarre telephone-effect of the sound that the narrator comes to describe: 'I did not hear it at all when I first arrived, although it must certainly have been there; I must first feel quite at home before I could hear it; it is, so to speak, audible only to the ear of the householder...'⁵² The 'I' is haunted by the ear, the whistling and the burrowing of the other. This other is variously figured as 'some animal unknown to me', a kind of double ('someone of my own kind, a connoisseur and prizer of burrows, a hermit, a lover of peace'), and as death: 'I know that my term is measured, that I do not have to hunt here forever, and that, whenever I am weary of this life and wish to leave it, Someone, whose invitation I shall not be able to withstand, will, so to speak, summon me to him.'⁵³ In its panic, anxiety and pleasure, 'The Burrow' presents the animological experience of the impossible. It recounts an allegory of the trace or difference within the ear of the householder who recounts: this trace is at the origin but will never have been lived in the present. It is the condition of having a burrow, of being in the burrow that is the text. Death, the one whose invitation cannot be withstood, is as unthinkable here as it is in *Aporias* when Derrida suggests that man has no more of a relation to death or to the 'name' of death than animals have.[54] One can call death a mole or call death through a mole, as Hamlet might appear to; or as Shakespeare's play might appear to, with all its labour of removing ground, delving and gravedigging (the fossorial and the fossor), relentlessly moving around the figure of death preparing its 'feast' in its 'eternal cell' (V.ii.370); or as George Herbert might appear to in his poem 'Grace' ('Death is still working like a mole, / And digs my grave at each remove . . .'[55]) – but the itinerancy of the trace will always already have burrowed deeper or elsewhere.)

(Final tunnel or *afterw.rd*. When it comes to secrets, 'nonmanifestation is never assured'.[56] I recall here Derrida's meditation on the question of whether animals can keep secrets. It is in 'How to Avoid Speaking', when he questions the 'somewhat naive philosophy' according to which 'animals are incapable of keeping or even having a secret'.[57] It is because 'the nonmanifestation is never assured' that it becomes necessary 'to reconsider all the boundaries between consciousness and the unconscious' and 'between man and animal'.[58] In an essay on *Hamlet* and *Mémoires: for Paul de Man*, published in *Diacritics* in 1990, I referred to the mole in the context of the promise and what Derrida calls 'a kind of irremediable disturbance or perversion' of 'the performative as promise': it is this that accounts for what he describes as 'the *unbelievable*, and comical, aspect of every promise'.[59] Isn't this also the experience of the non-assurance of the non-manifestation of a secret? As that which haunts, as that which comes from the future, would the mole already have been 'in' *Spectres of Marx*? And would it be my mole or that of my telepathic friend Jacques Derrida or the mole of the other? When Derrida sent me a copy of *Spectres of Marx*, I wrote (2 March 1994) thanking him and, in a letter that included some remarks on molluscs (about which I was then writing) and a certain hedgehog, I also wondered about the possible communication between the *Diacritics* essay and *Spectres of Marx*. In his reply (6 March 1994) Derrida wrote: 'I am going to reread your text from *Diacritics* 1990 to see if it has made a mole-like progression in the unconscious of my memory' ['Je vais relire votre texte de *Diacritics* 1990 pour voir s'il a fait un chemin de taupe dans l'inconscient de ma mémoire']. The letter is typewritten or word-processed, but in pen he makes two alterations: originally he says 'mon mémoire' and changes the 'mon' to 'ma'; and around the word 'taupe' he adds, either side, the little claws or 'fossors' of quotation marks.)

Side Tunnels

1. Friedrich Nietzsche, *Daybreak: Thoughts on the Prejudices of Morality*, trans. R.J. Hollingdale (Cambridge: Cambridge University Press, 1982), p. 1.
2. Harold Bloom, *The Western Canon: The Books and School of the Ages* (London: Macmillan, 1995), p. 448.
3. Hélène Cixous, 'Sorties', in *Modern Literary Theory: A Reader*, ed. Philip Rice and Patricia Waugh, 3rd edn (London: Edward Arnold, 1996), p. 140.
4. This text was originally presented at 'L'animal autobiographique: Autour de Jacques Derrida' at Cerisy-la-Salle, in July 1997. It was first published in French (trans. Ian Maclachlan and Michael Syrotinski), in *L'Animal autobiographique: Autour de Jacques Derrida*, ed. Marie-Louise Mallet (Paris: Galilée, 1999), pp. 547–62. 'Mole' was first published in English in *The Uncanny* (Manchester: Manchester University Press, 2003), pp. 241–55. In what follows, I hope that the uncanniness of the mole might (as it were) speak for itself, in particular in terms of the relations between the human and the animal, and in terms of deferred action or after-effect, writing, foreign body, secretiveness, solitude and death. Apparently 'by chance', immediately after writing 'Mole', in the summer of 1997, I began work on what I thought would be a very different project, a short account of the writings of E.M. Forster; but I quickly realised that it would be necessary to begin from the fact that, while they were students at Cambridge, Lytton Strachey had nicknamed Forster 'the taupe' (or 'mole'). Focusing on the mole-like and the uncanny, *E.M. Forster* (Plymouth: Northcote House/British Council, 1999) thus became a sort of extended supplement to the present text.
5. I borrow this word from John Lennard who in turn takes it from Erasmus. See John Lennard, *But I Digress: The Exploitation of Parentheses in English Printed Verse* (Oxford: Clarendon, 1991), pp. 1, 249, n. 1.
6. Jacques Derrida, 'Freud and the Scene of Writing', in *Writing and Difference*, trans. Alan Bass (London: Routledge and Kegan Paul, 1978), p. 214, translation slightly modified. See 'Freud et la scène de l'écriture', in *L'écriture et la différence* (Paris: Éditions du Seuil, 1967), p. 317.
7. Derrida, 'Freud and the Scene of Writing', p. 214.
8. Sigmund Freud, *The Interpretation of Dreams*, trans. James Strachey et al., Pelican Freud Library Vol. 4 (Harmondsworth: Penguin, 1973–86), pp. 211–12.
9. Ibid., p. 212, n. 1
10. See *The Complete Short Stories of Franz Kafka*, ed. Nahum N. Glatzer (London: Minerva, 1996), p. 470.
11. *Franz Kafka*, ed. Glatzer, p. 171.
12. Jacques Derrida, 'White Mythology: Metaphor in the Text of Philosophy', in *Margins of Philosophy*, trans. Alan Bass (Chicago: University of Chicago Press, 1982), p. 246.

13. Martyn L. Gorman and R. David Stone, *The Natural History of Moles* (London: Christopher Helm, 1990), pp. 10, 19.
14. Derrida, 'Freud and the Scene of Writing', p. 203
15. Jacques Derrida, *Archive Fever: A Freudian Impression*, trans. Eric Prenowitz (Chicago: University of Chicago Press, 1996), p. 80.
16. Gorman and Stone, *The Natural History of Moles*, p. 1.
17. Jacques Derrida, 'Passions: "An Oblique Offering"', trans. David Wood, in *On the Name* (Stanford: Stanford University Press, 1995), p. 26.
18. As I hope will become clear from the reading of *Hamlet* advanced in this essay, I would contend that Shakespeare's text (1600–1) effectively offers an earlier construal of 'mole' as 'false conception'.
19. Derrida, 'Freud and the Scene of Writing', p. 197
20. Ibid., p. 197.
21. Ibid., pp. 226, 227, 229, italics original.
22. Jacques Derrida, 'The Almost Nothing of the Unpresentable', trans. Peggy Kamuf, in *Points ... Interviews, 1974–1994*, ed. Elisabeth Weber (Stanford: Stanford University Press, 1995), p. 79.
23. Cf. *Of Grammatology*, trans. Gayatri Chakravorty Spivak (Baltimore: Johns Hopkins University Press, 1976), p. 162, and Weber, ed. *Points ... Interviews*, p. 48. Across the decades Derrida has followed the furrows of Freudian conceptuality and the contents of the Freudian archive about which he observes: 'These classical and extraordinary works move away from us at great speed, in a continually accelerated fashion. They burrow into the past...' (*Archive Fever*, p. 18).
24. Derrida, 'The Almost Nothing of the Unpresentable', p. 84.
25. Jacques Derrida, *Spectres of Marx: The State of the Debt, the Work of Mourning, and the New International*, trans. Peggy Kamuf (New York: Routledge, 1994).
26. References to Shakespeare's play are to the *Arden Hamlet*, ed. Harold Jenkins (London: Methuen, 1982).
27. Derrida, *Spectres of Marx*, p. 93
28. Ibid., p. 85
29. Ibid.
30. Ibid., p. 139
31. M.M. Mahood, *Shakespeare's Wordplay* (London: Methuen, 1957), p. 117.
32. J. Dover Wilson, *What Happens in Hamlet* (Cambridge: Cambridge University Press, 1935), p. 78.
33. Derrida, *Spectres of Marx*, p. 18
34. James Joyce, *Ulysses* (Harmondsworth: Penguin, 1969), p. 190.
35. Ibid., pp. 188, 189.
36. Derrida, *Spectres of Marx*, p. 7.
37. Jacques Derrida, 'The Time is Out of Joint', trans. Peggy Kamuf, in *Deconstruction is/in America*, ed. Anselm Haverkamp (New York: NYU Press, 1995), p. 29.
38. Derrida, *Archive Fever*, p. 84
39. Ibid., p. 61.
40. Derrida uses the Bonnefoy translation of 'beaver' as 'visière': see *Spectres of Marx*, p. 29. 'Beaver' is indeed the nearest word to 'visor' in Shakespeare's

text. In a note to the Arden edition Harold Jenkins writes: 'Originally the beaver was drawn up from the chin and the vizor let down from the forehead. But in 16th-century helmets beaver and vizor had ceased to be distinct, and either word was applied to the whole face-guard, which "could be pushed up entirely over the top of the helmet" (Planché, *Cyclopaedia of Costume*, i.39), thus leaving the face free' (*Hamlet*, p. 195).

41. Derrida, *Spectres of Marx*, p. 8.
42. Sir Thomas Browne, *Pseudodoxia Epidemica* [1646], Vol. I, ed. Robin Robbins (Oxford: Clarendon Press, 1981), Chapter XVIII, 'Of Moles, or Molls', p. 233.
43. Cf. Derrida, *Spectres of Marx*, p. 185, n. 10.
44. Karl Marx and Frederick Engels, 'The Eighteenth Brumaire of Louis Bonaparte', in *Collected Works*, Vol. XI (New York: International Publishers, 1979); *Marx-Engels Werke*, ed. Institut für Marxismus-Leninismus beim ZK der SED (Berlin: Dietz Verlag, 1969), VIII, 196.
45. Georges Bataille, 'The "Old Mole" and the Prefix *Sur*', in *Visions of Excess: Selected Writings, 1927–1939*, ed. Allan Stoekl (Minneapolis: University of Minnesota Press, 1985), p. 35.
46. Derrida, *Spectres of Marx*, p. 105
47. Ibid., p. 85.
48. See my *Telepathy and Literature: Essays on the Reading Mind* (Oxford and Cambridge, MA: Blackwell, 1991), p. 146. I explore further the notion of dramaturgic or theatrical telepathy, specifically in relation to *Hamlet*, in 'Night Writing', in *The Uncanny*, pp. 112–32.
49. See Derrida, 'Passions', p. 27.
50. *Franz Kafka*, ed. Glatzer, p. 325
51. Ibid., p. 331.
52. Ibid., p. 343
53. Ibid., pp. 347, 337, 334.
54. See Jacques Derrida, *Aporias*, trans. Thomas Dutoit (Stanford: Stanford University Press, 1993), p. 76.
55. *The Poems of George Herbert* (London: Oxford University Press, 1961), p. 52.
56. Jacques Derrida, 'How to Avoid Speaking: Denials', trans. Ken Frieden, in *Languages of the Unsayable: The Play of Negativity in Literature and Literary Theory*, ed. Sanford Budick and Wolfgang Iser (New York: Columbia University Press, 1989), p. 18.
57. Derrida, 'How to Avoid Speaking', p. 17.
58. Ibid., p. 18
59. Nicholas Royle, 'Nuclear Piece: *Mémoires* of *Hamlet* and the Time to Come', *Diacritics* 20.1, Spring 1990, p. 47 (citing Derrida, *Mémoires: for Paul de Man* [New York: Columbia University Press, 1986], p. 94). In the *Diacritics* essay I also refer to the mole in a footnote (p. 41, n. 2), and in particular to Ned Lukacher's remarkable chapter entitled 'Shakespeare in the Ear of Hegel' in his book *Primal Scenes: Literature, Philosophy, Psychoanalysis* (Ithaca, NY: Cornell University Press, 1986), pp. 178–235, in which, I suggest, 'Lukacher plays Molecatcher, following the cryptic movements of this "figure of a figure" through [Shakespeare's play]'.

Index

Abraham, Nicolas and Maria Torok, 60, 61
Aeschylus, 16, 31n
Agamben, Georgio, 106–12, 119, 120, 121
'animal question', 1–2, 3, 4, 18, 25, 42, 106, 107, 110, 112, 119, 120, 121, 181
animot, 26, 35, 36, 37, 38, 39, 42, 43, 48–9
anthropocentrism, 106, 119, 179
anthropomorphism, 4, 187
anthropophagy, 61
Aristotle, 105, 108
auto-affection, 56, 58, 75, 179
'autobiographical animal', 63, 181, 187
autobiography, 27, 28, 62, 180
autopsic gaze, 91, 93, 98, 99
autopsy, 90–5, 96, 97, 98, 99–102

Bennington, Geoffrey, 14–15, 23, 24, 135
Bentham, Jeremy, 73, 119
Berenbaum, May, 58, 67n
Bernstein, Charles, 77–9

carno-phallogocentrism, 55, 59, 61
Carroll, Lewis, 4
Cixous, Hélène
 'Contes de la différence sexuelle', 155n, 43n, 157n,
 Index Cixous, 1
 Insister à Jacques Derrida, 32n, 160, 174n; see also *Insister of Jacques Derrida*, 32n, 53n, 79n, 174n

Jours de l'an, 153
L'Amour du loup et autres remords, 36, 43, 50n, 132–7, 138n, 140n, 141n, 156n; see also 'Love of the Wolf'
L'Ange au secret, 170
'Letter-Beings and Time', 156n, 163, 175n
Le Voyage de la racine alechinsky, 143, 154n, 155n, 156n, 157n
'Love of the Wolf' 45, 50n, 52n, 126, 129, 130, 132–3, 150
Manhattan, 144, 146, 155n
'Savoir', 157n, 171, 175n
Si près, 145, 175n
'Tales of Sexual Difference', 66n, 148, 149, 152; see also 'Contes de la différence sexuelle'
The Blindfolded Fiancée or Amelait, 142–54, 155n, 156n
'The Cat's Arrival', 3, 7n
'The Laugh of the Medusa', 138n, 139n
Three Steps on the Ladder of Writing, 32n, 33n
'Writing Blind', 22
Coetzee, J. M., 117–19, 120
counter-fable, 100, 101

Dasein, 96, 111, 114, 117
death, 1, 2, 4, 10, 12, 15, 16, 22, 23, 28, 29, 48, 60, 62, 63, 65, 90, 91, 92, 93, 94–7, 99, 101–2, 113, 120, 137, 145–6, 149, 153, 164, 165, 188

deconstruction, 2, 3, 17, 20, 25, 28, 29, 35, 42, 43, 50, 54, 55, 57, 62, 70, 71, 74–5, 76, 81–2, 142, 183
Defoe, Daniel, 35, 36, 46–7, 48, 112–14, 115, 117–19, 120
Derrida, Jacques
  'A "Madness" Must Watch Over Thinking', 33n
  'And Say the Animal Responded?', 2, 7n, 77
  'Ants', 64–5, 66n, 68n, 69n, 156n, 157n
  Archive Fever, 81, 87n, 179, 183, 190n, 191n
  'A Silkworm of One's Own', 157n, 160, 170–4, 175n, 176n
  'Between Brackets I', 31n, 33n
  'Che cos'è la poesia?', 5, 8n, 87n
  'Dialanguages', 19
  'Différance', 54
  '"Eating Well" or the Calculation of the Subject', 6n, 7n, 58, 59–61, 66n, 76n, 68n, 69n
  'Edmond Jabès and the Question of the Book', 27, 33n
  Edmund Husserl's Origin of Geometry: An Introduction, 34, 35, 38–41, 44, 50n, 51n, 52n
  'Faith and Knowledge', 81, 85n, 87n, 95
  'Force and Signification', 29
  'Force of Law', 73
  For what tomorrow–: A Dialogue, 104n
  'Freud and the Scene of Writing', 18, 31n, 177–8, 179–80, 190n
  'Geschlecht II, Heidegger's Hand', 50, 53n, 121n
  Glas, 3, 19, 73, 85n
  'How to Avoid Speaking', 188, 191n, 192n
  'Khōra', 17, 18, 31n
  'Limited Inc a b c . . .', 70, 79, 81, 83n
  Of Grammatology, 32n, 63, 69n, 106, 121n, 140n, 190n
  Of Spirit, 114, 115, 122n
  Politics of Friendship, 30n, 31n, 135
  'Psyche: Invention of the Other', 78, 86n, 159, 174n
  'Punctuations', 37, 50n
  'Shibboleth: For Paul Celan', 43, 52n
  'Signature Event Context', 30n, 55, 71, 79, 83n
  Signsponge, 71–81, 83n, 84n, 85, 86, 87n, 88n
  Spectres of Marx, 155n, 156n, 181–2, 183–5, 189, 190n, 191n
  'Telepathy', 159, 174n
  'The Almost Nothing of the Unpresentable', 190n
  The Animal That Therefore I Am, 2–3, 6n, 26, 27, 33n, 34, 35, 36, 50n, 54, 55, 60, 62, 66n, 73, 84n, 87n, 95, 99, 100, 102, 105, 106, 119, 121n
  The Beast and The Sovereign Vol. I, 53n, 89–96, 102n, 104n, 106–7, 108–9, 110, 124, 125, 129, 138n, 139n, 140n, 141n, 156n
  The Beast and The Sovereign Vol. II, 50n, 52n, 53n, 103n, 112–15, 117, 119–21, 122n, 123n, 132, 134
  'The Force of Mourning', 99
  The Gift of Death, 19
  The Post Card: From Socrates to Freud and Beyond, 8n, 52n, 69n, 88n, 156n
  The Work of Mourning, 104n
  'Tympan', 19, 54–9, 61–2, 64, 66n, 67n, 68n
  'Typewriter Ribbon: Limited Ink (2)', 62–3, 65, 66n, 68n
  'Unsealing ("the old new language")', 33n
  'Why Peter Eisenmann Writes Such Good Books', 31n
Descartes, René, 2–3, 7n, 21n, 63, 96, 105–6, 110, 121n, 122n
Dick, Kirby and Amy Ziering Kofman, 33n, 34, 50n
Dickinson, Emily, 166–8, 175n
différance, 57, 74, 81, 167
dream, 6, 12, 13, 15, 17, 18, 20, 21, 24, 25, 29, 64, 159, 160, 161, 163–4, 166, 167–8, 171, 178

ear, 3, 55, 56–9, 60–1, 62, 64, 154, 187, 188
eating, 61, 64, 65, 132, 162, 177

fable, 58, 64, 78, 90, 91, 92, 94, 98, 99
fraternity, 129, 135–7
Freud, Sigmund, 18, 31n, 32n, 94, 95, 100, 124, 142, 177–8, 179, 183, 190n

gaze, 89, 90, 92, 95, 99, 101, 102, 105, 131; *see also* autopsic gaze
gender, 115, 124, 125, 136, 137, 143

Hegel, G. W. F., 35, 40, 42, 43, 44, 55, 57, 73, 80
Heidegger, Martin, 44, 47, 96, 102n, 103n, 105, 106, 108–9, 111, 112–15, 117, 119–20, 122n
Hobbes, Thomas, 106, 109, 127, 131, 137
Horn, Roni, 1
Husserl, Edmund, 37–9, 40, 41, 42, 43, 44, 45

incest, 63, 65
introjection, 60, 61, 64

Kafka, Franz, 31n, 142, 145, 146, 147, 148, 149, 152, 154n, 156n, 178, 187, 190n, 191n
Kant, Immanuel, 15, 30n, 107, 115–17, 122n
khōra, 17, 18, 19, 20, 21, 24

La Fontaine, Jean de, 89–90, 125, 132
Lacan, Jacques, 4, 45, 77, 79, 105, 129, 130, 136
law, 4, 10, 15, 17, 60, 63, 65, 77, 108, 109, 110, 116, 124, 126, 128, 129, 131, 132, 136, 137, 180, 183
Leavey, John P., 34–5, 37, 42, 45, 50n, 51n, 52n
Leiris, Michel, 55, 56, 58–9, 66n, 67n
Levinas, Emmanuel, 43, 44, 60, 107–8

limitrophy, 35, 36, 38, 54, 59, 61, 62, 64, 65
Loewenstein, Rudolf, 45, 52n

machine-event, 62
MacSweeney, Barry, 15, 30n, 31n
Mallarmé, Stéphane, 22
Marin, Louis, 99, 101, 102n
meat, 59, 60, 61, 65
Merleau-Ponty, Maurice, 43–4, 52n
Milton, John, 167, 168, 169
mourning, 91, 95–102
murder, 2, 16, 73, 96, 99, 103n, 136, 147
myopia, 154

Nietzsche, Friedrich, 88n, 189n
non-anthropocentric, 119, 120, 121

performative, 60, 78, 100, 106, 185
Petton, Luc, 24–5, 32n
phallogocentrism, 55, 57, 59
phenomenology, 37, 41, 42, 44, 45
Plato, 17, 19, 20, 24, 28, 31n, 32n, 81, 132, 140n
Plautus, 127–8, 131, 137, 139n
Ponge, Francis, 71–6, 78, 79, 80–1
Proust, Marcel, 14
psychoanalysis, 57, 60, 65, 179

reaction, 3, 19, 62, 77, 113, 136
repetition, 2, 27, 29, 99, 100, 145, 147, 165, 174, 186
response, 2–3, 36, 62, 77, 170
Ris-Orangis, 48–9
Rousseau, Jean-Jacques, 62, 63, 65, 69n, 108, 114, 121n, 128, 129, 130–2, 136, 137, 140n
Royle, Nicholas, 3, 4–5, 7n, 55, 66n, 142, 143, 145, 154n, 155n, 157n, 159, 162, 175n, 192n

sacrifice, 1, 11–12, 60, 62, 65, 94, 95, 96, 134–5, 136, 169
sericulture, 171, 172, 173, 174
sexual difference, 3, 55, 58, 126, 134, 150, 151, 152

Shakespeare, William, 24, 142, 144, 148, 151, 163, 166, 179, 181–4, 186, 188
Shelley, Percy Bysshe, 21, 22, 23
signature, 13, 20, 23–4, 25, 42–3, 70–2, 73, 75, 79, 80, 81, 82
sovereignty, 47, 89–96, 98, 99, 100, 101, 102, 106–7, 109, 111, 113, 114–15, 117–18, 120, 121, 125
spectre, 100, 145–7, 151
Spivak, Gayatri, 107, 115–16, 119, 122n, 123n
suffering, 9, 71, 73, 97, 119, 120, 125, 185

telephone, 55, 64, 164, 187
Tennyson, Alfred, 23

trace, 3, 5, 25, 26, 27, 58, 63, 70, 71, 74, 76, 91, 100, 133, 136, 151, 152, 178, 180, 183, 187, 188
Tsvetaeva, Marina, 125, 129, 130, 131, 133–7, 141n
tympanum, 56–9, 61, 63

vegan, 61
vegetarian, 61, 68n
violence, 42, 54, 56, 58, 59, 61, 81, 95, 107, 114, 120–1, 127, 129, 136
Vivien, Renée, 135, 136, 137

Wordsworth, William, 32n

Yeats, W. B., 23

EU representative:
Easy Access System Europe
Mustamäe tee 50, 10621 Tallinn, Estonia
Gpsr.requests@easproject.com